47375

| Red Crow, Warrior Chief |

/ Red Crow, Warrior Chief /

Hugh A. Dempsey

University of Nebraska Press
Lincoln and London

This edition authorized by Western Producer Prairie Books, Saskatoon, Canada. Published simultaneously by University of Nebraska Press, Lincoln and London.

Printed and bound in Canada by Modern Press, Saskatoon, Canada

Book and cover design by Ray Statham/Statham Design Inc.

Library of Congress Cataloging in Publication Data

Dempsey, Hugh Aylmer 1929-
    Red Crow, warrior chief.

    Bibliography: p. 237
    1. Red Crow 2. Siksika Indians—History.
3. Siksika Indians—Biography. 4. Kainah Indians—History
5. Kainah Indians—Biography. I. Title.
E99.S54R423   970.004'97 [B]   80-51872
ISBN 0-8032-1657-2

|Contents|

/ Preface /

From 1870 to 1900, Red Crow was head chief of the Blood tribe, a part of the great Blackfoot nation. As a warrior, diplomat, and statesman, he dominated the affairs of the largest reserve in Canada for more than two decades, keeping his people at peace, yet never letting them surrender their pride and dignity.

He was an important native leader and a significant Canadian, yet he has been virtually ignored in the pages of history. There are good reasons for this. On one hand, his reserve was isolated from the mainstream of Canadian society, so his work passed relatively unnoticed. Also, his career parallelled in time and area that of Crowfoot, an equally important Blackfoot chief. Crowfoot, however, had the questionable advantage of a reserve on the main line of the CPR, where he met journalists, dignitaries, and others who came to appreciate and record his eloquence and grace. He also had such publicity-conscious friends as Father Lacombe and Cecil Denny. So while Crowfoot railed publicly against the Mounted Police for their duplicity, searched his soul to decide whether or not to join the Riel Rebellion, and died a broken man, Red Crow forged ahead quietly to build a proud and self-reliant tribe.

Red Crow did not share the same doubts or misgivings as Crowfoot and perhaps that made him a less romantic figure. Rather, he was a true warrior chief who brought to his councils all the wisdom and strength he had gained on the warpath. His judgments were swift, assured, and decisive.

This book was not written, however, in an attempt to compare the careers of these two men. Red Crow was a strong and romantic enough figure to stand scrutiny without comparison, and the results of his wise counsel are still evident today on the Blood Reserve of southern Alberta.

Many people have assisted me during the twenty-year research for the book. Most notable were Frank Red Crow, the chief's adopted son, and Jim Shot Both Sides, head chief of the Blood tribe and adopted great-grandson of Red Crow. Others include such informants as Jack Low Horn, Jim White Bull, Laurie Plume, Charlie Pantherbone, Dan Chief Moon, Mrs. Rosie Davis, Percy Creighton, Archie Big Swan, George Calling Last, Mortimer Eagle Tailfeathers, and John Cotton. I also must express my appreciation to the Blood Tribal Council, which has encouraged me in this project and has checked the final result.

Special tribute also must go to my late father-in-law, Senator James Gladstone, who was my interpreter for most of the interviews and who added his own knowledge of the chief.

Thanks go to John C. Ewers of the Smithsonian Institution, to the late Claude Schaeffer, and to Esther S. Goldfrank for providing copies of some of their interviews. Other valuable help came from the Glenbow-Alberta Institute Archives, the Public Archives of Canada, Montana Historical Society, Provincial Archives of Alberta, the Oblate Archives, RCMP Museum in Regina, and Blackfeet Indian Agency, Browning, Montana.

Most of all, thanks go to the Blood tribe for allowing me to share this part of their history with the rest of the world.

1

/ Fish Eaters /

Red Crow was born to a family of chiefs, to the aristocracy of the Blood tribe. His father, Black Bear, *Kyiosiksinum*, was a chief, as were his uncle, Seen From Afar, *Peenaquim*, and his grandfather, Two Suns, *Stoô-kya-tosi*. Their band was one of the largest of the tribe, and over the years it became the richest.

At the time of Red Crow's birth in 1830, the Bloods wandered over a vast territory of northern Montana and southern Alberta. Their summer ranges were usually west of the Cypress Hills and their favorite wintering camps were on the Belly River, the Highwood, and along the Porcupine Hills. South of the Bloods to the Missouri River were the Peigans, while north as far as the Saskatchewan River ranged the Blackfoot tribe. Together, the Blood, Peigan and Blackfoot tribes comprised the great Blackfoot nation, a fierce nomadic people who spoke one language and shared one culture. Their staff of life was the buffalo. It provided meat for food, skin for clothing, and a reason for their belief in the Sun spirit.

About 100 years before Red Crow was born, the Bloods had acquired their first horses. Until that time, the dog had been their only beast of burden as the nomads moved from place to place in pursuit of the buffalo. Tepees had been small — only large enough for a dog to haul on a travois — and the people had feasted and starved according to the movements of the buffalo herds. But the horse had freed them from their pedestrian existence. Like an eagle set free from its nest, the Bloods had used the horse as their wings to carry them to every part of their domain, and beyond. Within a generation, their whole way of life had become adapted to the four-footed beast and they rode as though the animal had always been a part of their world. No longer did they need to wait patiently to drive buffalo over a cliff; with their buffalo runners they could dash among the shaggy beasts, picking out fat cows and bringing them thundering to the ground with well-placed shots from their bows. And within a few years, they acquired the white man's gun, cutting the barrel short so the hunter could reload at full gallop, simply by pouring in a load of powder from a horn around his neck and spitting a lead ball from his mouth into the barrel.

With the horse and the gun came freedom and power. And now that they had leisure time between hunts, the Bloods developed complex religious rituals, often adapted from ceremonies introduced from other tribes. The Sun Dance came to them that way, as did the medicine pipes and a host of religious bundles. Of all the events, the Sun Dance was the main festival of the year, a time when bands large and small gathered in a great camp to reaffirm their faith in the Sun spirit. During the days while the camp was assembled, warrior groups took the opportunity to perform their dances; the society of women, the *Motokix*, re-enacted the rites to honor the buffalo; and even the Mosquitoes, the clan of young boys, danced for the benefit of the camp.

The free time also let them devote their attentions to war, for not only had the Bloods and Blackfoot become mobile, but their enemies had as well. There were constant incursions into the Bloods' hunting grounds, while at the same time, the rich horse herds of enemy tribes became the goal of aspiring young warriors. To the Bloods there was a significant difference between "stealing" and "capturing." To take something from a friend was theft which could be punishable by death; but to capture a horse from an enemy camp was a feat of courage and honor to be proclaimed with pride around the campfire.

By the time Red Crow was born, the Bloods had fully adapted to the horse and the gun. There were no white man's forts within their territory, yet the Hudson's Bay posts at Rocky Mountain House and Edmonton were within ten days' journey of their camps. And a year after Red Crow was born, the Americans built their first trading post, Fort Union, among the Blackfoot on the Upper Missouri River. For the next four decades, the Blackfoot tribes astutely played the British off against the Americans, always holding out for the best prices and taking their buffalo robes, dried meat, horses, and furs to the company which offered the widest range of trade goods.

At the time of Red Crow's birth, the leading chief of the Blood tribe was Bull Back Fat who had assumed that position after Spotted Calf was killed in 1812. And during the two generations before that, another two chiefs named Bull Back Fat had also led the tribe.[1]

Like many of the Plains tribes, the Bloods were divided into many small bands, often held together through family relationships. Each had a distinctive name, such as All Tall People, Lone Fighters, or Black Elks, chosen as the result of some incident or characteristic of its members.

2

During the early part of the nineteenth century, the leadership of the Bloods was firmly in the hands of the Buffalo Followers band, which was controlled by the Bull Back Fat family. Red Crow's parents, on the other hand, belonged to the Fish Eaters, a minor band of the Bloods which played no significant role in the political life of the tribe. Yet in 1832, when Bull Back Fat agreed to end a twenty-six-year feud with the Americans, caused by the killing of a Peigan by the Lewis and Clark expedition in 1806, he unknowingly took the first step towards the decline of the Buffalo Followers and the ascendency of the rival Fish Eaters. After meeting the American Fur Company officers, Bull Back Fat agreed to a peace treaty and to trade at Fort Union or at a new fort at the confluence of the Marias and Missouri rivers.

Prior to this time, the Bloods had traded exclusively with the British at their forts in the north, but the Americans on the Missouri soon proved to be more convenient and offered better prices than their northern competitors. With a good navigation system along the Missouri river, the American Fur Company could easily import more kinds of trade goods, while the Hudson's Bay had to use sailing ships from Britain and a difficult inland canoe route from the coast. In trade guns and blankets the British maintained their superiority, but for many other commodities, the Americans had more variety at lower prices.

The opening of the southern trade led to a major change in the political structure of the Blood tribe after the chief trader of the Americans, Alexander Culbertson, married a girl named Holy Snake or *Natawista*,[2] whose father, Two Suns, was leader of the Fish Eaters band. He was also Red Crow's grandfather. By this time, Two Suns was an elderly man who had turned the leadership of the band over to his son, Seen From Afar, and it was from this warrior that Culbertson obtained permission to wed the girl.

The courtship of Natawista was a classic frontier romance, even though it may have been based upon the mundane realities of the fur trade economy. Alliances between traders and the daughters of chiefs were a common feature of the fur trade and a sure way to obtain the friendship and allegiance of a group of trading Indians.

In this instance, Culbertson saw *Natawista* when she was at the trading post but when he asked for her hand in marriage, her father demurred.

"I am going to make you prove that you are worthy to have my daughter," said Two Suns. "At this time, this moon of next summer, if you are still without a woman, that will be evidence that you love her and she shall be your woman."[3]

Culbertson agreed, and a year later when the Bloods realized that he would fulfill his promise, *Natawista's* female relatives prepared a complete dowry for her, including buckskin costumes, a new lodge, backrests, parfleche bags of dried meat, saddles, and fourteen horses. On the appointed day, an entourage of Fish Eaters rode into the fort, singing a greeting song. The cannon thundered its welcome and, after a pipe had been smoked, Culbertson presented Two Suns and his band with guns, blankets, tobacco, and other goods; he also gave his bride a beautiful wardrobe of silk, woollen, and cotton clothing. *Natawista* became the lady of the fort. Later, in 1847, she moved to the newly-built trading post of Fort Benton and made it her home for many years.

The impact of the marriage upon the Fish Eaters band was immediate and impressive. Although already recognized as a prominent and aggressive warrior, Seen From Afar soon became rich with the white man's trade goods and horses. On occasions, wagonloads of presents were sent to the chief as Culbertson used the family alliance to cement trading relations with the tribe. By the time Bull Back Fat died in the late 1840s, Seen From Afar was recognized as a second head chief of the tribe.

This young warrior embodied all the qualities that were expected of a successful Plains Indian leader of the nineteenth century. Blood informants considered him the greatest chief they ever had, a man who outshone even his nephew Red Crow when it came to decisive leadership.

On one occasion he saw a buffalo bull which had become trapped in a coulee during the winter. Large snowdrifts had blown in on each side, forming sheer walls. As Seen From Afar and his friends watched, the buffalo ran back and forth, driving its horns into the snowbanks.

"I think I'll go down after the bull," Seen From Afar roguishly told his comrades.

"No!" they cried. "You don't have a rifle. You'll be killed!"

But Seen From Afar ignored them. He slid down the snowbank and landed on the back of the buffalo bull. The animal was so terrified that it broke through the snow barrier and Seen From Afar laughingly dismounted as it galloped away.[4]

On another occasion, Seen From Afar and his companions were passing some bushes when they saw a bear. As his friends fled, Seen From Afar took off everything except his breech-cloth and knife and lay on his back across the trail. A few moments later the bear approached and stopped when it caught the human scent. Seeing the body, the bear put its paw on the man's chest to see if he was alive. At that moment, Seen From Afar shouted and jumped to his feet, frightening the bear and sending it scurrying down the path.[5]

Seen From Afar, besides being a reckless warrior, was deeply involved with native religion. In 1832, two years after Red Crow was born, the chief and his wife Pretty Woman had travelled down the Missouri River by steamboat to visit the Mandan Indians. They remained there all winter, and when they returned home, Seen From Afar brought with him the Longtime Medicine Pipe which even now is one of the most respected religious articles in the Blood tribe. At the same time, his wife learned the rituals of the Mandan women's society and, bringing back the leader's medicine bundle, she formed the sacred *Motoki* society among her people. This holy organization of women has survived the years and remains active in the tribe today.

But Seen From Afar's most noteworthy contributions were made as a warrior, as a leader, and as a wealthy man. And both his wealth and his leadership can be directly attributed to his relationship with trader Alexander Culbertson. As an Indian informant stated:

"One reason *Peenaquim* was chief was that his brother-in-law, Mr. Culbertson, used to give him all kinds of gifts and made him the richest warrior among the Bloods. He used to have whole rings of tobacco, bags filled with arrowheads and many other things. When he went out hunting or on the war path he would cut a great pile of sarviceberry sticks and arrow shafts and carry them with him. He even took a big wad of sinew to tie the arrowheads on the shafts.

"When he travelled, *Peenaquim* carried his own sweat lodge on his travois. The old men of the camp would come to him and say: '*Peenaquim*, I want to take a sweat bath. May I borrow your lodge?' And the chief would answer: 'Go ahead, take it. But be sure to bring it back when you are finished.'

"*Peenaquim* was a generous man. When the Bloods went out hunting buffalo, some of them would not have the proper horses — maybe just a couple of old pack animals. They would go to *Peenaquim* and say: 'May I use one of your horses to hunt buffalo?' And *Peenaquim* would answer, 'Sure, take that one over there.' When the man came back after the hunt he would take the horse and plenty of meat to *Peenaquim*'s lodge, but instead of accepting the meat, the chief would say: 'Keep your meat; I have enough of my own. And use my horse whenever you need it to go hunting.' "[6]

During Seen From Afar's rise to leadership, he faced opposition from some members of the Buffalo Followers band. Although his relationship with Bull Back Fat remained cordial, others resented his wealth, his influence, and his impressive war record.

One of his most notable confrontations took place with a prominent war chief named Big Snake. Both Seen From Afar and Big Snake were members of a war party that attacked a camp of Crow Indians. During the raid, Seen From Afar snatched a gun from the back of an enemy mule and, in the melee, Big Snake tried to take the gun away from him but was unsuccessful. Frustrated, Big Snake cursed Seen From Afar and told him he would have only bad luck from that time forward.

After this incident, Seen From Afar went on several raiding expeditions but was unsuccessful each time. Then, when on a foray against the Crows, he dreamed that his spinster sister, Sacred Woman, could lift the curse that had been placed on him. Abandoning his companions, he immediately set out for the Blood camps on the Belly River where he took his favorite horse and medicine pipe to his sister's lodge. She told Seen From Afar to prepare a sweat lodge and, after he had rubbed himself with sagebrush, she painted his face and he went through the sweat ceremony.

Sacred Woman told him that on the following day he should leave on a raid but should capture only a white horse which he would find in an enemy camp. She said that he would meet Big Snake, who would be on his way to trade at Fort Edmonton, and that the horse should be given to him as a gift. Everything turned out just as Sacred Woman predicted, and when the two men met, Big Snake gladly accepted the four-footed gift.

Seen From Afar realized that the giving of the horse automatically lifted the curse, but his sister had warned him not to take any presents from Big Snake in return. Later, when they were back at their camp, Big Snake invited Seen From Afar to a feast during which he tried to give him a weasel-tail suit. However, much to Big Snake's chagrin, Seen From Afar refused and the spell remained broken.[7]

In spite of its supernatural undertones, the story reflects the feeling of hostility and resentment which Seen From Afar encountered within the tribe, particularly from such bands as the Many Fat Horses, All Tall People, and the Marrows who owed their allegiance to the Buffalo Followers and to Bull Back Fat.

During most seasons of the year, the Blood bands were scattered across their hunting grounds, some travelling with the Peigans or the

Blackfoot in search of buffalo. Those who followed Seen From Afar tended to hunt in the southern part of the territory, often accompanied by the Peigans. The chief's favorite hunting area was in the vicinity of the Milk River, north to the South Saskatchewan, and east to the Cypress Hills. The Buffalo Followers, on the other hand, preferred to range beyond the South Saskatchewan, north to the Red Deer, and west to the Highwood River. There were no clear-cut boundaries and the bands moved according to their needs, often dictated by the location of buffalo herds, the availability of ripe berries in season, the replacing of worn tepee poles in the mountains, the danger of enemy incursions, and problems created by intertribal quarrels.

In many ways, Red Crow's birth occurred at an opportune time for a person with warrior and leadership abilities. By 1830, the Bloods were rich in horses, masters of a vast hunting ground, proudly aloof from the white traders, and just entering their golden age of prosperity and cultural life. And before Red Crow reached manhood, his band had gained dominance within the tribe, his own family had become wealthy and influential, and his uncles, Seen From Afar and Big Plume, *Omuxsapop*, were inspiring examples of the prestige and wealth to be gained on the warpath.

By 1830, the Bloods numbered about 4,500 persons, the Peigans 5,000, the Blackfoot about 4,500, and the Small Robes (a Peigan offshoot) about 2,500.[8] In all, the Blackfoot nation, not including the allied Gros Ventre and Sarcee tribes, had a population of some 16,500 persons occupying a broad, rolling prairie bounded on the north by the Battle River, the south by the Missouri, the west by the Rocky Mountains, and the east by the Cypress Hills. Within the entire northern region there were no white men's forts, nor did an enemy hunting party venture without fear into this forbidden land of the Blackfoot.

For Red Crow, 1830 was a good year to be born.

2

/ Early Years /

The Fish Eaters camp was pitched at the confluence of the Oldman and St. Mary rivers in the heart of the Bloods' hunting grounds when Red Crow was born.[1] Red Crow's mother, Handsome Woman, was one of Black Bear's several wives but Red Crow was the only boy of that particular union. He had three younger half-brothers, Kit Fox, Sheep Old Man, and Not Real Good, as well as two full sisters — both of whom remained childless—and several half-sisters, including Revenge Walker[2] and Paper Woman.[3]

At the time of his birth, Red Crow was given the baby name of Captured the Gun Inside, commemorating a war experience of his grandfather Two Suns. Names were family possessions, often given as a result of visions or victories on the warpath. The name given a girl at birth remained with her for the rest of her life, but a boy kept his baby name only until manhood, when he had an opportunity to earn a new one of his own.

During his early years, Red Crow was under the care of his mother and his "near mothers" — Black Bear's other wives. But as soon as he was old enough to talk and to understand, there were several men in the band ready to give him the lessons he would need during his development towards manhood. As the oldest of four boys and nephew of the band chief, he had a favored position among the children in the camp. People knew that by helping Red Crow they would be pleasing his father and his uncle, Seen From Afar.

But Red Crow was never a spoiled child; there were too many warriors in the family, too many men who were fiercely proud of the rising role of the Fish Eaters clan.

While Black Bear may have helped to instruct his son, the task was left primarily to the boy's elderly grandfather Two Suns, to his uncle Big Plume, and to a close friend, White Wolf, who later took the name of Rainy Chief. The latter two men were about twenty years older than Red Crow and their task was to train him in the intricacies of war. To the grandfather fell the duty of telling the boy the heroic stories of

Kutoyis and Blood Clot Boy, and the sometimes humorous, sometimes sad tales of *Napi*.

The stories were not told for mere entertainment, for almost every *Napi* story had a meaning or a lesson. *Napi*, a mythological being who personified all the strengths and weaknesses of man, yet at the same time possessed supernatural abilities, experienced many adventures which could teach a young listener how to avoid errors in his own life. The hero tales, on the other hand, provided goals for a budding young warrior and emphasized how he must always place confidence in his spiritual protectors if he were to overcome the myriad of evil forces surrounding him. A man's own ability was not enough in a world dominated by Nature.

Red Crow was still just a boy when he received his first spiritual protector. One of his teachers had shown him how to make his own bow and arrows and how to hunt small game. One day, just when the camp was being struck, Red Crow set out with his bow and wooden-pointed arrows. Seeing a gopher some distance away from the camp, he crept towards it, but the animal scurried into its hole before the boy could fire a shaft.

Determinedly, Red Crow said to himself, "I must kill this gopher. I'll wait until he comes out." Patiently he lay beside the hole, but the gopher failed to appear. By this time the camp was already moving away, but Red Crow stubbornly refused to go until he had killed his prey. At last the young boy slept and the gopher came to him in a dream.

"My boy," it said, "you can't kill me with arrows, you must catch me with your hands. Go away and I'll come out to eat. I'm getting hungry."

Then the dream gopher gave Red Crow some advice for his future life. "When you go against an enemy," advised the spirit, "take a blade of grass and stick it in your hair. Then you'll never get hit. The only time you will be in danger is if the enemy captures you by hand. If a bullet strikes the blade of grass, you will be wounded."[4] The gopher also warned Red Crow never to offer a piece of his body to the sun, as some warriors did. If he did, bad luck would follow.

When Red Crow awoke, the camp was gone, but resolutely he followed the instructions of his dream. Moving away from the hole, he saw the gopher come out to eat, but because it had now become his spiritual helper, he decided to leave it alone. Instead, he trotted down the coulee, following the fresh ruts of the loaded travois until they led him to the new campsite of the Fish Eaters clan.

In his later life, Red Crow always followed the instructions of his spirit guardian, placing a blade of grass in his hair before going to war. Only once did he disobey any of the taboos; just before leaving on a raid, he cut off a lock of hair and left it as an offering to the Sun. And true to the gopher's prediction, bad luck came when the war party was surrounded and Red Crow barely escaped with his life.

But in the 1830s and early 1840s, warfare was still in Red Crow's future. During those years he saw the three men he idolized — Big Plume, Rainy Chief, and Seen From Afar — constantly going on raids against their enemies. Sometimes Seen From Afar did not come back for months at a time; after successfully concluding one attack, he would send a young boy home with his captured horses and set out in search of another hapless enemy.

While Red Crow was still a child, Seen From Afar and Rainy Chief took part in one memorable raid which became part of Blackfoot folklore. They were co-leaders of a war party which discovered a Crow village; there they saw that the horses had all been gathered in the camp circle and the Indians were performing a war dance. Arrogantly, Seen From Afar produced his hand mirror and flashed signals to the Crows, revealing his presence to them. When Rainy Chief expressed his concern for the young boys in their party, Seen From Afar disdainfully replied:

"We'll let the young people watch us. We alone will fight the Crows. The young ones can load our guns."[5]

The leader of the Crows had had a dream the previous night, warning him of a disaster which faced his camp. When he saw the flashing lights, he cautioned his people not to respond, but the young Crow warriors protested: "We are not women! We can't let them flash lights at us. If we ignore them, our enemies will make fun of us."

When the Crow warriors dashed to the hill, they were surprised to see only two men waiting for them. Rainy Chief was tall and lithe, while Seen From Afar was short and looked almost like a boy. When the Crows attacked, the bullets and arrows flew all around the Blood warriors, but none struck them. Rainy Chief and Seen From Afar, on the other hand, shot down one Crow warrior after another.

At last, the reluctant Crow chief who had had the dream raised his shield and spear and attacked Rainy Chief. Charging on horseback, he intended to run the Blood down, but Rainy Chief jumped aside at the last moment and shot his opponent dead. Then he scalped his enemy, stripped his body of its clothes, and let the horse gallop back to the camp. A second chief of the Crows, seeing his leader dead, attacked Seen From Afar, but he too was killed.

As night was falling, a Crow who could speak Blackfoot crawled forward and shouted: "Who are you?"

"We are the Bloods," responded Seen From Afar proudly. "I am Bull Collar and my comrade is White Wolf."[6]

A gasp arose from the Crows, for the two chiefs who had been killed were also named Bull Collar and White Wolf. Fearful that supernatural forces were protecting the Bloods, the Crows withdrew and, under the cover of darkness, the raiding party safely escaped to its own land.

With adventures like this being told and retold around the campfires, there was little doubt in Red Crow's mind that when he reached manhood, he too would follow the war trail of his uncles and their comrades. Bold, yet respectful, he hovered near his favorite relatives as they told of raiding the Crow camps, attacking a Cree war party, or destroying a band of Kootenais which had had the temerity to cross the mountains to hunt in Blackfoot lands. He was thrilled by the excitement which pulsated through the audience, particularly in the Sun Dance ceremonies, when even the wizened old patriarchs cackled and wheezed as they remembered ancient battles.

Yet other events were taking place in Blackfoot country during those years. They were important events. Bull Back Fat had established friendly relations with the Americans in 1832, and their fort at the mouth of the Marias River had become a focal point for all the tribes. When it was burned down, a new one, named Fort McKenzie, was opened in the summer of 1833. There factor David Mitchell carried out a lucrative trade with the Bloods and Peigans, drawing off much of the business that had formerly gone to the British.

Farther north, the Hudson's Bay Company did not sit idly by and let the Americans steal their trade. They realized that most of the Blackfoot and a large number of Bloods, particularly the Buffalo Followers, ranged far enough north that it was still convenient for them to take their robes to the Saskatchewan. But the Peigans were the best beaver hunters in the nation, and it was their trade that the British wanted to keep.

Accordingly, a fort named Peagan Post was built on the upper waters of the Bow River, west of the present city of Calgary. The river was unsuitable for navigation so everything at the new fort had to be brought in by packhorses. In order to keep expenses to a minimum, the Hudson's Bay Company decreed that only the Peigans would be permitted to trade at the Bow River fort, while the Bloods and Blackfoot would have to make the longer journey to Fort Edmonton.

The Fish Eaters and more southerly Bloods were not concerned, as they had no intention of travelling northward anyway. But the Buffalo Followers were angry at the favoritism shown the Peigans and advised their brother tribe to boycott the fort. When the Peigans ignored the advice, some of the Blood war chiefs intercepted them on Badger Creek. The Peigans announced that they were determined to go north, a violent argument erupted, and a number of Peigans were killed. Appalled by the intertribal conflict, the Peigans abandoned their plans to go to the Bow River fort and a few months later the post was closed because of a lack of trade.

As a result, the Americans' Fort McKenzie continued to prosper. In 1834-35, for example, its winter trade amounted to 9,000 buffalo robes, 1,020 beaver pelts, 2,800 muskrats, 1,500 prairie dogs, 200 red foxes, 180 wolves, 40 otter, 19 bear, and 390 dried buffalo tongues.[7] And the Bloods were among its best customers.

When Red Crow was seven years old, another event occurred which affected every lodge in the Blackfoot nation. It began innocently enough early in 1837 when a number of passengers travelling from St. Louis on the American Fur Company steamboat St. Peter's became infected with smallpox. At the mouth of the Little Missouri, a Blackfoot Indian boarded the boat and travelled with it to Fort Union, where he transferred to a keel boat bound for Fort McKenzie. Before he reached his destination, he and two other passengers had come down with the dreaded disease.

At Fort McKenzie, Alexander Culbertson tried to delay the boat downriver and to keep it in isolation until the onset of winter, when he hoped that the cold weather would eradicate the sickness. However, a large camp of Bloods and Peigans had been waiting for days for the trade goods and threatened to attack the boat if trading did not begin immediately. Reluctantly, Culbertson ordered the boat to proceed to the fort.

The Blackfoot had experienced smallpox epidemics before, particularly in 1781-82 and in 1801, but none was a virulent as the one which swept the northern Plains during 1837 and 1838. Within two weeks of the boat's landing, twenty-six Indian women in the fort and one trader had perished. Meanwhile, out on the plains the pestilence was killing the Bloods, Peigans, and Blackfoot by the hundreds. Two months after the ill-fated visit of the steamboat, Culbertson went to a Peigan camp of about sixty lodges at the three forks of the Missouri.

"Not a soul was to be seen, and a funereal stillness rested upon it. ... Soon a stench was observed in the air, that increased as they advanced; and presently the scene in all its horror was before them. Hundreds of decaying forms of human beings, horses and dogs lay scattered everywhere among the lodges. . . . Two old women, too feeble to travel, were the sole living occupants of the village. All who had not died on the spot had fled in small bands here and there, frantic to escape the pestilence which pursued them at every turn, seizing its victims on the prairie, in the valley, among the mountains, dotting the country with their corrupting bodies, till thousands had perished."[8]

At the confluence of the Oldman and St. Mary rivers, where Red Crow had been born, so many Bloods perished that the site was named *Akaisakoyi*, or "Many Dead."[9]

In telling of the tragedy, Chief Factor John Rowand of the Hudson's Bay Company summarized the events: "It was on the 11th November when I first heard of the raging Sickness from a party of Circees who I had to supply with what Medicine I had; at that time they told me they might be one Hundred Tents of them, who I am sorry to say are already reduced to only thirty. Such a reduction in so short a time speaks for itself.

"The accounts we have about the Blood Indians, who were the first attacked with the Sickness & who were supposed to be about four hundred Tents of them alone, are now also reduced to a very small number. Those same Indians, I must confess, have pillaged and killed many a poor unfortunate white man across the Rocky Mountains and when they found an opportunity; however, if the accounts we have is correct, very few of these miserable Indians are living now.

"The Sickness they complain of begins with a dreadful pain in head, back, neck and bleeding at the Nose, which they say carried them off in two or three days at most."[10]

By the time the epidemic had run its savage course, the Blackfoot nation had suffered some 6,000 casualties, or almost two-thirds of its members. Yet in spite of this terrible ordeal, the Bloods who recovered continued to gain in wealth. The number of buffalo robes they traded increased each year, and their horse herds grew larger. Even the population, so badly decimated, rapidly increased in the next decade, during a stable period marked by plentiful food and no further epidemics.

As for Red Crow, these were simply growing-up years. He saw the calamitous smallpox epidemic, but came through it unmarked. Only eight years old at its termination, he was still learning to ride, to shoot, and to fulfill all the requirements of a young warrior. Even the games he played, like spin top, were based upon the exploits of war.

These were the lessons of Red Crow's childhood. War. War. War. And he was an apt pupil.

3

/ Novice Warrior /

Red Crow was in his early teens when he first went to war, and at the end of his career he could boast that he had been involved in thirty-three raids against enemy tribes, the Crow, Shoshoni, Cree, and Nez Perce. He killed at least four men and one woman, captured innumerable horses, shields, and religious objects, took enemy scalps, and counted "coups" on many dead bodies. It was a glorious, exciting time, when he faced death over and over again and responded literally with a laugh or a defiant curse.

In his first three summers on the war trail, Red Crow went from boy to man, from an untried neophyte to a young warrior. In his first raid, he went along only as a servant and had little chance to demonstrate his ability or prowess in battle. Like other boys going out for the first time, he carried wood and water, tended the fire, and when in enemy territory, he helped build tepee-like war lodges out of small trees and branches, providing the men with a place where they could rest at night without fear of discovery. Red Crow's first war party was large, and when it discovered an enemy camp of Crees, the more seasoned warriors succeeded in capturing several horses. But boys like Red Crow were given no chance to take part in the raid itself and when it was over they went back home afoot. That was Red Crow's first taste of war.[1]

But because it was his first act as a warrior, no matter how unspectacular, he was permitted to abandon his baby name of Captured the Gun Inside and receive a new one. The choice, which was not his own, was Lately Gone, *Manistapo,* a name which he hated and one which he tried for years to get rid of. Yet it stayed with him until he was finally granted permission to take the name of Red Crow, or *Mekaisto.* This was an honored name in the tribe; it had previously belonged to a relative who had gone on a raid in the winter of 1826 and had been killed when trying to enter an enemy camp.[2] The "crow" part of his name referred to the winged raven, not the Crow tribe; throughout his life he felt no kinship towards his enemies to the south, and not even his name could be linked to that enemy tribe.

An entire year passed before Red Crow ventured onto the warpath a second time. On this occasion, a Blood named Middle Painted Lodge let him to go along as a servant and, although he was given no chance to join in the attack, he was given a horse by one of his relatives who had been successful in the raid.

That was the last time Red Crow willingly went to war as a servant. Already proud and haughty, he was determined to be a warrior in his own right. Let others make fires and carry water for the raiders; he was from a family of chiefs, a family of warriors. Let the cowards and striplings sit in the camps; he would go to raid his enemies who were rich in horses and claim his proper share of the spoils.

Shortly after returning from his second raid, he got his chance. Red Crow heard that a Blood named One Spot was forming a large war party at a camp near Fort Benton. With a number of other young friends he joined the raiders and they set out for the Yellowstone River and Fort Sarpy, where the Crows often camped. Scouts sent ahead said that the trading post was busy with the enemy and that many lodges were pitched nearby.

One Spot saw at once that the raid would be a difficult one and that his party was too large to approach undetected. As a result, he told the very young and the very old to go back home. He explained that the ground was muddy, that travelling would be hard, and that the inexperienced would tire easily and thus be a danger and a nuisance to the others.

Red Crow and his two companions were among those ordered back, but they refused to go. At first One Spot tried to reason with them, then angrily cursed them and stalked away. The boys paid no heed to the threats, but followed in the wake of the war party as it advanced to a high bushy ridge and built three war lodges of timber and brush a few miles from the trading post. Once inside these lodges, the warriors could light small fires and remain undetected, even from several yards away.

As punishment for their failure to turn back, the boys were ordered to butcher and pack an entire buffalo carcass which the hunters had killed. Then, when a nearby rocky hill was to be transformed into a defensive fort in case it was needed during the retreat, the boys were put to work piling stones. They were also sent to carry water for the men, and whenever one of the youths sat down, an older warrior found some chore for him to do. After the work, torment, and humiliation failed to dissuade the boys, they were simply ignored. Red Crow, angry yet determined, suffered the indignities in silence. He had joined the expedition to be a real warrior and nothing would stop him.

On the morning of the raid, a large hunting party of Crows passed close to the hidden Blood camp and there was fear that they had been discovered. Quickly, the three boys were pushed into a shallow hole so they would be out of the way in case any fighting started. However, the Crows did not discover the camp, but killed a few buffalo nearby, butchered them, and prepared to pack the meat to their camps. Throughout the operation, the boys were kept in the hole while the warriors tried to frighten them with stories about the approaching enemy.

At last the Crow hunters left and the warriors began to prepare for their attack. They painted their faces, examined their weapons, and planned their strategy. The three boys were told that they could take part, but they had to go by themselves and none of the experienced warriors was permitted to help them. In fact, as Red Crow wryly observed: "We three were treated like stray pups following a camp. No one had a pleasant word for us; nothing but offensive torments and insults were bestowed upon us."[3] However, instead of discouraging Red Crow it made him more determined than ever to take part in the attack.

When the Bloods approached the village, they saw it was a large one that stretched for miles along the river. After sunset, One Spot dispatched a destitute young warrior to go into the camp first, both to act as scout and to have a chance to take some horses before the others got there. A short time later, he came back with three horses and was sent on his way home.

The war party split up into small groups, with Red Crow and his two companions being left to their own resources. Completely inexperienced, they went upstream until they came to a likely group of Crow lodges. As they crawled toward them, they met a warrior named High Sun, an older brother of one of the boys. Apparently taking pity on the trio, High Sun led them along a route which brought them close to a corral beside the Crow tepees. Telling the others he would scout ahead, he entered the camp and returned a few minutes later with a beautifully ornamented spear which he had taken from a tripod beside its owner's lodge. The spear handle was covered with buckskin and decorated with crow feathers. Hanging from it was a stuffed crow's head which could be removed and worn in the owner's hair when he went to war.

High Sun then went back to the enemy village, brought out a large grey horse, and told the boys to follow him, as he was going to the rendezvous. They had gone only a few paces when Red Crow suddenly realized that all they had done was act as lookouts for High Sun while he made his raid. They still had nothing. Angrily he summoned the other two to a hurried conference, but when they told High Sun they were going back to the camp, the older warrior persuaded his brother to remain with him in return for a rifle.

Red Crow and his companion went back to the enemy lodges and crept towards the corral. On their way, Red Crow noticed a number of medicine bundles, shields, and ceremonial objects hanging from tripods and decided he would rather have these than horses. When he told his friend, there was a whispered argument in the centre of the camp. At last, each decided to go his own separate way. Red Crow approached the nearest lodge and took a shield and a number of fringed parfleche bags from a tripod, as well as a horse which was tethered in front. At the next tepee he found another shield and some more bundles, and although their tripod was leaning against the side of the tent, he carefully lifted the war objects off, one by one. Then, spreading his robe over the horse's back, he tied the bags together in pairs and slung them over the animal. The two shields he tied around his neck, letting them hang down his back. During this whole time, he was cautious but calm as he went silently about his work. Then, just as he was leading the horse from the camp, he discovered another animal tied near a lodge, so he took it too.

To add to his dangerous situation, Red Crow found that the war bundles he had taken were covered with bells, and any quick movement would cause a jingling that would awaken the entire village.

Passing the corral, Red Crow saw that his companion had gone, so he slowly led the horses away from the camp until he felt it was safe to mount. Then, astride the animal which was loaded with the bundles, he made for the Blood war camp on the ridge. Everything went well until he was some distance from the Crow village when his newly-adopted mount stubbornly decided to go back home. When Red Crow tried to control it, the horse pranced up and down, setting off a wild jingling of bells that caused it to buck the young raider over its head and onto the ground.

Although he lost his second horse in the confusion, Red Crow had kept a firm hold on the bridle of his own animal. Afraid to mount him again in the darkness, he led the horse far out onto the prairie until it calmed down. At daybreak, as he was nearing the Blood war camp, Red

Crow was at last able to remount, and he saw for the first time that he had captured a fine buckskin. As they approached the rendezvous, Red Crow's horse grew nervous again and began prancing sideways, showing first one side of its body and then the other to the Blood scouts. At last Red Crow rode into the camp and, with the horse prancing, the bells jingling, and the shields flopping on his back, he felt an exhilarating sense of superiority and pride. The scowling looks of envy he received from the seasoned warriors made up for all the indignities he had suffered before the raid.

Unloading his bundles, Red Crow excitedly opened them one by one to reveal his trophies. The first contained a man's complete outfit, including a highly ornamented shirt and leggings. Others had beaded objects, women's trinkets, and valuable costumes. Most of these he generously gave away, reserving for himself the buckskin horse and the two shields. One shield in particular was a beautiful specimen, fringed with eagle feathers and painted with a mountain lion design. There was a bullet hole through it and blood spattered on the inside.

Red Crow learned, with some satisfaction, that most of the older warriors had come back to the camp empty-handed; they had found the Crow horses too securely corralled to be taken. Red Crow had been the most successful raider of the expedition.

That night, the Bloods left their secret camp and travelled northward to Fort Benton. Without pausing, the exultant Red Crow continued on to the Belly River where he was welcomed to the lodges of his older relatives and invited again and again to tell of his daring exploits inside the Crow camp. Surely here was a warrior who would bring honor the the entire nation. Fearless, intelligent, and proud, he was already displaying the qualities of leadership for which his family had become famous. Still a young teenager, Red Crow made no more raids that year but, more than ever, he was anxious to devote all his attentions to the warpath. He could understand why his uncles Big Plume and Seen From Afar had gloried in the adventure of war. The idea of danger, of hardship, and of possible death only sharpened the sense of excitement which he felt after the thrilling experience of the Crow raid.

In the following summer, Red Crow experienced both the stimulations and the disappointments of the warpath. And this time there was no question of his going as a servant or being sent home with the boys. Although still in his teens, Red Crow had become a proven and successful warrior. Anxious to pursue this exciting life, he took the opportunity to join a large raiding party of Bloods, Blackfoot, and

Sarcees organized by Old Sun, a renowned Blackfoot warrior. This man, a chief of All Medicine Men band, had led war parties since he was a youngster and continued to do so until he was halted by old age. Where many Blackfoot went on raids only until their twenties, there were men like Old Sun who never ceased to crave the glory of war. In spite of wives, family, and responsibilities in their home camps, they were always ready to leave everything behind for the lure of battle and personal gain.

Because of Old Sun's reputation, a large number of men had voiced their intentions to accompany him. Unlike many war parties, this one was to be highly mobile, with everyone travelling on horseback. Now that Red Crow was a proven warrior, he was invited to go on the raid by his uncle Big Plume. After all his years of learning the intricacies of war from his older relative, it was a signal honor actually to be asked to join Big Plume as a partner. Together, the two Bloods went to the Red Deer River, where they found the Blackfoot warriors just setting out for the north.

The mixed raiding party had almost reached the North Saskatchewan River before it discovered any Crees. Then the scouts signalled that they had sighted three hunters, so some of the men took their buffalo robes and, covering themselves, moved along a nearby ridge, imitating the actions of a buffalo herd. Taken in by the ruse, the three hunters galloped to the hill, only to be met by the Blackfoot warriors. One of the Crees fired hurriedly at the attackers, striking a Blackfoot in the shoulder. In the hand-to-hand fighting which followed, Big Plume suffered a knife slash across his back. In a few moments, however, all three Crees were lying dead on the hillside.

Some Bloods picked up the enemy guns as trophies, while a Blackfoot took a Cree bow and arrows and Red Crow snatched a white Hudson's Bay blanket from one of the bodies. At that point, he also tore his first scalp from the head of a slain enemy.

He returned home in triumph, but within a few days he learned that Morning Writing, chief of the All Tall People band, was leading a small party into Crow country. Without hesitation, Red Crow joined the eight or nine others as they set out on foot for the south, and he was with them several days later when they found an enemy camp. On his first foray, he succeeded in taking three horses, which he tethered to some bushes. Returning for more, he was no sooner in the camp than there was a flurry of shouting and gunfire. He learned later that a Blackfoot had taken a skittish race horse from in front of its owner's lodge; instead of leading it out of the camp, he had tried to mount it and the noise had awakened the Crows. The owner sprang from his lodge and fired a wild shot but the raider slipped to the ground and escaped with only a bullet hole in his robe.

Red Crow ran from the camp as fast as he could, but it was impossible to go back to the place where he had cached the three horses. Instead, he ran for the hills where he met four companions and together they started for home the way they had come — afoot. En route, they met a small party of Crows and had a short running battle with them, but by the time they reached the Blackfoot camps, they had neither scalps nor horses to show for their efforts.

This was the first of many raids from which Red Crow returned empty-handed. The risks were great, and the fact the party had been discovered and all members had reached home safely was considered to be a feat in itself.

Red Crow was disappointed by his failure but was determined to set out again as soon as possible. During this period — the summer months of the late 1840s — the plains were alive with small war parties. The Blackfoot were raiding the Crees, the Peigans were attacking the Shoshonis, the Assiniboines were raiding the Blackfoot, and the Bloods were crossing the mountains to attack the Nez Perce and Pend d'Oreilles. Most war parties were small and in search only of horses, but sometimes a larger force set out, prepared to destroy an entire camp in its quest for revenge and booty.

Only three days after Red Crow's return from the unsuccessful raid on the Crows, he left again with his uncle Big Plume in a raiding party led by an older relative named Red Old Man, a famous shaman-warrior who had received his spiritual powers from a mouse.

They traveled southward on foot until they found a trail left by a moving camp of Shoshonis. While most of the raiders favored going on to the Crows, who were richer in horses than the Shoshonis, Red Crow, Big Plume, and three others decided to follow the travois trail. They had not gone far when they saw three horses that had strayed from the moving camp, but the animals were fat and wild and would not let the Indians come near them. Abandoning the attempt, they continued on the trail and two days later they caught up with the Shoshonis just as they were starting to move again.

Red Crow and the others saw at once that it was a large camp. Later in the day, when they prowled around the abandoned village, they found a stray horse which had been left behind. Using the old cayuse for scouting, they followed the fresh trail of the enemy westward over the mountains.

That night, when the Shoshonis pitched their camp, the Bloods were close behind. After darkness had settled over the valley, the last bustle of nighttime activities had ceased, and the dogs had settled down, the Blood warriors quietly crept toward the tepees in search of horses.

Red Crow grabbed the first animal he could find, but in the darkness he didn't realize until too late that it was an unbroken colt. As he placed the rope around its neck and tried to lead it away, the colt suddenly reared and stampeded toward the village. Not wanting to lose his only rope, Red Crow held on. He was dragged along the ground and was only a short distance from the sleeping lodges when the choking effects of the noose finally caused the colt to collapse. Quickly, Red Crow slipped the rope loose and turned the animal free, thankful that he hadn't been pulled among the lodges where the noise would have alerted the entire camp. As it was, no one had been disturbed by the brief encounter.

Still determined, Red Crow went back to the Shoshoni horse herd and cut out a small bunch grazing some distance away from the others. Driving them on foot, he had gone only a short distance when a Shoshoni warrior suddenly appeared from one of the lodges and herded the rest of the animals into the centre of the village. As he did so, he shouted in Shoshoni for everyone to look after their horses and to picket or hobble them for the night.

Breathlessly, Red Crow watched and kept his small herd under control. When he realized that the animals hadn't been missed, he continued to drive them on foot until he was far enough away to mount one and to herd the others along to a prearranged meeting place. Once there, Red Crow found that his companions were gone. Guessing that they had been frightened by the camp crier, he left the captured herd behind and set off along the route he expected they would take. A short time later, when riding through a coulee, he heard whispered voices, but when he approached his friends, they scampered away in fear. Angrily Red Crow ignored the danger and shouted to them in Blackfoot that he was not the enemy. Sheepishly, they hurried back to the rider and were taken to the captured horses.

A count revealed that Red Crow had picked up forty horses, so he divided these among his companions, reserving the best one for himself. The five jubilant warriors then set out for home, but during the night their luck ran out when a flock of prairie chickens suddenly exploded from the bushes in front of them, sending the horses in a wild stampede. There was no way they could control the herd in the darkness and within a few seconds they were left with only the horses they were riding. Red Crow wanted to make another raid on the sleeping village, but his comrades wouldn't hear of it. After a long argument, Red Crow and Big Plume decided to go back alone and to let the three others leave for home. Sending their own captured horses back with the rest of the party, Red Crow and his uncle set out on foot and were not surprised to find that the stampeded horses were now with the main herd in the middle of the Shoshoni village.

Undaunted, the pair crossed the river to the camp and circled around it, hoping to find a way of cutting some horses from the bunch. However, they discovered a night guard on the far side, so they abandoned that idea in favor of looking for strays on the prairie. After a brief search, they found three, and although one got away and ran to the camp, they were able to capture the other two. Mounted, the pair were now able to make a better search and found nine more horses scattered about the prairie. One was a particularly fine brown with eagle feathers tied to its mane. Turning loose his mare, Red Crow mounted this animal and the pair joyfully rode northeast, driving their small captured herd before them. Once on the trail, they moved steadily for the rest of the night and all next day, hoping to catch up with their comrades. Near sundown of the second day, they arrived at a point where the rest of the war party had agreed to meet them and a flash of a mirror let them know that their friends were there; a short time later the reunited party was on its way again, travelling until dawn. Then Red Crow slept for the first time in three days, and several hours later they continued on their northern journey. On their way, they caught up with Red Old Man and the others who had gone to the Crows. They had been unsuccessful in their quest and were making the long walk home. Not wanting to leave their fellow tribesmen, Red Crow and his friends dismounted and drove their horses before them as they walked along the trail.

Red Crow remembered where they had seen the wild horses on the way in, so when they reached that spot, he and his uncle mounted and gathered the three strays into the herd. By this time, their war adventure should have been over but it wasn't. Instead, while crossing a river during a heavy rainstorm, they observed a large Nez Perce village on the other side. Because of the weather, the presence of the war party had not been detected.

Red Crow, still anxious for excitement, immediately proposed that they should make a horse raid under cover of the heavy rain. The elders said it was foolhardy to hit a camp in broad daylight while others argued that if the rain stopped, the entire war party could be discovered.

Undeterred, Red Crow set off alone. Before he had gone far, Big Plume caught up with him and tried to convince him to return. Instead, Red Crow persuaded his uncle to join the raid. In disgust, Red Old Man and the others started out for the Missouri, promising to deliver Red Crow's Shoshoni horses to the Fish Eaters camp.

After the others had gone, Red Crow walked boldly into the Nez Perce village and roped a bald-faced bay, while Big Plume caught a buffalo runner. Both men knew that the Nez Perce bred some of the finest horses in the region, so any raid on their camp brought valuable booty along with war honors. Satisfied that they had performed a daring deed by capturing two horses from an enemy camp in broad daylight, the pair set out along the trail, overtaking the main party a few miles away.

When Red Old Man and the others heard how easy the raid had been, they had second thoughts about the venture, and most of them decided to return to the enemy village. Only Red Crow, Big Plume, and the others from the Shoshoni raid chose to go home. All had plenty of horses from the two forays.

On the following day, Red Crow saw a small herd of buffalo near the trail but when he went to kill one, he was alarmed to see them stampeding towards him. Then the sound of gunfire let him know that the herd was being pursued by hunters. Turning his horse loose, Red Crow went into hiding and saw a hunter kill a buffalo nearby. Moments later, a woman and boy joined the man, and together they skinned and butchered the slain beast. After they had gone, Red Crow examined the carcass, and judging by the way it had been skinned, he realized that the Indians must have been members of the Blackfoot nation. Running after the trio, he learned that they were Peigans but when he tried to find his companions to let them know they were among friends, he discovered they were gone. He suspected they had fled when they heard the hunter's gun.

Red Crow stayed with the Peigan camp on White River that night and left on foot the next morning for the north. Eight days later, he reached Fort Benton where he finally caught up to his companions. Angry at the way they had deserted him on the trail, he collected his horses, presented one to his uncle, Alexander Culbertson, and set out alone to search for his family in the Fish Eaters camp. On the Milk River he met some Blackfoot who said that his relatives were camped farther down along the same stream, and a short time later, after several weeks of travel, he returned to his father's lodge with seven captured horses and some thrilling tales about his raids on the Shoshoni and Nez Perce camps.

Red Crow had proven himself a brave and competent warrior. But he also revealed that he had no patience with fools or cowards — even if they were relatives or leaders of war parties. If he disagreed with them, he spoke his mind, and if their actions were not to his liking, he did as he pleased. In these, the first of his many war experiences, he set a pattern which remained unchanged through much of his life. Red Crow was proud, arrogant, and aggressive. He was like that as a warrior, and he would be like that when he became a chief. He had the potential to be a leader of men, but in his early years he would accept only his way; this attitude would change in time, but such were his intelligence and wisdom that his way often proved to be right.

The Bloods were noted for their pride. They acted as though they were, as one observer noted, "the cream of creation," and it was this very attitude which made them feel inferior to no one, enemy or ally, Indian or white. It was a kind of pride that the Indians would need in the years ahead.

4

/ On the Warpath /

By the late 1840s and early 1850s, the constant raids by the Blackfoot along the Upper Missouri posed serious problems for American traders, missionaries, and enemy Indians. Although traders had established winter outposts at Willow Round, Flat Wood, and Milk River, all within Blackfoot country, they found the forts in Crow territory almost impossible to maintain. As trader Edwin Denig complained,

"Scarcely a day passes but the Crow country is infested with more or less parties of Blackfeet[1] who murder indiscriminately anyone who comes within their reach. At Fort Sarpy so great is the danger that no one ventures over a few yards from his own door without company and being well-armed."[2]

Of course, the Bloods did not feel welcome at Fort Sarpy, even when they came in peace. As Red Crow observed: "We did not call at this post, because the white men there did not like us; they were in the habit of shooting at us whenever we gave them a chance."[3]

In 1851, the Crows had even refused to attend the Fort Laramie Treaty to receive their annuities because of "the risk of passing through a country beset by their deadliest enemies, the Blackfeet and Blood Indians of the north."[4] Similarly, Father Jean De Smet complained in 1846 that the Flathead Indians, across the mountains, were "greatly reduced by the continued attacks of the Blackfeet."[5]

Yet as long as the Blackfoot had horses, guns, plenty of buffalo, and warriors willing to risk their lives for personal gain and glory, there was little the traders could do. Even the threat of cutting off the American trade would have been meaningless, for the tribes could always go to the British.

Within the Blood tribe, a few subtle shifts had taken place in the political structure. With the death of Bull Back Fat, the leadership of the Buffalo Followers had gone to his son, also named Bull Back Fat. But some of the band wanted the old chief's son-in-law, Father of Many Children, to assume control. When this failed to happen, a number of families chose to follow Father of Many Children and, although no actual rift developed, the latter group became a sub-band within the Buffalo Followers clan.

This was not unusual; over the years, bands were constantly uniting or dividing, according to the type of leadership being offered. But in this instance, the action weakened the position of the Buffalo Followers at a time when the Fish Eaters were playing a dominant role in tribal affairs. Bull Back Fat, still the nominal leader of the Buffalo Followers band, was a respected political chief who, like his father, favored keeping peace with the white traders and with other tribes. But more and more, the warrior leadership of Seen From Afar and his flamboyant family was creating a climate which encouraged frequent raids against enemy tribes.

By this time, Red Crow had completed half a dozen attacks against the Crees, Crows, Shoshonis, and Nez Perces. He was not concerned about the fur traders or tribal politics, for his only interest was in war. In the fall after his long raid to the Shoshonis, he camped with his uncle, Seen From Afar, on the Waterton River near the Rocky Mountains, while the main part of the tribe was hunting farther south. Because of the experience he had gained, Red Crow decided to form his own war party and when he announced the news, four young men volunteered to go with him.

Now, with the responsibility of leadership, Red Crow believed he needed more than daring and luck if he was to succeed. On the way south, when they reached the Bear River, he went away by himself in search of a vision. That night he had a dream in which he saw a large herd of horses near a place called Big Butte. Next morning he told his followers that he was taking them to that place and, as they approached it, they saw a big camp of Crows. After sunset, Red Crow went into the village first and took a large gray mare. Afterwards, the party went to a nearby ridge, where they made a brush camp in the trees.

For three days they spied on the Crows, until at last Red Crow went out again, this time taking a black stallion and a pinto. For another four days the Bloods watched, and then the entire war party went down but succeeded in picking up only two more horses, one of which was taken by Red Crow. This meant there was one horse for each raider, so Red Crow loaned three of those he had captured and the party continued to the slopes of Big Butte. Earlier Red Crow may have believed that the horses in the Crow camp were the ones he had seen in his dream, but once they arrived at the butte, he observed a scene which was identical to his vision and there, in the foreground, was a herd of horses just as he had dreamed.

To reach the herd, the Bloods had to cross a river which, in the fall of the year, was frozen and slippery. In order to make a safe pathway, they spread dirt over the ice and were just about finished when they were joined by a war party of Blackfoot. Without waiting or helping, the Blackfoot darted over and took a number of horses from the herd while Red Crow and his friends worked until their dirt bridge was finished. By the time they approached the herd, they found out that the supposed "enemy" camp was actually a party of Peigans and Bloods who had just raided the Crows and were on their way home. Red Crow explained to them that they had just been "raided" by their own people, who were now racing back to the north with their booty.

Disappointed with the abortive attack, Red Crow decided he would lead some Bloods and Peigans who wanted to go farther south. The four horses he had captured he sent back by a young man, giving him one animal for his trouble, and instructing him to present one to Seen From Afar, one to a female relative, and the fourth to a woman who had made his moccasins for the journey. He also sent a message that he would not go home until he had captured a large herd of horses, even if it took him until the following summer.

There were four in the new party besides Red Crow but they were soon joined by twelve others. Again reacting to the responsibility of being a leader, Red Crow slept and fasted alone for several days, until at last he dreamed of a mountain with a large number of horses nearby. Leading his party to the spot in Wyoming, he found a Shoshoni camp, with horses grazing on the surrounding prairie.

On the first night, Red Crow took six horses and sent them back with two young boys. On his second attempt, he rounded up a large herd and when he joined the others, he went to his friend Eagle Ribs, afterwards a tribal chief, and said: "Take your choice of all these horses, my friend, for you are a married man and I am single."[6]

When all but four of the raiders had come back to the camp, Red Crow gave away the rest of his horses, keeping only two for himself. Then the warriors set out for their homes; the four missing men had not returned, so the Bloods concluded that they had been killed by the enemy.

En route north, Red Crow was leading the party when he saw a number of hobbled horses by the trail. Realizing that an enemy camp must be near, he collected four of the animals and added them to the two which he already had. For the next three or four days, the party moved rapidly through enemy land, with one of Red Crow's captured horses playing out and being abandoned along the way.

At the Yellowstone River they saw a Crow village, and although they swung wide to avoid it, their tracks were seen. They were being followed by a large enemy force when a blizzard covered their trail. Shortly afterwards they reached a Peigan camp where Red Crow was pleased to find Seen From Afar and a number of other relatives. An entire winter had passed since he had left his uncle on the Waterton River, and when he finally rode into the friendly camps he was ragged, tired, and glad to be back.

But not for long.

The following day when he learned that Red Old Man had organized another war party he could not resist the temptation to leave again. This party was so large that it didn't even take the precaution of travelling at night. Rather, it sent scouts forward and along its flanks, watching for signs of the enemy, while the main force walked leisurely along during the day and slept at night.

Several days later, while scouting the forward point for the raiders, Red Crow noticed several buffalo running in the distance and heard the faint echo of musket shots. When he passed along this news, the Bloods and Peigans painted their faces according to their own personal war medicines and set out towards the sounds of the gunfire. Approaching quietly, they observed five Shoshoni hunters busily engaged in butchering a carcass. Joyfully, the raiders swooped down upon the hapless party, who quickly dashed towards a nearby hill. Then, just as the pursuers were coming within range, a large number of enemy Indians suddenly exploded over the ridge and raced towards them.

Realizing that they were outnumbered, the Bloods and Peigans wheeled about and beat a hasty retreat. They were all afoot, while a number of the Shoshoni were mounted, and soon the horsemen caught up with the stragglers. Two Bloods and a Peigan were the first to be struck down and killed while another man was about to be overtaken when he screamed for help.

Red Crow and a few others immediately turned back, causing the enemy to pause, and during that moment of hesitation the endangered warrior was able to join the main party. Although they were in an exposed position, Red Old Man decided to make a stand, and in the fight which followed, he was the only one wounded when a ball struck him in the thigh.

The Shoshoni, satisfied at having killed three enemy without sustaining any losses themselves, gleefully withdrew from the scene, singing and chanting their victory songs. When it was safe to leave, the dejected war party carried Red Old Man to a grove of trees where they made a crude stretcher of willows and buffalo robes. With six men taking turns, they carried him in shifts from the southern Yellowstone country to the Snowy Mountains in central Montana, where they left him in a secluded wooded coulee with a man to look after him. The rest of the party then pushed on to get horses and help for the wounded leader. They had not gone far when they met a large war party of Peigans travelling with horses and women. Some of them immediately went for Red Old Man and saw that he was safely taken to his home camp farther north.

The remainder of the war party held a council and decided to retrace their route to the Shoshonis. None of them wanted to go home empty-handed and in disgrace, and all were anxious to get revenge for their ignominious defeat. Red Crow set off in advance of the party, and a few days later he caught up with the Shoshonis who were moving camp. Watching them all day with his field glasses and determining where they would camp for the night, he went back to the main party and guided it to the spot.

Quietly, the Bloods and Peigans approached the campfires, but were surprised to find that their enemy had slipped away during the night. Suspecting that a war party might be near, they had ringed the site with campfires and had moved to a new spot.

Angry that the Shoshonis had outwitted them, the war party sent scouts scattering throughout the area in search of the camp. It was too dark to pick up the trail but after scouring the countryside, the scouts discovered the village hidden along a small branch of the same stream on which the decoy camp was located.

Although the warriors wanted revenge for the slaughter of three of their party, they were primarily in search of horses, not a confrontation which might result in more killings. In recounting their war honors, the death of an enemy did not rate high on their list. Rather, the skill and courage required to perform a war deed was a more important basis for recognition. To capture an enemy's gun was the highest honor, followed by the capturing of a bow and quiver, shield, medicine bundle, or any accoutrement of war. Only after these brave deeds did the scalping of an enemy merit distinction. The taking of a horse, almost a commonplace act, had a low rating, for it was performed as much for economic reasons as for gaining a good war reputation.

Yet the Bloods and Peigans were angry enough at the Shoshonis that they were not prepared to take the horses by stealth. Instead, they went boldly among the herds and each man took all he could control. The enemy quickly learned of the raid, but when they tried to defend their camp, a Peigan shot and killed one of their leading men. As the remaining Shoshonis held back, the victorious Bloods and Peigans galloped away with their captured horses. They returned home in triumph and blackened their faces as a sign of victory when they finally approached their camps.

In the fall, after Red Old Man had recovered from his gunshot wound, he sent out word from his camp near the mouth of Two Medicine River that he was organizing another raid. Red Crow and a friend, Long Hair, joined the older relative, and with a number of warriors they travelled to Fort Benton and then south to the Yellowstone River. Passing close to Fort Sarpy, they had reached the Lonely Mountains when they ran into a heavy storm.

Realizing that the Crows wouldn't be expecting any raids in the deep snow, they scouted the region until they found an enemy camp and, true to their expectations, the horses were grazing loose outside the village. Campfires and tracks showed where the boys guarding the herds had rested during the day, but by nightfall all were sound asleep in their lodges.

The horses were hard to catch so the raiders herded them to a nearby river, to a sheet of glassy ice near a watering hole. There Red Crow roped and mounted a black-eared gelding which had slipped and fallen, but as soon as it was on its feet it bucked him off and got away with the warrior's rope.

Five horses were still on the ice, so Red Crow hurried back and grabbed a gentle one by the tail and headed it into a deep snowbank. As it struggled to its feet, he mounted and hung onto the mane as the horse galloped away to catch up with the rest of the herd which the Bloods were taking north. Some distance away, the raiders paused, giving Red Crow a chance to grab his rope hanging from the gelding and change mounts. He then turned back and rounded up the other four horses left on the ice.

The men travelled all that night and the next day to get clear of the Crows' hunting area. On the second night, while they were encamped, they saw a light to the north of them, which one man identified as a campfire. However, four boys scouted ahead and came back saying it was only a star.

Next morning they discovered their mistake, for as soon as they struck the trail, they ran into the tail of a huge Crow war party that was crossing their path. It was so large that the Bloods could not see the front of the procession. Although surprised by the small band of raiders, the Crows, who were afoot, quickly spread out to surround them. Off to one side was a low ridge with a bare strip where the snow had been blown away; the Bloods galloped for that spot and gained the low ground before their attackers reached them. Seeing that the Bloods were now in a position where they could easily ride away, the Crows did not press the attack, but proceeded on their way. All they captured was a small colt which the Bloods had abandoned in their flight across the prairie.

Red Crow had taken six horses during the raid while Red Old Man had been even more successful, acquiring two mules which were highly prized by the Blackfoot. Later, in a demonstration of generosity, the leader presented both of them, a bobtail and a split-ear, to Alexander Culbertson. When Red Crow finally reached the Fish Eaters camp on Sun River, winter had settled on the countryside and his raiding was finished for the year.

One of Red Crow's most frequent companions during these exciting days was his uncle, Big Plume. Although several years older, he was Red Crow's *tuka*, or war partner. It was the duty of such partners to look after each other in times of danger and to work as a team when capturing horses or raiding an enemy camp. If both men were armed with guns, they might take turns at shooting, so that one would always have a loaded weapon in case of a sudden attack.

In having Big Plume as his companion, Red Crow had an apt teacher. Wild and truculant, he was the personification of the wild warrior chieftain who neither gave nor expected mercy. And although his brother-in-law Culbertson was a white man, he had no hesitation in attacking trappers or traders if the circumstances were favorable.

In 1854, for example, a British sportsman named George Gore made an extensive tour through the Upper Missouri region, slaughtering large numbers of game animals on the trail. At the end of the season he camped on Tongue River in Crow territory which, in the eyes of Big Plume, automatically associated him with the enemy. Accordingly, during the winter Big Plume led an expedition to attack the camp, but unknown to him, a war party of Peigans had been there first, taking twenty-one horses. When Big Plume made his raid, the Britisher's men were on guard and the Blood warrior was shot and wounded.[7]

Successfully eluding the whites who pursued him for many miles through the deep snow, Big Plume finally made his way to Fort Benton. There, ironically, the wound made by a white man was treated by Big

Plume's sister, the wife of another white man. The warrior remained for several weeks until *Natawista* nursed him back to health.

A few years later, Big Plume was camped on the Oldman River with Red Crow's sister, Revenge Walker, and ten lodges of Fish Eaters, when they received a surprise visit from five white men on a hunting expedition. They proved to be Eastern tourists who were travelling for pleasure and had drifted into Blackfoot country.

They seemed to have no fear of the Bloods but casually pitched their camp a few yards from them on the opposite side of the stream. When Big Plume went to their tents, he was kindly welcomed and remained with them until after dark. Although the travellers could speak no Blackfoot, they communicated through signs. Next morning, Big Plume and his party had breakfast with the hunters and then, as they were leaving, the warrior suddenly drew a knife and stabbed the leader in the chest. Moments later, the other four men were dead and scalped.[8]

To Big Plume, any stranger in his land was an enemy, whether Indian, white, or half-breed.

As part of a warrior family, Red Crow had no reason to be friendly with the whites, but he never admitted raiding their camps or wagon trains. When he accompanied Big Plume, it was usually to attack enemy tribes in the constant quest for horses.

After he came back from the two raids with Red Old Man, Red Crow sought out Big Plume and the pair of them set out in search of Crow villages. A day's travel south of the Missouri, they were overtaken by a number of young Peigans who had heard they had left and were determined to go with them. As they continued south, Red Crow observed a moving camp of Indians. Keeping them in sight with his spyglasses, he noted where they camped for the night and then went back to inform Big Plume and the boys. By the time the moon was glistening in the prairie sky, the raiders were scouting the village, finding to their dismay that all the horses had been secured within the centre of the Crow encampment. While they watched, Red Crow saw three horses stray from the herd, so he quickly caught two while Big Plume took the other. These they led across a river and tied in the trees so they could return to capture more. Back at the camp, five more horses drifted away but as the Bloods went to pick them up, they were suddenly attacked by a number of Crows. Too late, Red Crow and Big Plume realized that they had fallen into a trap, that the horses had been deliberately released from the herd to draw them into the open.

Amidst a flurry of arrows and gunshots, the two Bloods dashed for the river and successfully gained the other side, where they mounted their captured horses and, driving the others before them, rode off into the night.

The Peigan boys were nowhere to be seen, but later the two Bloods learned that they had fled at the first sound of gunfire and had walked back home.

Red Crow and Big Plume made a formidable pair, daring and fearless. They liked going to war together, but the older Big Plume had wives and children to be concerned about. Besides, several families recognized him as their leader and he was in the first stages of forming his own band. In 1856, the clerk at Fort Benton noted that he "Traded with Big Feather [Big Plume] Blood Indian party, exactly 400 Robes"[9] separately from Seen From Afar's followers, who did not arrive until the next day. By 1870, Big Plume was listed as the leader of the Scabbies band, with fourteen lodges of 168 people.[10]

In the early 1850s, Red Crow had no such responsibilities; he was simply a wild young warrior who had no concern for camp life or the responsibilities of the household. Particularly during the summer season, his only interest was in war. During the balance of the year, he was a good hunter and participated actively in the religious activities of the tribe.

And whenever he visited Fort Benton with other members of the band to trade buffalo robes or horses, he joined with those who got gloriously drunk on whiskey. Both Big Plume and Seen From Afar also enjoyed their periodic debauch at the fort. Their whole way of life was tipped towards excess in everything they did. And that included drinking.

But these were mere diversions for Red Crow. His interest was in war.

5

/ A Seasoned Warrior /

The name "Big Snake" seemed to spell bad luck for the Fish Eaters. First, Seen From Afar had a running feud with a Blood leader by that name, then Red Crow had the misfortune to go on an ill-fated war party with another chief named Big Snake. The two were not related, for the latter man was from the neighboring Blackfoot tribe. But the name seemed jinxed.

His war party had gone undetected into Crow country but after unsuccessfully scouting one village, Red Crow and the others had been discovered by alert warriors and attacked. Afoot and completely unprepared for battle, the mixed war party of Bloods, Blackfoot, and Peigans lost four men before Big Snake led them to what he considered a defensive position. In fact, it was a hollow vale in the hills, completely vulnerable to attack and a perfect position for the Crows to wipe out every member of the party.

In one onslaught when a Crow was shot and killed, Red Crow dashed forward, grabbed the man's black horse, and rode away in search of a better fortification. He could see that more and more Crows were arriving at the scene and if his people did not get out of the coulee, they would soon be annihilated. Galloping along the slope, he found a natural fort not too far away and rode back to urge his friends to run for it. Some were afraid, but at last they followed the warrior to the rock-strewn slope.

The move had been unexpected and all the party reached the rocks safely, except for one straggler who was forced to find refuge in a narrow crevice. However, he was not seen and remained in the hiding place throughout the battle.

The fight lasted for the entire day, with the Crows making four mass charges on the new position. But Red Crow had chosen the defences well and the enemy was driven back with heavy losses. At one point, when the advancing line was within ten feet of the fortification, Red Crow jumped out from the rocks, at the same time pulling back his bow in a threatening manner. Hurriedly, the enemy fell back.

"A Crow called out in the Blackfeet language," mused Red Crow, "enquiring who we were. I replied that I was a Blood. He assured me that not one of us would live to tell the story of this fight, for said he, 'We have you securely and you cannot escape.' We laughed at this and taunted them to do their best, telling them that they could not hurt us, though they were as numerous as trees."[1]

The final charge was made just before sundown, after which a ring of campfires was lit around the entire fort. Derisively, one of the Crows shouted that they were going to starve the raiders out, then kill them to avenge one of their chiefs who had been slain. The Bloods ridiculed the Crows, saying, "Do your best; you're quite harmless and we have no fear of being hurt."[2]

After dark, the raiders made several attempts to escape, but each time they were observed in the light of the campfires and driven back. At last, Red Crow remembered a trick which his teachers had shown him. Selecting a large pine tree standing in their rock fortress, he set fire to the upper branches, and soon a heavy black smoke was billowing down the slope. Before the Crows had a chance to suspect its purpose, the war party followed the smoke until they reached the safety of some bushes below. Red Crow led the escape and as he left he noted with satisfaction that the Crows were still busy watching the burning tree.

By dawn, the raiders were far from the scene, and a few days later they found the main Peigan camp in the Bearpaw Mountains. Red Crow, who had gone along only as a member of the war party, had emerged its leader. Big Snake, on the other hand, was accused of cowardice and bad judgment, and his life was threatened for the way he had handled the expedition.

Red Crow bore graphic evidence of the vicious battle. His coat was tattered by bullet and arrow holes and when he unbraided his hair, a huge lock came loose in his hand, cut off by a Crow bullet.

Big Snake was humiliated by the accusations of cowardice and begged Red Crow to go with him on another raid so that he might redeem his honor. Reluctantly, the Blood warrior agreed and they set out quietly one night for the south. When word flashed through the camp next morning that the two warriors had gone, about fifty young men hurriedly left camp to join them. Five days later, the large war party reached Owl's Head, a distinctive landmark in central Montana, from which vantage point Red Crow saw two men chasing buffalo. When he reported the incident, four scouts went to investigate, but returned empty-handed, claiming that Red Crow had sent them on a fruitless search. Angrily, Red Crow slipped away alone, discovering the carcass of the bull buffalo which the mysterious hunters had killed. As he was examining it, he was joined by Big Snake, who had guessed Red Crow's mission.

After searching for most of the night the pair finally found the Crow camp, but Big Snake was reluctant to lead the attack as he feared that the criticism he had received might have weakened his supernatural power. Instead, Red Crow went ahead first, discovering five horses in a nearby coulee. As Big Snake was a married man, Red Crow gave him three, but reserved the best two for himself.

Mounted, the two warriors then circled the village, rounding up three more animals before heading north. Because the young men had insulted Red Crow by refusing to believe that he had seen the hunters, he would not go back to their war camp, but proceeded straight for the Missouri River.

He was disgusted with the performance of Big Snake, believing that he still showed cowardice in the face of the enemy. On the trail, in an attempt to make amends, Big Snake offered to trade his sacred black-covered medicine pipe for a bay horse which Red Crow had captured. The Blood accepted the offer and shifted the bundle to his own mount.

Later in the journey, the pair found another dozen stray horses and Red Crow, who was first on the scene, cut out the best ones for himself. Now, with each man driving several horses before him, they were ready to go home. As they travelled, Red Crow's captured animals proved to be more spirited than those of Big Snake but although he had a hard time keeping them together, his companion never offered to help. Finally, when Red Crow's horse was almost played out from trying to control the herd, he angrily cantered over to the Blackfoot warrior.

"Here, take back your sacred pipe," he exclaimed, "I don't want it. I have on this trip given you four horses and thought that you would help me drive mine. The animal I gave you is back with my horses. Get him and give me the one you are riding."[3]

Big Snake tried to dissuade Red Crow, but the Blood was adamant. The return exchange was made and, chastened, Big Snake began to help with his partner's herd.

Reaching the Bearpaw Mountains, Red Crow saw a war party of three Crees coming towards them. Hurriedly the horses were cached and the two warriors hid along the trail to ambush the unsuspecting party. When the trio reached Big Snake's position, Red Crow waited expectantly for the attack. But it never came; instead, the three Crees suddenly turned and darted away to safety.

Upon investigation, Red Crow learned that his clumsy companion had gone to check the horses and had exposed his position to the Crees before he could get back. In their haste to escape, they had abandoned some of their goods, but Red Crow wanted no part of them; not so proud, Big Snake picked up a striped Hudson's Bay blanket coat, moccasins, and rope. It was the last time Red Crow ever accompanied Big Snake to war.

The experiences which Red Crow gained on the warpath made him an authority on the subject. He knew all the taboos, requirements, and obligations both of the leaders and of the members. As he explained:

"Before and after starting, young men would not eat meat of the lower rib of a buffalo nor the shank of the animal, because should they do so, the corresponding parts of their own bodies would suffer and thus bring ill luck upon the party. Smoking was seldom indulged in, for it had a tendency to cause thirst and a shortness of breath.

"Each member of a party took whatever medicine outfit he possessed, such as war bonnets, shields, cross belts, and fancy clothing, all of which would be carried upon the back of the owners. Each member of a war party would take 10 or 15 pairs of moccasins and no cooking utensils were used, as the packed food was dry meat and any meat killed would be cooked over a fire on sticks."[4]

Red Crow also explained the actual procedure followed on the warpath. They normally left at daylight without ceremony, with two to four scouts travelling ahead of the party. When they saw signs of an enemy, the scouts signalled their own people by running in circles. Once this sign had been observed, the warriors stood in a semicircle and sang while the scouts approached and stated what they had discovered.

If the enemy was near, everyone dressed in his best clothes and prepared for the attack. Early morning was the most favored time to strike an enemy camp, but night was preferred for a horse raid. When horses were taken, the individual kept all he acquired and was under no obligation to share his booty with others, even if they were still afoot and had to walk back.

When the war party returned home, they entered the camp quietly and without fanfare if they had been unsuccessful. If any of their members had been killed, an advance scout arrived at a hill near the camp, held a hand outstretched and made a motion as though placing, something on the ground. Each such motion signified one dead member of the party. If they had been victorious, all the raiders painted their faces black and went into the camp firing guns. Captured horses were painted and trophies given away as soon as the warriors were among their friends.

Red Crow knew the ways of the war trail from first-hand experience, particularly in hand-to-hand combat and in killing an enemy. In all, five members of enemy tribes fell to him during his warring days. One death occurred during a raid under the leadership of a warrior named Marten. With the rest of the war party, Red Crow had been prowling through Crow territory for several days. After an attempt to ambush two horsemen had failed, Red Crow saw a single rider leaving Fort Sarpy. Lying in wait with his companions, the Blood warrior was the first to attack, shooting and killing the traveller. The man's gun he gave to a young relative, while the horse went to a Peigan in the party. Red Crow was matter-of-fact about the killing. "The man we killed was a good looking fellow," he observed, "with very long hair. He had a new white blanket tied behind his saddle; no doubt he had just bought it."[5]

During another prolonged adventure, Red Crow killed two of his enemies. On that occasion, Red Crow and a man named White Wolf from another village were co-leaders of a war party which located a Crow camp near Lonely Mountain. The party split in two, Red Crow leading his group through a backwater to the horse herd. Just as they approached the animals, a Crow who had been lying in ambush near a log saw them.

"As I looked at him," said Red Crow, "he slowly arose to his feet, gun in hand, which he cocked as he reached the upright attitude. My gun was already cocked and ready for instant use, and there we stood looking at each other for some little time. Without taking our eyes from each other for an instant, the Crow and I slowly began to back away from each other. My adversary backed towards the nearest lodge and as soon as he reached its immediate locality, he, with a spring, got behind it and took to his heels."[6]

Discovered, the Bloods fled from the village and regrouped in their secret camp. White Wolf then proposed that they attack the village the following night, but Red Crow protested, saying that it would be too well protected and that the crow birds sitting near the Blood warriors were a bad omen. When his objections were ignored, Red Crow's pride left him no recourse but to join the others. As they neared the camp, four men went to check ahead while Red Crow took another three to · scout from a nearby hill. Just as they took their positions, a massive party of Crows galloped from the trees to attack the main party below. Caught in the open, the horse raiders didn't have a chance and within minutes, the leader White Wolf, together with three other Bloods, Gambler, Singing Back, and Many Gifts to the Sun, and two Blackfoot, Good Young Man and Many Tail Feathers, were killed. A seventh man was badly wounded.

Only one Blackfoot managed to reach the hill, giving Red Crow a total force of five men. As they ran, a mounted Crow bore down on the Blood leader but before he could fire, Red Crow dropped the enemy's horse with an arrow in its kidneys. A second horse suffered a similar fate. Then, breaking through the Crow lines, the five men gained the safety of tall timber and eventually reached home.

Seeking to avenge the killing of the six warriors, within a few days of his safe return Red Crow joined another party led by Blackfoot chief Big Road and went back to the same area. By this time, there was snow on the ground, and although the raiders found a secret war camp used by the previous Blood party, their tracks were seen and the fort surrounded. Logs had been piled three feet high around the lodge, but in spite of this, the first Crow volley broke the leg of Weasel Horse and the arm of Medicine Shield.

As the Bloods and Blackfoot had been unprepared for the surprise attack, a Blackfoot medicine pipe bundle had been left hanging from a tree. One of the Crows dashed out to capture it, but as he was returning to safety another Crow tried to grab it away from him. While they were scuffling, Red Crow took careful aim and shot one of the men dead.

During the fight, a bullet struck a log near Red Crow's head and a splinter of wood gashed his forehead. "I do not consider that I was wounded by the Crow," stated Red Crow, "for his bullet did not touch me. This was the only time in my life that my blood flowed in battle. I still boast that no enemy ever struck or wounded me."[7]

The attack continued into the night, with the Crows building a large fire nearby. At one point, an enemy made the mistake of walking between the fort and the fire, silhouetting his entire body. Red Crow promptly shot and killed him.

Next morning, the Crows tried to trick the raiders into thinking they had left, but when this didn't work they besieged the fort for another two days before finally withdrawing.

In spite of the harrowing experience, Red Crow was unwilling to go back home until he had picked up some horses. Accordingly, with a small group of men he went to another Crow village, passing the grisly remains of a scalped Blackfoot who had been killed the previous day.

Unfazed, Red Crow witnessed the scalp dance taking place in the enemy camp and, while everyone was watching it, he ran off most of their horse herd and at last returned home in triumph.

Red Crow had demonstrated that he would show no mercy to an enemy; but he was also willing to risk his life for his comrades. The opportunity arose on one occasion when Running Rabbit led an expedition to the south. Red Crow was asked to scout ahead with two other men — Rough Hair and Flying White Buffalo. All three were lying on the edge of a hill, observing the country with field glasses, when the Crows suddenly came up behind them. As the three began to run, one of them was wounded and cried for help. Disregarding his own safety, Red Crow went back to his comrade and slowly walked him along while bullets flew all about them. Finally, another ball struck the warrior in the hip and he was unable to move.

As the wounded man was placed in a sitting position, he begged his comrade not to leave, so Red Crow stayed with him, dodging and moving about to avoid being hit. Taking courage at seeing only two men, one badly wounded, a short, dark-faced Crow dashed forward to wrench the gun out of the injured man's hand. Instantly, a dozen Crows set upon the hapless victim, but Red Crow rushed forward, firing a wild shot and sending them scattering.

At that moment, just when the situation seemed hopeless, the main Blood party arrived and drove back the Crows, killing two in their flight. After it was over, Red Crow went back to see his wounded friend. He was dead.

6

/ Treaty With the Long Knives /

During the early 1850s, when Red Crow's life was occupied by a continuous series of battles and raids, other events were taking place which would ultimately affect the future of his tribe.

The first of these was a treaty with the United States government — or "Long Knives" as the Blackfoot called them. This took place at Fort Laramie and was negotiated in 1852, ostensibly with all of the Plains tribes in United States territories. Unfortunately, word of the great council reached Fort Union too late for Alexander Culbertson to choose delegates from the Blackfoot and Gros Ventre tribes. In spite of this, a large hunting reservation for the Blackfoot was designated on the advice of Culbertson, Indian superintendent D. D. Mitchell, and Father Jean De Smet.

The treaty recognized Blackfoot territory as a vast area south of the Missouri River to the source of the Yellowstone — a region, interestingly enough, which did not include the true Blood, Peigan, and Blackfoot hunting grounds north of the Missouri.

Immediately following the treaty, proposals were made for the construction of a railroad from the Mississippi River to the Pacific coast, and in 1853 the United States government began surveys to determine which was the best route. The northern proposal, from St. Paul, Minnesota, to Puget Sound, would pass directly through the Blackfoot area.

Isaac I. Stevens, governor of Washington Territory, was placed in charge of the survey, while Alexander Culbertson became his special agent. Realizing that any survey parties sent out by the government would immediately be attacked by the warlike Blackfoot, Culbertson arranged to contact the various chiefs and to explain the situation to them. When Red Crow's aunt *Natawista* learned of the mission, she demanded that her husband include her.

"My people are a good people, but they are jealous and vindictive," she said. "I am afraid that they and the whites will not understand each other; but if I go I may be able to explain things to them. I know there is danger, but my husband, where you go I will go, and where you die, I will die."[1]

The involvement of *Natawista* in the successful negotiations added to the prestige and influence of the Fish Eaters who by now had almost reached equal status with the Buffalo Followers, in spite of their smaller numbers.

The result of the survey activities was a decision to hold a formal treaty council during October of 1855. In order to notify the tribes about the negotiations, James Doty was despatched to contact as many Blackfoot bands as possible. On his return, he estimated that the Bloods consisted of 270 lodges, the Blackfoot 290 lodges, and the Peigans 290 lodges.[2] Of these, the Blackfoot estimate, gained only from hearsay, was probably high.

Doty located the main Blood bands of Fish Eaters and the Buffalo Followers in the region west of Cypress Hills. He also found small bands on the Oldman and Bow rivers, some camped with Peigans or Blackfoot.[3] But it was clear from his survey that most of the Bloods were together under Seen From Afar and Bull Back Fat.

The 1855 treaty was called primarily to establish peace among the tribes in the area. Besides the Bloods, Peigans, and Blackfoot, those represented included the Gros Ventre, Flathead, Pend d'Oreille, Nez Perce, and Cree tribes. Significantly, no members of the Crow tribe were there.

If Red Crow attended the council — and he likely did — it was only as a twenty-five-year-old warrior whose uncle was the chief. Much of the business covered in the treaty would have held little interest for him, such as the establishment of a new common reserve for the Bloods, Peigans, and Blackfoot in an area bounded by the source of the Musselshell River, the International Boundary, the Rocky Mountains and the mouth of the Milk River. A further area south of the reservation was set aside for ninety-nine years as a common hunting ground for all tribes.

In addition, the treaty called for the Indians to live in peace with each other and with the United States government. It called for unrestricted passage by white people through the territory, and permission to build missions, schools, Indian agencies, and military posts. In exchange, the Blackfoot were to receive $20,000 annually in goods and provisions, with another $15,000 set aside for education and agriculture. The treaty also limited the availability of intoxicating liquor and provided for compensation for those who suffered losses through Indian attacks.

The only part of the treaty which might have had any significance for Red Crow was the provision for a peace treaty with neighboring tribes. But as the Crows were not a party to the agreement, this primary enemy was still fair game.

Seen From Afar, one of the major participants in the negotiations, doubted whether the Bloods were ready for peace in any form. "As far as we old men are concerned," said the forty-five-year-old chief, "we want peace and to cease going to war; but I am afraid that we cannot stop our young men. The Crows are not here to smoke the pipe with us and I am afraid our young men will not be persuaded that they ought not to war against the Crows. We, however, will try our best to keep our young men at home."[4]

When the chiefs were designated to sign the treaty on behalf of the Blood tribe, the shift in political influence was revealed. Seen From Afar, leader of the Fish Eaters, was the most prominent Blood signatory of the group, and the only representative of his band. Bull Back Fat, nominally chief of the Buffalo Followers, was third to sign, following after his brother-in-law, Father of Many Children. Thus the split in the Buffalo Followers band was formalized in the treaty. The document was also signed by Many Spotted Horses, leader of the turbulent Many Fat Horses band, and by Calf Shirt of the Lone Fighters. Both of these bands had been closely associated with the Buffalo Followers, if not actually offshoots of them. The other major signator, Medicine Calf, was a warrior leader of the Many Tumors band.[5]

Although the Buffalo Followers band still accounted for the major segment of the Blood tribe, the leadership of the Fish Eaters under Seen From Afar, and the chief's obvious influence through Culbertson, had placed his band in the superior position.

In a practical sense, the treaty had very little effect upon the Bloods, except for providing them with annual annuities. Within ten days of the signing, Blood war parties were back raiding the Crow camps, and during the winter they killed five Assiniboines — a tribe which, like the Crows, had been absent from the treaty.[6]

Red Crow tried to honor the treaty where it applied to tribes which had been present at the signing. For example, he led a mounted war party of seven men into the Cypress Hills where they observed a single Cree rider. Mistaking a Blood scout for one of his own, the man rode right into the enemy camp and was taken prisoner. However, when Red Crow saw that he belonged to a tribe which had signed the treaty, he only took the man's rifle and set him free. This was a singular act for a man who in the past had shown no mercy to an enemy; it was, however, a significant measure of the effectiveness of the treaty.

Yet the peace could not be maintained indefinitely between such inveterate enemies as the Crees and Blackfoot. Some time after the signing, the Crees raided a Blood camp on the Red Deer River, and Red Crow immediately organized a war party of seven "to see what we could do in the way of retaliation."[7]

Travelling northeasterly, they sighted a solitary man on the trail and when he was surrounded, he was found to be an unarmed Cree. Disgusted at the man's cowardice, Red Crow turned him over to the younger warriors, who argued heatedly whether to kill him or release him. In the end, Red Crow painted the man's face black, figuratively gave him to the Sun as a gift, and released him.

"I guess he had never heard of one of his people falling into the hands of the Bloods and living to tell about it," he laughed. "No doubt, he wonders to what good circumstances he owed his really remarkable escape. I do not think that he would ever have guessed the truth — *that he was not worth killing!* "[8]

Continuing their journey, the war party came to a camp of Assiniboines, with whom the Bloods at that time were at peace. Although greeted coolly, the warriors were invited into the village, where they learned the Cree horse raiders whom they were pursuing were also camped.

On the first day, while Red Crow was visiting in the lodge of an Assiniboine chief, an old man holding a large knife came in and sat near the entrance where he began chanting. When Red Crow was told that he was seeking vengeance for four sons who had been killed when trying to raid the Blood camps, he scoffed at him. "What are you talking about?" he asked indignantly. "Did I tell your sons to come and steal my horses? Did I ask them to come a way down there and get killed?"[9]

On the following day, Red Crow attended a war dance put on by the Cree raiders, even though the Bloods were warned by a friendly Assiniboine that they would probably be killed if they got too near. As they watched, the enemy warriors danced close to the Bloods, pointing their guns and acting in a threatening manner. Then, when the drumming ended, they began to recount their war exploits, taking particular delight in relating their victories over the Bloods, Blackfoot, and Peigans.

One Cree who could speak Blackfoot uttered the name of a Blood that he had killed and described the horse the man was riding. This was too much for Red Crow to bear:

"I got mad at once, peeled out my knife and walked into the circle, shouting, 'You are no good! You are no good!' I then began to sing and yell and count coups at them. I told them that I have killed three Crees in one day. It was a lie on my part, but I was an eye witness of the event that I referred to, so I was able to discuss it to their satisfaction. They thought I spoke truly. I only wanted to make them angry because they had succeeded in making me so. I told them lots of lies about the Crees that I had killed, scalped, and taken guns from.

"The women all began leaving the camp, taking their children away to the bush. On a pole in the dancing circle was an H.B.C. flag, and on the ground beside it was a bow and thirty arrows. I went and, with a yell, cut loose the flag and took possession of the bow and arrows. Then, turning my back upon the Cree dancers, I told them once more that they were no good and stalked away with their flag."[10]

Later, when he challenged the Crees to fight the seven Bloods in the village, there was no response, and the party left as haughtily and arrogantly as they had come.

The 1855 treaty may have promised peace, but as long as there were young warriors like Red Crow, there was no way the provisions could ever have been enforced.

By this time, Red Crow was a stocky man in his mid-twenties, with a solid build which fitted him well for the warpath. He believed in keeping himself fit to endure the long walks to enemy territory, the days of constant vigil, and the moments of hand-to-hand combat when sheer physical strength was needed.

Like his uncle Seen From Afar, Red Crow was not a tall man, standing about five feet nine inches. Neither was he handsome and, in fact, he was always sensitive about his appearance. As a young warrior who had accomplished tremendous feats against his enemies, he could have been a "dandy," sitting in full view of admiring girls and combing his long black hair. Or dressing in his finest regalia and proudly parading around the camp during a quiet afternoon. But Red Crow did none of these things, for he was too conscious of his looks, considering himself ugly. He had wealth and prestige, but possessed too much pride to expose himself to ridicule.

Although the role of a warrior was in keeping with his family's tradition and placed him on an equal footing with Seen From Afar and Big Plume, yet among his own brothers, none was so dedicated to gaining honor through war as was Red Crow. His younger brothers, Kit

Fox and Sheep Old Man, were handsome men with limited war records who could glory in the reputation of their prestigious family. For Red Crow, however, dedication to war seemed almost to be a compensation for his plain appearance. Perhaps others did not see him that way, but for such a proud and sensitive man, his only shortcoming seemed to be his lack of handsome features. However as a warrior, he had few peers. His reputation was such that his partners were often older men like Rainy Chief, whereas the usual custom was for warriors to travel with companions their own age. Most warriors would have been disdainful about taking a younger partner, but because of Red Crow's war record his one-time teacher was pleased to be with him.

Red Crow was first married during the mid-1850s, to Water Bird, or *Ohkipiksew*, a daughter of Calf Shirt, great warrior leader of the Lone Fighters band.[11] It was a union of two wealthy families and whether dictated by love or politics, its result was to solidify the position both of Red Crow and of the Fish Eaters band. Perhaps he was referring to his own situation when he commented that "The usual custom was for parents of the girl to choose a young man whom they think desirable for a son-in-law."[12]

Similarly, Red Crow described the procedure when the children of two wealthy families, such as his, were married.

"If these people are well-to-do," he stated, "they will send their daughter away with a complete lodge and its furniture, horses, saddles, travois, robes, fine garments, and the best of everything that they and their relatives can produce.

"When all is ready, sometimes after weeks, even months, of preparation, the damsel's father and mother take her and the horses and property to the lodge of her intended. The bride rides one horse and leads another, drawing a loaded travois. Arrived at their destination, someone comes out of the lodge and takes the horses and unpacks the goods. The bride at once enters and seats herself next to her husband, and her parents take their departure for home."[13]

According to Red Crow, a return payment was made on the following day when the relatives of the groom tried to outgive the givers by offering more and better horses than those that came with the girl.

As was the custom, Red Crow's first bride became his main wife, or his "sits beside him" woman. But the Blackfoot tribes were polygamous, partly for economic reasons and also because of the shortage of men through incessant warfare. If a man was rich, he often took five or six wives, sometimes sisters, so they could tan hides, feed guests, and perform the many household tasks of wood gathering, making and decorating clothing, and caring for the children.

A short time after his first marriage, Red Crow took a second wife, the daughter of a Blood named Sun Old Man. Unlike his first wedding, the second had no political undertones, as Sun Old Man was simply a member of the Many Children band. Yet this second union had a great impact upon Red Crow's life, for it presented him with his first son in a most unexpected way.

Not long after the marriage, a sickness swept through the camps and among those who died were Sun Old Man and his wife. Orphaned by the tragedy was their young boy, Crop Eared Wolf. Tearfully, Red Crow's young wife asked if her younger brother could be taken into the family. Red Crow readily agreed, adopting the boy as his own and raising him to follow in his footsteps. Born in 1845, Crop Eared Wolf became a herder and guard of his adoptive father's horses and eventually established his own impressive war record.

Although Red Crow later had children of his own, Crop Eared Wolf was always his favorite. In fact, Red Crow probably saw much of himself in the boy — a fearless fighter, good ceremonialist, not very tall and somewhat plain, he embodied many of the leadership traits which Red Crow also possessed.

Crop Eared Wolf took part in five raids during his lifetime, but unlike Red Crow, he did not escape unscathed. In his first raid against the Sioux, he was shot in the chest while leading a horse out of the enemy camp. In his next raid he killed a Cree on the South Saskatchewan River, capturing three horses and riding gear. After that, he killed and scalped a Crow Indian, took two horses and a mule from the Sioux, and killed a woman in a raid on a Cree camp near the Cypress Hills.[14] On at least one of these raids, he was accompanied by his famous warrior father. Red Crow continued to go to war during his early married years for he could always find members of his close-knit family to look after his herd and to provide meat for his lodge while he was away. As a wealthy man who seemed to grow richer with each successful raid, he could afford to hire horse guards. If there was sickness in the family, Red Crow's religious uncle, Scalp Robe or *Motokani*, could always be called to help.

And quietly in the background during all this period was Red Crow's father, Black Bear. Much older than Seen From Afar, he too had once been a great warrior but now lived as a quiet and respected family leader. Although overshadowed by his younger chieftain brother, Black Bear maintained strict leadership of his own small family unit.

Red Crow had no political aspirations at this period, for the Fish Eaters already had an overabundance of leaders in the three brothers, Seen From Afar, Big Plume, and Black Bear. Rather, Red Crow's interests were in warfare, ceremonialism, and horse breeding. He was not a leader, but simply a wealthy young warrior with a growing family.

7

/ Unsettled Years /

The signing of the 1855 treaty with the Americans brought about a number of changes in the southern hunting grounds during the next few years. The pact opened the way for government and missionary activities, bringing more and more white people into the Upper Missouri region.

As far as the Fish Eaters were concerned, the most important event was the retirement of Alexander Culbertson from the fur trade in 1858 and his decision to leave the country. Culbertson had amassed a fortune of some $300,000 and, taking his Blood Indian wife with him, he moved to Peoria, Illinois. There they purchased a magnificent nine-room mansion with hundreds of acres of lawns and gardens. Red Crow's aunt exchanged the buffalo-skin tepee and the adobe dwellings of Fort Benton for drawing rooms, carriage houses, servants, and stablemen.

While Culbertson's departure may not have had a direct effect upon the political stability of the Fish Eaters, who now dominated the Blood tribe, the family was to miss the steadying influence of the trader during the coming confrontations with white settlers. Over the years, Seen From Afar had remained suspicious of the white man, in spite of having a white brother-in-law. On one occasion in 1846, when visited by Father Nicholas Point, the Blood chief responded to the stories of Christianity with the skeptical comment:

"What the Blackrobe tells us is the truth? How is it that he tells the truth when the truth has never come from the mouth of a single white man?"[1]

His cynicism was confirmed in his dealings with United States government Indian agents. Although the treaty had stipulated the distribution of $20,000 in goods annually, the presents were often shoddy or impractical. The calico cloth proved to be flimsy; the face paint was inferior to the type handled by the traders; and such items as fish hooks, coffee, and thread were of no practical use to the Indians.[2]

Yet more troublesome than the broken treaty promises were the increasing numbers of whites who arrived during the early 1860s. A false report of gold in the summer of 1862 even sent eleven experienced miners through the heart of Blackfoot country, almost to the North Saskatchewan River. The unsettled conditions caused some of the Blackfoot tribes to gravitate more to the north, but there they found that during their years on the Upper Missouri, the Crees and Assiniboines had consolidated their positions near Fort Edmonton and Fort Pitt. Formerly a trading party could go to either British trading post with only minimal danger of attack, but now they found the last fifty miles swarming with their enemy.

Their northern troubles started in September 1860 when Old Sun, a leading chief of the Blackfoot, was killed going to trade at Fort Edmonton.[3] In retaliation, a Blackfoot revenge party struck a Cree camp, slaughtering twenty of its inhabitants.[4]

Just as the white man was blamed by the Bloods and Peigans for their problems on the Upper Missouri, so did the Blackfoot and Sarcee blame the British for the death of Old Sun. The result was described by one of the traders:

" .. the Blackfeet who have always come in large numbers to the Fort armed, brought no provisions or anything else, [they] came apparently only to get Rum and threatening to kill the people ... the Blackfeet have been un-bearable for the last 3 years or more, always getting worse & worse, destroying our crops, stealing our Horses & doing everything they could to annoy us, in order to provide a quarrel so as to kill us. They now threaten openly to kill whites, Halfbreeds or Crees wherever they find them, and to burn Edmonton Fort. All this is owing to the Blackfoot Chief that was killed here last fall by the Crees."[5]

Late in 1862, another party of Blackfoot leaving Fort Edmonton was attacked, suffering one dead and another wounded, while early in 1863, a Blackfoot family was set upon by Assiniboines in sight of the fort, their dogs killed and goods stolen.

The situation on the American side was no better, except that the confrontations were taking place between the Indians and settlers, rather than with enemy tribes. Late in 1863, the chief factor at Fort Edmonton believed that the events in the south would eventually drive all the Blackfoot north.

"The Fur traders at Fort Benton find it more profitable to sell their wares to the Miners than to throw it away on the plain Indian Trade, and as the Indians find their treatment altered, they will in all probability be driven up this way and trade with us."[6]

The first of the Blood chiefs to return to the British was Red Crow's old teacher, Rainy Chief, who arrived at Fort Edmonton in April 1864. Although his party came through unscathed, another mixed band of thirty Bloods and Blackfoot who went there in the same month wasn't so fortunate. No sooner had they finished their trade and were leaving the post than they were raided by a war party of Crees. In the attack, one Blood was killed and the horse herd stolen.

In the south the problems between the Blackfoot and the Americans finally erupted into open warfare in the spring of 1865. By this time, the Bloods were spending most of their time on British soil, travelling to Fort Benton only to trade, or to the Crow on horse raids. When an epidemic of measles swept through the camps in that year, it caused scores of deaths and was blamed on the presence of the whites. This caused the simmering resentment to explode and provided a perfect excuse for a war party of Bloods to raid the residents of Fort Benton in April 1865, triumphantly netting forty horses.

In retaliation, two of the town's frontiersmen vowed to kill the next "hostile" Indian who came to the village. The man proved to be a Blood chief who arrived in May and was promptly murdered, his body being thrown into the Missouri River. When the news of the chief's killing reached the Blood camps on the Belly River, a revenge party was formed. Its function was exactly the same as any revenge party retaliating against an enemy tribe: to kill as many people as possible. The victims did not need to be the actual perpetrators of the original deed; the fact that they were from the same tribe was sufficient. This time, the enemy was the white man, and any fair-skinned victim would be appropriate. Normally, such a revenge party might discover a lone prospector or trapper and be satisfied with his death. This time, however, the captain of a Missouri sternwheeler had been carrying out plans to establish a trading post at the mouth of the Marias River and had dispatched ten woodcutters to the site to begin work.

Red Crow's father-in-law, Calf Shirt, was the organizer of the revenge party and, according to one observer: "The chiefs of the Fish Eaters, Fat Horses and Black Elk bands marshalled about 200 men, led by their chiefs ... Medicine Sun, Un-es-tina [White Calf], and Big Snake."[7] When the scouts discovered the embryo fort on April 23, the Bloods initially decided to pass it by and to concentrate on the settlers closer to Fort Benton. However, when the woodcutters opened fire, the raiders swept into the camp and killed them all.

The Montanans were shocked by the wholesale killing, proclaiming that a "Blackfoot war" had started, and they were partially correct, for it proved to be the first of many skirmishes in the hardening relations between the Americans and the Blackfoot during the next four years. News of the raid travelled quickly, with the Montanans taking steps to organize a volunteer army to launch a counterattack. Similarly, the British traders soon heard of the incident, commenting: " . . . the Slave Indians have killed eleven American miners (*sic*) somewhere near Fort Benton and are determined to kill the Americans on every opportunity."[8]

The records do not show if Red Crow took part in the raid, but with the Fish Eaters involved, he likely was there. Red Crow at this time was thirty-five years old, with a reputation for being a fearless warrior in battle. The enemies of the Blood tribe were his enemies, regardless of whether they were Indian, half-breed, or white. Besides, when the raiders returned to their huge camp on the Belly River after killing the woodcutters, they immediately set out on another war expedition to chastise the Crees in the north. And Red Crow admitted that he was in the second raid, so there can be little doubt that he took part in both.

In later years, Red Crow related his war experiences to a white trader, but he was careful to mention only those battles which took place with enemy tribes. To extol his prowess in killing white settlers would have been politically unwise during the reservation years.

The second raid took place because of an incident which happened at the time the Bloods were busy attacking the woodcutters. Far to the north, a small camp of Sarcees had been raided by the Crees and one of their leading chiefs had been killed. As a result, when the Blood raiders returned from the south, a deputation of Sarcees was waiting for them, calling for a grand council of the Blackfoot, Bloods, Peigans, and Sarcees to see if a revenge party could be formed.

Red Crow described the procedure: "If one of the tribes in the confederacy was injured by hostile tribes, their chiefs went to the camp of their friends — that is, to the other tribes of the Blackfoot nation — and told the story of their grievance and solicited assistance, at the same time presenting an ordinary plain pipe filled with tobacco and lit. The friendly chiefs, if in sympathy, smoked the pipe and promised support in war."[9]

In this instance, the Bloods were flushed with the success of their Montana raid and enthusiastically agreed to join the expedition. One of their prominent warriors, Bull Shakes His Tail, was chosen as leader, and Red Crow volunteered to be an advance scout. For the first time, he was accompanied into battle by his twenty-year-old son, Crop Eared Wolf.

Travelling northeast, the party discovered a Cree camp near Round Timber and some of the younger warriors had to be restrained forcibly when they wanted to make a frontal attack. Instead, when intelligence was received that there was a sheltered trail which led almost to the edge of the village, their leader chose this route for their advance. Red Crow described the scene:

"We covered the fronts of our light-coloured horses with buffalo robes and made the party look like buffalo. We walked our horses towards a certain hill that was between us and the camp. Several times we had to take to open prairie, but we walked slow, like buffalo, and all lowered our heads and horses' necks, and reached the hill, behind which all of us painted and made ready for action.

"I crawled to the top of the hill, leading my horse, and saw the Cree men away running buffalo. Near us and between us and the camp were ten people who had been getting water and were now on their way back to the village. I signalled to the men and continued watching the water-carriers, there being two women on ahead, then six women and a mounted man, and a single woman bringing up the rear — nine women and one man, all loaded with water kegs.

"As soon as I saw our party behind the hill mounting, I sprang on my horse and started down the opposite slope after the women. I had a good start of any of our party and was soon close behind the water-carriers, who had heard nothing and were slowly plodding along. Soon, however, our big party came around the hill and in sight, and as they broke into a run, all yelling, the women looked behind. Throwing water kegs in every direction, they ran for their lives.

"I rode up alongside of the hindmost woman and shot her dead with my flintlock and called to Eagle Head to take her clothes and scalp. The man who was mounted escaped to camp, but the nine women were all killed."[10]

Close behind Red Crow was his son Crop Eared Wolf who shot another woman in the breast, killing her instantly. A few moments later, they discovered another group of women also bringing home water and these were surrounded and slaughtered. Red Crow was satisfied with the one killing, but for the rest of the massacre he rode around the outside of the action, driving back any who tried to escape. In the end, every woman was killed.

As the chief factor at Fort Edmonton reported on June 17, " . . . a war party (eighty in number) of Slave indians have been down country, fell in with a camp of Crees or Stonies, not certain which, and killed twenty-nine of them, principally women and children going for water."[11]

As the Bloods started for home, they were pursued by the Crees. "We went slow," recalled Red Crow, "allowed them to catch up to us, then turned and charged them, killing their leader."[12] In the fight, however, Crop Eared Wolf was shot in the leg and walked with a limp for the rest of his life.

The violence which erupted during the spring of 1865 in Blackfoot country continued unabated throughout the year. Six prospectors camped on the Oldman River were killed by Bloods, while farther south another Blood war party on the Dearborn River killed Charles Carson, a nephew of the famous Kit Carson. And near the end of the year, a major intertribal battle at Three Ponds resulted in the deaths of twelve Blackfoot and twenty Crees, besides wounding Father Lacombe, an Oblate missionary who was in the Blackfoot camp when the fighting started.[13]

In an attempt to halt the bloody confrontations which were occurring on the Montana frontier, the Americans presented a revised treaty to the Bloods, Peigans, and Blackfoot, reducing the size of their reservation and opening the southern part of the hunting grounds for white settlement. At the same time, annuity payments were increased to $50,000 annually for a period of twenty years.

As far as the Bloods were concerned, the treaty was a farce. The only Blackfoot to attend, a man named Fish Child, was not even a chief, while the Bloods were represented only by a number of Buffalo Followers who happened to be in the area at the time. Although Bull Back Fat and Father of Many Children signed for the Buffalo Followers, neither Seen From Afar nor any of his minor chiefs were present. According to one native informant: "In 1865 there were many Bloods around the South Peigan Agency. Big Nose, a South Peigan, said they would get another treaty at Fort Benton, so these Bloods went along and signed this treaty. But they were not representative of our tribe."[14]

It soon became obvious to the American government that the revised treaty had no popular support, for the attacks on miners and traders continued unchecked. When authorities in Washington learned of the situation, they refused to recommend ratification of the document.

In 1866, the Bloods were involved in several more killings, while their allies, the Peigans, under Bull's Head attacked the government's Sun River farm and killed one of the attendants. The chief's goal had been to obtain revenge for three Peigans who had been hanged by prospectors on Sun River.

Seen From Afar was concerned about the hardening of relations in Montana so in the summer of 1866 he kept his band in British territory, and for the first time in many years he tried to take his trade to Fort Edmonton. The Buffalo Followers, who normally ranged farther north than the Fish Eaters, went to the post in August, trading some 845 pounds of dried meat, 168 buffalo robes, 14 horses and other sundry articles. However, the expedition had been fraught with trouble, starting with a Cree who stole a horse from outside the gate while the Bloods were trading. Four days later, another Cree war party waiting in ambush opened fire and killed a number of men.

When Seen From Afar and the Peigan chiefs heard about the harrassment, they refused to travel through the Cree-infested country to reach Edmonton. At the same time, not wanting to venture into the hostile region along the Missouri, they went north as far as the Battle River and sent a messenger to the fort asking that a trading expedition be sent out to their camp. On October 11, a train of thirty Red River carts, manned by fifteen Cree half-breed employees of the fort, set out on the perilous journey.

At this time, there was a significant difference between the enemies of the Blackfoot nation in the north and those in the south. While the Bloods and Peigans had no love for the Cree half-breeds, they saw their real enemies to be the Americans. The Blackfoot and Sarcees, on the other hand, cared little about the conflict on the Missouri but despised their northern enemies.

The Bloods and Peigans were pleased to see the trading party arrive. Red Crow's family and others in the camp had amassed a good supply of dried buffalo meat during the fall hunt and were anxious to trade it for much-needed supplies. Although a number of Blackfoot camped nearby greeted the half-breeds with hostility, the traders proceeded directly to Seen From Afar's lodge where the chief smoked a pipe of peace with them. Pointedly, the only Blackfoot to smoke was Crowfoot, a young chief.

The trading began with the southern tribes and about twenty-five horses and a supply of dried meat had been exchanged when an angry mob of Blackfoot led by Big Eagle and Big Swan intervened. Pillaging the carts of all their goods, the Blackfoot were about to attack the Cree half-breed traders when Seen From Afar intervened. Claiming that the men were there at his invitation, he offered them the protection of his warriors and stood alone in the clearing, openly defying his Blackfoot allies. At that point, he was joined by Crowfoot, who berated his tribe for their actions, exclaiming, "You people are dogs! The whites should sweep you off the face of the earth."[15] Then, with guards provided by the Fish Eaters and Crowfoot, the traders left the carts and returned empty-handed to Fort Edmonton.

After the abortive attempt to negotiate a treaty in 1865 had failed, the United States government tried again three years later, this time making a concerted effort to see that the Indian leaders were all present. The provisions were similar to the proposals of 1865, offering added annuities in exchange for a smaller reservation.

The leading southern Blood chiefs were present, including Red Crow's two uncles, Seen From Afar and Big Plume, and his father-in-law, Calf Shirt, from the Lone Fighters. By this time, Bull Back Fat was dead and his brother-in-law, Father of Many Children, did not attend, as the Buffalo Followers normally hunted in British territory. After the treaty had been signed by the Bloods and Blackfoot, the document was sent to Washington but, like its predecessor, it was never ratified.

Until the International Boundary was surveyed in 1874, the Bloods were active participants in the United States treaties and were considered to be "American" Indians. "Not until the line was fixed," said an informant, "were we cut off the lists."[16] But it was clear that the Bloods were beginning to spend more and more time on the British side. The vast buffalo herds near the South Saskatchewan, plus the open hostility of the Montana settlers, made it both necessary and advisable for the Bloods to congregate in their traditional campsites along the Belly and Oldman rivers.

By the late 1860s, Red Crow's role was still that of a warrior. In times of danger he was among the first to defend the camp or to take revenge against an enemy. Now that he was in his thirties, he did not go to war as much; he already had a large horse herd, family, and prestige.

As a wealthy man, he had several wives during his lifetime. Besides Water Bird and Crop Eared Wolf's sister, he married Spear Woman, *Sapapistatisaki*; Pretty Woman, *Anaohkitsi*; Longtime Pipe Woman, *Misumakoyinmaki*; and a Stoney named Lazy Woman. In later years, his favorite wife was Singing Before Woman, *Ikaenikiwaki*, who was twenty-two years younger than he.[17] From these marriages he had at least three boys and four girls, as well as several adopted children.

But Red Crow was not yet a peaceful family man, as his uncle Seen From Afar had become. Over the years, he had seen the chief change from a fearless warrior to a quiet leader who presided over the councils of his tribe. Perhaps he was still a warrior at heart, but now that he was almost sixty, he seemed more concerned with protecting his camp and settling disputes within the tribe. Red Crow, on the other hand, could still see only the glories of war.

In the spring of 1866, a mixed party of Bloods and Blackfoot attacked what they thought was a small Cree camp at the edge of the Red Ochre Hills. The warriors killed two women, who had been cutting wood, and were following a snow-filled coulee to the top of the hill when they were ambushed. The lodges they had seen were part of a larger camp, and soon the Crees surrounded the coulee and slaughtered dozens of Indians in the snow.

When the survivors straggled back to the Blood camp on the Red Deer River, a grand council of the Bloods, Blackfoot, Peigans, and Sarcees was held, with the result that a large revenge party was formed, with Red Crow as one of its prominent members. They travelled southeast, and as they approached the South Saskatchewan, two scouts named White Calf and Eagle Head went ahead, returning with the scalp of a pregnant Cree woman they had killed. They reported the location of the Cree village, and a small segment of the revenge party swept into the camp at daybreak, then appeared to retreat in the face of heavy fire. Believing that the raiding party was a small one, the Crees charged across the plains towards the fleeing Blackfoot, but suddenly found themselves surrounded by scores of warriors who poured from the nearby hills and coulees.

Red Crow was in the midst of the attacking party. Picking out three Crees, he raced after them and when one stopped to fire a wild shot, Red Crow took careful aim and killed him. A young relative picked up the dead man's rifle, while Red Crow took a fine painted buffalo robe. When the battle was over, scores of Crees were dead and Red Crow's brother-in-law, Insect Wild Ear, was the only victim from the revenge party.[18]

On another occasion, the Fish Eaters were hunting near the Sweetgrass Hills in early autumn when a war party of nine Crees stole a number of horses from a Peigan camp farther south. Not realizing where the Bloods were camped, the raiders passed near them on their way to the Cypress Hills and were noticed by an observant scout.

The morning had been frosty and foggy, and Red Crow had just returned from hunting buffalo when the scout rushed into camp, announcing the presence of the enemy party. Red Crow had left his buffalo runner saddled and tied to the lodge, so he was mounted in an instant and off in pursuit. He was soon joined by his uncle, Seen From Afar, his father-in-law, Calf Shirt, Big Snake, Many Spotted Horses, a number of other Bloods, and seven Peigans who had been pursuing the raiders.

They had no trouble finding the trail in the frost-covered grass and when the path split, Calf Shirt's men took one route, while Seen From Afar, Red Crow, and five others followed the second one. When the morning fog lifted, Red Crow set off on the flank to scout and from a hill he saw a Cree skinning a buffalo. He signalled the other Bloods and Peigans with a mirror, and they rushed upon the camp, finding eight other sleeping warriors and a ninth, a young boy, doing the butchering. When the Crees jumped to their feet, Red Crow, who was armed only with a knife, urged his party to attack, but some of the Peigans were afraid of the risk and held him back.

Moments later, when the Crees were mounted, Red Crow tore away from those restraining him and was in hot pursuit. Then, just as he was closing in on two stragglers, the Crees decided to make a stand and the Blood warrior was forced to retreat. On the open prairie, the Crees were quickly surrounded and, realizing that escape was impossible, they killed their horses to use a barricades. Throughout the day the Bloods and Peigans attacked on foot, then retreated in the face of heavy fire. At last, just before sundown, a rush was made on the barricades and the last of the Crees were killed in hand-to-hand combat.

In his anxiety to pursue the enemy, Red Crow had gone into the fray unarmed, except for his knife. As a result, he did not kill any of the nine, but he did capture a number of articles on the battlefield. On their return to the camp, all the warriors painted their faces black and celebrated the occasion, for they had killed nine Crees without losing a man.

The five years of conflict with the Americans came to a tragic culmination during the winter of 1869-70, after a prominent Montanan, Malcolm Clark, was shot and killed by Peigans. Claiming that fifty-six whites had been killed and more than a thousand horses had been stolen by Bloods and Peigans in that year alone, the United States marshal appealed for help from the military. In response, Colonel E.M. Baker conducted a mid-winter attack on the Peigan camp of Heavy Runner, believing it to be that of Mountain Chief who was accused of harboring the man who had killed Clark.[19]

After the raid on the morning of January 23, 1870, there were 173 men, women, and children dead on the prairies. Remembered as the Baker massacre, the killings so shocked the Blackfoot tribes that any thought of retaliation was forgotten. The "Blackfoot war" that had started with the blood of ten woodchoppers, ended with the death and dispersal of an entire Indian camp.

8

/ Whiskey /

Although the Bloods had been trading with white men for more than 100 years, Red Crow seldom saw them within his tribe's hunting grounds along the Belly River. Although the tribe was pressed from the south by American traders and from the north by the Crees, the rolling plains within view of the Belly Buttes seemed to be isolated from the realities of the world around them. Near the Buttes, the land was thick with buffalo; the river bottoms offered ample firewood and campsites; and the eagle soaring overhead seemed to symbolize the harmonious relationship between man and nature.

This idyllic isolation ended during the summer of 1869, when two Montana traders came north to open a trading post. By this time, industrialists in the eastern United States had discovered the value of buffalo hides for making machinery belts; the skins were tough, durable, easily obtained, and new techniques made tanning easier. Until that time, the shaggy robes had been in only limited demand for clothing and blankets.

Also during the 1860s, the end of the Civil War brought many adventurers to the Upper Missouri country, men who were looking for a quick dollar. Whiskey had always been a stock in trade for the old British and American companies, but now it became the principal commodity in dealings with Indians. Yet as long as they were doing business in Montana, diligent marshals and sheriffs had managed to keep the illicit trade under control.

In 1869, two Sun River merchants, John J. Healy and Alfred B. Hamilton, realized that if they could move their trading operations north of the forty-ninth parallel, they would not be subject to American law. The northern territory was ostensibly under British control but was in the process of being transferred to the newly-formed Dominion of Canada. During the interim, a legal vacuum existed, with absolutely no form of law enforcement north of the border in the valuable buffalo ranges of the Bloods and Blackfoot.

When Healy set out for the north, he was well prepared. Not only did he have an ample stock of whiskey and repeating rifles for sale, but he had married the daughter of Many Spotted Horses, the influential Blood leader of the Many Fat Horses band. Lavishing on his father-in-law $300 worth of trade goods, Healy received permission to build Fort Whoop-Up near Red Crow's birthplace, a favorite wintering ground of the Bloods at the confluence of the Oldman and St. Mary rivers.[1]

Yet the existence of the fort was initially only a minor irritation when compared with another unwelcome visitor to the northern plains.

Smallpox.

First signs of the dreaded disease appeared in the late summer of 1869 when some Blackfoot purportedly stole a blanket from a smallpox patient on a Missouri River steamboat. Quickly the disease spread through the Blackfoot nation and by fall it had struck almost every camp and every lodge.

Sir William F. Butler, sent out by the Canadian government to investigate the conditions in the West, painted a poignant picture of the disaster.

"By streams and lakes, in willow copses, and upon bare hill-sides, often shelterless from the fierce rays of the summer sun and exposed to the rains and dews of night, the poor plague-stricken wretches lay down to die — no assistance of any kind, for the ties of family were quickly loosened, and mothers abandoned their helpless children upon the wayside, fleeing onward to some fancied place of safety."[2]

Seen From Afar was on a trading expedition to Fort Benton when the epidemic started and his first concern was for his favorite daughter, Otter Woman, who was camped on the Belly River. Just before leaving for the north, the chief had four dreams in which he was told he would be spared from the plague as long as he stayed on the Missouri. On the fourth morning, the great Blood leader rode through his camp, shouting:

"My people! My children! The Sun looks down upon me. I am going away. My dreams have told me not to cross the Milk River Ridge; four times I have been told. But I have no power to stay here. I must go to my daughter. My people! I will not see you again. Live good lives and do the best you can."[3]

Travelling with his wife, Red Crow's uncle reached the Belly River, where he found Otter Woman safe and well. He immediately turned about and went south with her but while they were camped for the night on the Milk River Ridge he began to complain of pains in his back. "I have the sickness," he said quietly. "I will die today."

Later, his grieving widow and daughter carried his body back to the Belly River, placing it in a scaffold burial just below the Belly's confluence with the St. Mary.

The Bloods were stunned by the news that their greatest chief was dead, even though John J. Healy wryly observed that it was "a good thing, as his death made the settlement of the north easier."[4]

The obvious candidate to replace Seen From Afar was one of his three brothers. However, Big Plume had already formed the nucleus of his own sub-band, while Scalp Robe was a ceremonialist and healer, never a political leader. In the end, the members of the Fish Eaters band chose Black Bear, Red Crow's father, to be the new chief.

A survey made by the American army during that winter revealed just how many Bloods were dying in the smallpox epidemic. Whereas in 1854 they had had a population of 6,800, they were now reduced to 2,544 persons. Of these, 264 were in the Fish Eaters band under Black Bear, while another 168 were followers of Big Plume. In all, some 924 persons were in the Fish Eaters or its offshoots. In the other bands, the Buffalo Followers under Father of Many Children had 336 persons; the Lone Fighters of Calf Shirt, 288; the Many Tumors of Medicine Calf, 336; the Many Fat Horses under Many Spotted Horses, 276; and the Black Elks, 216.[5] Clearly, Seen From Afar had elevated the Fish Eaters in his lifetime to a leading position within the tribe.

The tragedy of his uncle's death deeply affected Red Crow. He had always admired Seen From Afar as a great warrior and leader. While his own father was quiet and dignified, his uncle had been like a wild and untamed spirit. Black Bear was a good man and a good father, but he did not inspire the tribe in the way that Seen From Afar had been able to do. Even as he grew older and more reserved, Seen From Afar had still commanded the respect and devotion of everyone around him.

Black Bear's leadership of the Fish Eaters band was sadly short. He kept them together during the tragic winter of 1869-70, when smallpox killed scores of his followers and whiskey from the new trading post created untold misery for the others. Then, early in 1870, he too began to show the terrible symptoms of the pestilence and in a few days, he was dead. He was one of the 1,200 members of the Blackfoot nation to perish in an epidemic which seemed to carry off so many of the chiefs.

Twice within a year the Fish Eaters band was without a leader. The succession of a chieftainship did not automatically go from father to son, nor did it even need to remain within the same family. Yet the children of chiefs were often rich, generous, and had learned how to govern. In the end, the people themselves made the decision, not by ballot, but by following the man of their choice when he moved camp.

The candidates for leadership of the Fish Eaters were limited. Seen From Afar had left no sons, while neither the Big Plume nor Scalp Robe families were seriously considered. The likely persons were Black Bear's two eldest boys — Red Crow and Sheep Old Man.

There was no doubt that Sheep Old Man, the younger of the two, aspired to the chieftainship. He was intelligent, wealthy, and generous and, although his war record could not compare to that of his older brother, it was still a credit to him and his tribe. Red Crow, on the other hand, was a forty-year-old veteran of the warpath. Shrewd, tough, proud, and rich, he had proven he could be merciless in dealing with an enemy, yet was a good family man, an excellent hunter, and a capable provider for the camp.

He was, in every sense, a warrior. Others may have gone to war, but their lives were balanced through their interests in hunting, gambling, or ceremonialism. Red Crow, too, participated in these pursuits, but they seemed to be mere interruptions to his career as a fighting man. He was a leader of his own warrior society — a group of young men of equal age who guarded the camp — and while he no longer needed to raid the enemy for horses, he was a willing participant in any retaliatory attacks on tribal foes.

He was an outgoing, friendly man when he was with his family and relatives, but more often he was found in the company of other warriors. Many comrades of his youthful raids had become chiefs, so his camaraderie and influence extended far beyond the Fish Eaters camps.

In the days following Black Bear's death, Sheep Old Man actively sought support from members of the band in a campaign to become leader of the Fish Eaters. He gave feasts in his lodge, loaned horses to the needy, reminded old friends of his past deeds, and urged his relatives to stand with him. Red Crow, on the other hand, remained aloof from the political manoeuvring which seemed to be taking place all around him. He sadly mourned the death of his father, and when he was asked by friends in the camp if he would lead them, he quietly agreed.

When the time came to move camp, the choice had been made. The

Fish Eaters, almost to the last lodge, chose to follow Red Crow. As a warrior he was stern and uncompromising; the people saw a need for the same qualities in their chief. Sheep Old Man also had leadership capabilities, but too often he had shown himself to be petty, spiteful, and vindictive.

Perhaps the traders had been glad when Seen From Afar died, for they knew he distrusted the whites and would not hesitate to meet them in battle. Yet in the spring of 1870, when Red Crow became chief of the band, he was potentially as dangerous as any warrior leader. While he did not hate the whites as his uncle had, he was an arrogant and fearless man who would face danger or death if the occasion arose. As a chief, he embodied all the qualities of endurance, strength, and decisiveness that had carried him through his turbulent young years.

Sheep Old Man was angry when the Fish Eaters picked Red Crow. Taking his brother Not Real Good and his sister Revenge Walker with him, he abandoned the camp entirely and moved to the opposing band, the Buffalo Followers. Because he was wealthy, he was welcomed by them and although he was not their chief, he hoped that eventually he would become their leader.

Encouraging him was his sister, who was known as a "manly-hearted woman." She rode like a man, hunted buffalo, and was an excellent shot. Married to Running Bird, she ruled her husband's life and wielded a powerful influence over other members of the family. Yet she could never dominate Red Crow, so relations between the two were often strained.

As a political chief, Red Crow found that he was now called upon to be mediator in intraband squabbles, as well as to keep a benevolent watch over the elderly and the widows in camp. Because he was rich, he could afford to loan horses to the needy, either when moving camp or for hunting, and as his family brought in more meat than it needed, the surplus could be distributed to the poor or the unlucky.

Whenever the band moved camp, it was Red Crow's responsibility to indicate the time of departure, usually by having his wives strike his own lodge. On the trail, if any question arose about hunting, watching for enemy war parties, or making an unexpected stop, he would call the leaders of the warrior societies together to discuss it with them. Once the matter was resolved, the warriors hastened to carry out the chief's instructions.

If important matters arose affecting the entire tribe, not just the Fish Eaters, a council was called of all the band chiefs in the vicinity. There, decisions usually were made by consensus, rather than by individual action. There was no single head chief of the Blood tribe; each chief was simply a leader of his own band. Besides his own following, however, Red Crow came to exert considerable influence over the Hair Shirts, Six Mouths, and Many Brown Weasels bands which had split off from the parent group. With the death of Bull Back Fat during the epidemic, the only other chiefs who had influence comparable to Red Crow's were Father of Many Children and Medicine Calf. Together, the three could rightly have been described as the head chiefs of the tribe.

The first test of Red Crow's leadership came in the autumn of 1870, while his smallpox-ravaged band was camped on the Oldman River, not far from Whoop-Up. Upstream from him were the Buffalo Followers and Lone Fighters, while a few miles on the other side of the fort were the main camps of Peigans who had fled across the line after the Baker massacre.

The Crees and Assiniboines knew that the Blackfoot tribes had been weakened by smallpox, so a large party under Piapot, Big Bear, Little Mountain, and Little Pine had set out to attack them. Camping within a few miles of Whoop-Up, they sent their scouts to reconnoitre, but in their haste to report the location of the Bloods, the scouts failed to observe the well-armed camps of Peigans farther along the stream.

Just before dawn, the huge enemy raiding party struck the Fish Eaters camp, killing a relative of Red Crow's and two or three women. Red Crow rallied his outnumbered warriors but was hard pressed until joined by Medicine Calf and Bull Back Fat. At this point, the battle might have been a standoff, both sides being relatively equal in warriors and firepower. But the sounds of gunfire brought the Peigans from St. Mary's River and by dawn the Cree-Assiniboine raid had turned into a rout. The Peigans, armed with American repeating rifles, soon cut down the Crees with their inferior muzzleloaders, and when the fight was over, dozens of Crees and Assiniboines had been slaughtered in the river and in isolated groups along the valley. Final estimates were that between two and three hundred Crees were killed, while the Bloods and Peigans lost about forty.[7]

In the months that followed his election, Red Crow found that leadership during the whiskey trading era was an impossible task. Like other chiefs, his authority became meaningless when faced with drunkenness, murder, and senseless internal strife. As more and more forts dotted the Belly River country, carrying such ominous names as Standoff, Slide Out, and Robbers' Roost, whiskey became the dominant part of Indian life. As a priest, Father Scollen, explained:

"The fiery water flowed as freely, if I may use the metaphor, as the streams running from the Rocky Mountains, and hundreds of the poor Indians fell victims to the white man's craving for money, some poisoned, some frozen to death whilst in a state of intoxication, and many shot down by American bullets." The Indians, he continued "sold their robes and their horses by the hundreds for it, and now they began killing one another, so that in a short time they were divided into several small parties, afraid to meet."[8]

There were many graphic examples to substantiate Scollen's description. In 1872, several families of Fish Eaters split off from the main camp because of discord resulting from whiskey. Two brothers, Many Shot and Young Sun, became the family leaders and were constantly hanging around the whiskey forts. At last, when they had nothing to trade, they waylaid other Indians and stole their liquor.

One day, while camped near Blackfoot Crossing, they were drinking with a Blackfoot chief named Bull Horn when an argument arose and Bull Horn's companion was killed. The fight attracted the attention of some other Blackfoot who were also drinking, and in their stupor they thought that their chief had been killed. By the time the two Bloods had returned to their camp, a drunken Blackfoot war party had descended upon it, killing most of their men and some of the women.

Similarly, the Many Fat Horses band was virtually destroyed through intraband dissension. The leader, Many Spotted Horses, remained aloof from much of the drinking, but one of his sub-bands, the Many Children, was notorious for its drunken brawls.

In 1871, the Many Children became jealous when Many Spotted Horses's daughter married No Chief and the young man became a favourite of their leader. A short time later, when No Chief went to the Many Children camp to pick up some whiskey, an argument developed between him and a man named Hairy Face. In the ensuing scuffle, No Chief shot and killed his attacker. Moments later, he was set upon by the dead man's drunken relatives and when it was over, No Chief had been killed, but not before seriously wounding Hairy Face's brother Big Snake and killing the man's father, Not Afraid of the Gros Ventres. As a result of the incident, Many Spotted Horses went to the Lone Fighters band and eventually became its leader.

The early 1870s were years of alcohol, fear, and bloodshed. One visitor to a trading post claimed that in a single winter, seventy Bloods had died through the direct influence of liquor. Some of the chiefs were convinced that the traffic would eventually wipe the entire tribe from the face of the earth.

In fact, an American who visited Whoop-Up in 1871 felt the same way. "Far from being an injury to the United States," he said of the whiskey traders, "they were a great benefit, as they keep the Indians poor, and kill directly or indirectly more Indians of the most warlike tribe on the continent every year, at no cost to the United States Government, than the entire regular army did in ten years! The Indians . . . were British subjects and had a right to exercise all the freedom of British subjects; and if the British subject sees fit to pay big prices for poor whiskey and get immensely drunk on the Saskatchewan plains, it is the subject's affair, and not that of the United States."[9]

A typical trader of that period, Joe Kipp, built his fort at the confluence of the Belly and Oldman rivers, in the heart of Blood hunting grounds. It consisted of a series of log houses, forming three sides of a square, with all the windows facing in towards an enclosed courtyard. While still under construction, the fort was fired upon by irate Bloods, but once it was finished, they became Kipp's best customers.

The trading room in the fort had a high, bulletproof counter, with shelves of tobacco and cloth behind it. Adjoining was one room for whiskey and another for piling the furs which had been bought.

"Although some whiskey was used in the Indian trade," observed a friend of Kipp's, "the greater part of the spirits sold was alcohol, properly diluted with water, the amount of the latter depending upon the condition of the purchaser. If he was sober, he got four parts of water to one of the spirits; if partly drunk the proportion was six to one, and if wholly drunk, it was eight or ten to one. To the alcohol and water a small amount of burnt sugar and oil of bourbon was added to give it a whiskey color and flavor."[10]

Other ingredients added at times were tobacco, peppers, molasses, ginger, red ink, castile soap, and bluestone.[11] In some cases, the liquor itself, if taken in excessive quantities, could kill but if not, the effects were such that many Indians froze to death while in a drunken stupor, or became involved in violent fatal disputes.

Red Crow drank as excessively as the others in his tribe. Just as he had thrown caution to the winds when he went to war, so did he cast aside all restraints when he drank. He was usually inclined to embark on a wild debauch for a few days and then remain sober for weeks afterwards, rather than drink steadily. But alcohol became a regular part of his life, just as it did with other members of his family. His uncle, Big Plume, was often drunk; his father-in-law, Calf Shirt, killed some of his own wives while intoxicated; and his brothers, Kit Fox and Sheep Old Man, were frequent visitors to the whiskey fort.

It was almost inevitable that the violence of the whiskey traffic would also enter Red Crow's lodge.

On one occasion, he had been to a trading post and had become quite drunk. During the night, some young men who were also intoxicated decided to come to his tepee to beat him up.

"Old Maycasto is too drunk to help himself," one of the Indians said, "and he has been pretty mean to us sometimes; we will tie him up and get even with him."[12]

One of the men made a move towards the sleeping chief, but Red Crow's warrior instinct had not deserted him and in his stupor he suddenly pulled his revolver and killed his attacker on the spot.

During another drinking orgy, two brothers who were relatives of Red Crow staggered in to visit him. After they were seated, one on either side of him, the chief offered his pipe to them to smoke, but the first one refused, pointing the stem disdainfully at Red Crow. At that point, the other brother drunkenly arose and fired a shot at his host, missing him but mortally wounding Red Crow's wife, Water Bird. Red Crow then shot and killed his assailant while the other man escaped into the darkness.[13]

In 1872, the tragedy of the whiskey trade struck again when Red Crow's uncle, Big Plume, was killed. He had been in his winter camp on Sheep River, not far from the big rock at Okotoks, when some drunken Blackfoot came looking for liquor. Big Plume tried to force the carousers out of his camp but in the melee he was shot and killed. The man who had taught Red Crow the intricacies of war and who had successfully escaped injury when raiding his enemies, perished from a wound inflicted by a member of his own nation. Sheep Old Man and Not Real Good, who were in the village at the time, tried to find the killers, but their identities were never discovered.

Most of Big Plume's followers joined Red Crow's band, but Sheep Old Man persuaded the dead chief's widows to come with him to the Buffalo Followers. After being cared for by him for some time, the widows eventually married him.

During the dissension within his family, Red Crow's youngest brother, Kit Fox, had remained with the chief. However, during 1872, Red Crow became convinced that the young man was having an affair with one of his wives. They were camped near a whiskey post at the mouth of the Highwood River one day when both men got drunk and had an argument about the chief's suspicions.

Realizing how sensitive Red Crow was about his appearance, Kit Fox taunted him about his ugliness and, to emphasize the point, he reached drunkenly across the campfire to strike him in the face. Fiercely proud, whether drunk or sober, Red Crow exploded in rage, grabbed Kit Fox by the hair, and pulled him to the ground. Then, picking up one of the stones from the fireplace, he smashed him on the head again and again until his brother was dead.

Still drunk, Red Crow dragged the body out of the lodge and left it lying outside, saying: "I'm sorry I had to kill my brother, but I had warned him not to touch my face."[14]

The killing caused an even greater rift between Red Crow and his family. As a result, their feud was often the source of gossip and speculation in the Blood camps.

A year later, when Sheep Old Man, Not Real Good, and Revenge Walker were camped near a trading post at Calgary, Red Crow and the rest of the Fish Eaters band arrived to trade for whiskey. By this time, Revenge Walker's husband had abandoned her and she was being courted by the trader at the fort, D. W. Davis.

That evening, while drinking in one of the tepees, an older relative of Red Crow's named Owns Centre Painted Lodge claimed that the chief had accepted horses from Running Bird for Revenge Walker's hand in marriage when she was still a little girl, but had victimized her by failing to give a similar number of animals in return when the marriage actually took place.

Revenge Walker was told the gossip the following day and, without checking the veracity of the story, she mounted her black horse and angrily rode over to her chieftain brother's lodge to confront him. Red Crow, however, had prudently left the camp in order to avoid a family quarrel. Claiming that Red Crow had become rich because of her dowry, Revenge Walker began shooting his horses and was stopped only when Sheep Old Man intervened.

"Now we will have trouble," Sheep Old Man told her. "We had better move our tepees away from our relatives."[15] So they went to the Highwood River.

A few days later, Sheep Old Man decided to go to Calgary for whiskey, and when he did not return, Revenge Walker sent Not Real Good to search for him. In the meantime, Sheep Old Man had met Many Dust and some other relatives and had stayed with them until he was roaring drunk. Then, when ready to continue his journey to the post, he warned the others not to follow him.

Not Real Good arrived at Many Dust's camp just after Sheep Old Man had left, so he quickly rode off in pursuit of his brother. In his befuddled state, Sheep Old Man thought he was being followed by the drunken Indians he had just turned away, so turning in the saddle, he shot his brother in the shoulder. Still not realizing what was happening, he then climbed off his horse and stabbed Not Real Good in the other arm. Only then did Sheep Old Man come to his senses enough to realize that he was assaulting his own brother.

As soon as she heard the news, Revenge Walker rushed to the side of her wounded brother. She wanted to pursue Sheep Old Man and to kill him, but she was unable to find his trail. Later, she discovered that he had fled from the area.

Revenge Walker stayed up all night tending her brother's wounds, and in the morning, the young man spoke to her.

"Niss,"[16] he said, "you have had trouble with Red Crow, our brother, and now you are having trouble with Sheep Old Man, our brother. Now there is only you and I. We have other relatives but they may not like us because we have been having trouble with our brothers. They may stick with them.

"Running Bird, your husband, has gone. You take my advice and marry the white man who keeps the store, Davis. They must have good medicine and I may then get better."[17]

"Brother," responded Revenge Walker, "you and I are only two. I don't want to see you die. I will do as you advise, even though I don't like to marry a white man."[18]

True to her word, Revenge Walker married D. W. Davis, and under his treatment Not Real Good recovered. In fact, a white visitor to the fort met the wounded man, stating that he was "a fine looking young fellow" with his thumb and wrist opened up by a knife slash and suffering from a bullet wound on the point of his shoulder.

"His wound was dressed by Mr. Davis," said the traveller, "and a bed made for him. He was at the post for several weeks, receiving every possible attention. He may have been quarrelsome, but he showed gratitude for the treatment received, as he sent Mr. Davis a present of a fine horse."[19]

And it was probably Revenge Walker the visitor was referring to when he described a young girl at the fort. "She had a dress of a very light colored and well turned buckskin. It was made to conform to the shape of the body. It was trimmed with the usual buckskin fringe, but had also a double row of elk's teeth in a semi-circle beneath the neck and quite a number on the sleeves. Taken all in all, it was quite a spectacular looking dress, and one that would have attracted attention anywhere."[20]

Red Crow had been saddened by the dissension in his family, so when he learned that Revenge Walker had married Davis, he decided to end the feud. He gathered up a number of tanned dresses and shirts and twenty horses and went to his sister. There he embraced and kissed her and asked her to forget their differences. When Not Real Good supported his brother, she relented; although the two never became close friends, the open hostility was at an end.

With the marriage of Revenge Walker, Red Crow now had a brother-in-law who was the chief trader for I. G. Baker and Company, and his aunt, *Natawista*, had returned from Illinois and had married another whiskey trader named Fred Kanouse. Alexander Culbertson had gone broke through gambling and in 1869 both he and his wife came back to Fort Benton. Finally they had split up and *Natawista* had come north to live with Red Crow. There she met Kanouse and became one of his Indian wives.

A man who saw *Natawista* at a dance was amazed at her appearance: "You should have seen her dress," he exclaimed. "It was the Dolly Varden style, a large figured chintz just short enough to display the gorgeous stripes of a balmoral petticoat which in its turn was also just short enough to show two very small feet clad in moccasins and the end of a pair of leggings beautifully worked in beads. She also had on a heavy black velvet loose-fitting overcoat and over this a most brilliant striped shawl, the stripes being about three inches broad and alternately red, blue, green, and red, with a narrow line of yellow between each colour. Her head gear consisted of a small plaid shawl. The other titled aristocrats were dressed also in gorgeous array, but perforce they yielded the palm to Madame."[21]

During the early 1870s, some of the enemy tribes considered the whiskey-weakened Bloods to be easy prey. More and more raids were made on their camps, and enemy buffalo hunters became openly defiant in entering Blackfoot country. But Red Crow — chief and warrior — was always ready to turn back a foe. In October of 1871, he learned that a party of Crows was in Blood territory on the upper waters of the Milk River. Organizing a force of some sixty warriors, he struck the unsuspecting camp in a surprise attack at dawn.

"The onslaught was so terrific," said trader George Houk, who came on the scene a day later, "that those of the Crows who were left alive fled, snatching the skins of their tepees and leaving the poles standing, not having sufficient time to take these with them."[22]

Although a few Bloods were wounded, none were killed, but the losses to the Crows were enormous. "On the prairie, were the bodies of horses by the score slain in the general slaughter of the Crows. Indian braves lay with their faces stretched to the sky with their scalps removed by the victorious Bloods."[23]

Houk claimed to have counted sixty dead Crows on the battlefield near the Benton Trail and said that "Red Crow was the greatest chieftain of them all, when compared with the rest of the chiefs of the Indian tribes."[24]

Another incident with intruders took place in 1872, when the Bloods encountered a party of some 100 half-breeds, 15 or 20 Crees, and a white man, John Kerr, in their territory. Throughout his life, Red Crow distrusted the Cree and Metis, and the encounter only confirmed his worst thoughts about them. The Fish Eaters met the northerners while buffalo hunting near the South Saskatchewan. During the trading, Edouard Dumont, brother of the famous leader Gabriel, bought a grey stallion from Red Crow in exchange for two cart horses and a quantity of other goods. However, Dumont had only one horse with him and promised to take the chief back to his camp for the other. The two men were riding together to the Metis village when one of Dumont's men rode up saying that trouble had broken out with some of the Blood women who claimed they had been swindled. At that point, Red Crow wanted to call off the deal, but was finally persuaded to spend the night at the enemy half-breed village and to return with the second cart horse in the morning.

About midnight a Cree warrior crept into Dumont's camp and, amid shooting and yelling, made off with the grey stallion. In the morning, Red Crow demanded his other cart horse, claiming that a deal had been made and that the stallion had been stolen from Dumont, not him. The half-breed, on the other hand, refused to go through with the agreement, and Red Crow angrily stalked back to his own camp.

Shortly after his return the Bloods decamped, and five young Crees who had spent the night with the tribe mysteriously disappeared and were never heard from again. "The Crees had met their end," observed the white trader, "for revenge must have run high on the frustrated chief's return."[25]

The years of the early 1870s were the most demoralizing ones ever experienced by the Blood tribe. The initial destruction caused by the smallpox epidemic, followed by the tremendous social and economic upheaval of the whiskey trade, created untold anguish and heartache. Bull Back Fat, the great leader of the Buffalo Followers, was murdered by a fellow Blood in a drunken quarrel; Red Crow's father-in-law, Calf Shirt, chief of the Lone Fighters, was shot and killed by whiskey trader Joe Kipp; and many other families were torn apart by strife and dissension. When Father Scollen travelled to their camps, he mourned, "It was painful to me to see the state of poverty to which they had been reduced. Formerly they had been the most opulent Indians in the country, and now they were clothed in rags, without horses and without guns."[26]

To Red Crow, the period was a devastating one. When it began he was a proud and arrogant warrior, but in the intervening five years he had killed his brother and two fellow tribesmen in drunken quarrels, and had seen the deaths of his father, two uncles, his wife, and his father-in-law.

It had been a shattering, traumatic experience, and although it had not shaken his deep-rooted pride, it had made Red Crow realize that the Bloods could never return to their old ways. They could defeat such enemies as the Crows and Crees, but they were no match for the massive destruction created by alcohol, smallpox, and the incursions of the white man.

Sometime during that period, Red Crow's attitude changed. Where previously he had believed that all problems could be settled quickly with a gun or scalping knife, he came to realize that these were no solutions for the changing times. Perhaps his responsibility as a chief provided him with a different viewpoint; perhaps the tragedy in his own family made him realize the futility of needless bloodshed; or perhaps he was simply growing older.

"I have had enough war and trouble in my time and know what it is," he observed with a note of sadness. "That is why I try to keep the young men quiet; they do not know what they say when they talk of war."[27]

9

/ Red Coats /

The chaos and demoralization on the prairies had not gone unnoticed in Ottawa. Even while the Canadian government was negotiating with Imperial authorities to gain control of the West, it realized that protection would have to be afforded its inhabitants. Until 1870, legal responsibility had rested with the Hudson's Bay Company which, although a no-nonsense corporation, had found it to be in its interest to maintain friendly relations with the various Indian tribes. The trouble in Blackfoot country had started just as the Hudson's Bay's responsibility was ending.

Yet even before the transfer had been made, the prime minister, Sir John A. Macdonald, had considered sending a body of mounted riflemen to Fort Garry — the largest settlement on the plains — from which point they could maintain law and order. By 1871, after the first plan had been abandoned, he watched the deteriorating conditions on the frontier with concern. "There must be organized ere long for the North West a Mounted Police," he said. "With emigrants of all nations flowing into that country, we are in constant danger of an Indian war, and that commenced God knows where it may end."[1] Reports by the Hudson's Bay Company, missionaries, and special investigators, finally caused the prime minister to dispatch the adjutant general of the Canadian Militia, Colonel P. Robertson-Ross, to make a personal inspection of the West.

When the officer reached Rocky Mountain House late in 1872, he was told that the Blackfoot tribes had "lost 221 of their people by death last year, 133 from disease and 88 from murders committed in drunken brawls and from the effects of liquor; so much for Yankee Whiskey Traders."[2] A major portion of the violent fatalities had occurred among the Bloods, with forty-six deaths from liquor. Of course, the bare statistics conveyed none of the tragedies of demoralization and debauchery which had become a way of life for the tribes. Yet Robertson-Ross's concise report of conditions resulted in the Canadian government passing an Act to establish a police force in the spring of

1873. By winter, the first contingent of the newly-formed North-West Mounted Police had reached Red River, and by the summer of 1874, a force of 300 men was prepared to make the 900-mile march west to Blackfoot country.

A missionary, John McDougall, was commissioned to notify the tribes that the Red Coats were on their way, but it is likely that he contacted only his own docile Stoneys and the neighboring Blackfoot who were camped on the Bow River. The Bloods found out they were coming, but no one in authority explained to them their motive or purpose. In Montana in the 1860s the arrival of a military force had meant disaster — first in protecting the white man so that he could illegally trespass on the vast Blackfeet Reservation, and later in slaughtering Heavy Runner's peaceful camp at the first light of dawn.

So when the tired and footsore contingent of police first entered Blackfoot country from the east, they were the object of fear and consternation. On one hand, stories had drifted down from the Blackfoot and Stoneys, saying that these men were coming in peace to drive away the whiskey traders. On the other hand, the Americans were spreading wild stories about the land being taken away from the Indians.

The result was that during the police's historic trek, no effort was made to contact them. As one officer noted while still on their journey, "Talks of our designs and rumours of our intentions have been circulated amongst them to such an extent, that they have been frightened away from us altogether."[3]

When at last the police reached the Oldman River and began to build their fort, the first message received from the Indians was: "What are you doing here? Do you mean peace or war?"[4] When finally assured that the missionaries, not the whiskey traders, had been telling the truth, curious Indians began drifting cautiously into the fort. When a Blackfoot named Three Bulls reported that men were selling whiskey farther north, the prompt action of the Red Coats in arresting the Americans was ample proof that they meant what they said.

For the first time in five years, the Belly River country was free of whiskey! Where only a few weeks earlier, the traders had been doling out the rotgut in exchange for buffalo robes and horses, now the land was as dry as the arid plains in summer. Not a drop of whiskey could be found north of the boundary line.

The first tribe to contact the Police officially was the Peigans, on whose land the force had settled. In a meeting between Colonel James F. Macleod, the commander, and Bull's Head — the chief who had attacked the United States government farm in 1866 — a friendly relationship was established. Bull's Head not only gave permission for the police to stay for the winter and to use the trees for logs and firewood, but he bestowed his own name, *Stamixotokan,* upon the soft-spoken officer.[5]

Sometime during November, before the bands went into their winter camps, the Bloods also met with Colonel Macleod. Red Crow and Medicine Calf were there, and it is quite likely that Father of Many Children and Many Spotted Horses, the other leading chiefs, attended as well. Colonel Macleod explained the procedure followed when he met such chiefs:

"Upon being introduced they all shake hands and invariably express their delight at meeting me. They then sit down, and my interpreter lights and hands the chief a pipe, which he smokes for a few seconds, and then passes to the others, and all remain silent to hear what I have to say.

"I then explain to them what the Government has sent this Force into the country for, and endeavor to give them a general idea of the laws which will be enforced, telling them that not only the white men but Indians also will be punished for breaking them, and impressing upon them that they need not fear being punished for doing what they do not know is wrong.

"I then tell them also that we have not come to take their land from them (an intimation they all receive with a great pleasure), but that when the Government wants to speak to them about this matter, their great men will be sent to speak to them and that they will know the intention of Government before any thing is done.

"The chief then stands up and shakes hands with every one and makes a speech, expresses his great delight at our arrival, tells how they were being robbed and ruined by the whiskey traders; that their horses, robes, and women were taken from them; that their young men were continually engaged in drunken riots, and numbers of them shot; that their horses were gradually decreasing in numbers, and that before long they would not have enough to chase the buffalo, and would have no means of procuring food — that all this was now changed, and as one old chief expressed, suiting the action to his words, 'Before you came the Indian crept along, now he is not afraid to walk erect.'

"After the chief has finished, I make him and his warriors a few presents of clothing and tobacco, and a further quantity of tobacco in proportion to the number of his followers."[6]

As Medicine Calf expressed his feelings, "Before the arrival of the

Police, when I laid my head down at night, every sound frightened me; my sleep was broken; now I can sleep sound and not afraid."[7] Similarly, Red Crow heard Macleod's words and believed him.[8]

After the meeting, the Bloods scattered into small bands to find winter quarters where they could hunt buffalo. Medicine Calf took his band north to the Highwood River, while Running Rabbit led twenty-seven lodges south of the line to Medicine Lodge Creek. The remainder camped along the Belly, with neither Red Crow nor the other chiefs having any desire to remain near the new police fort. As one Mounted Policeman explained during the winter, the Indians "are afraid of the traders and know the traders are afraid of us, so that in their eyes we are no common men."[9]

Even before the year was finished, the positive effects of the police presence were being felt. For the first time, horses were being imported from Montana, as the Bloods used their buffalo robes to build up their depleted herds, rather than to buy whiskey. The killings stopped, the camps were quiet, and a slow task of rebuilding began.

The few Bloods who went south of the line provided an interesting contrast. Not only were there local traders to contend with, but some of the Americans who had been trading on Canadian soil actually followed Running Rabbit and his band across the line. As a merchant on Birch Creek complained in January 1875: "I have this day been informed by Indians that on Medicine Lodge Creek, and in close proximity to several Camps of Indians, Six White Men have commenced building a house or houses for the purpose of illegal traffic with Indians, their principal stock in trade being whiskey. These White Men are from the North and have been driven to this side on the account of the presence of British Troops at their former field of operation."[10]

But in Canadian territory, the winter was a quiet one. The Blackfoot, under Crowfoot, visited Fort Macleod in early December and the chief, after establishing friendly relations with the commander, brought his band to spend the winter nearby. He was the only leader who immediately sought the benevolent protection of the police; even his fellow head chief, Old Sun, chose to winter in the north.[11]

When whiskey had been available, the Indians had ruined their lives for it, yet when the police halted the illicit trade, only a few made any effort to pursue the deadly brew. In fact, the last liquor to flow from the region was carried away in a mixture of humor and pathos. Shortly after their arrival, the police caught two whiskey traders and ordered that their large cans of alcohol be dumped into the Oldman

River. A number of Bloods watched incredulously as the liquid, for which some had once given everything they owned, gurgled into the clear water. Quickly, some of the warriors grabbed tin cups and stood in the water downstream, savoring their last, albeit diluted, taste of the rotgut as it splashed and bubbled its way toward the sea.

Like the others in his tribe, Red Crow had drunk whiskey to excess when he could get it, yet when it was gone he thanked the Police for taking it away and made no attempt to buy it from traders who were still operating in Montana. And throughout the rest of his life, he followed that same principle: if it was there he drank it; if not, he was content to do without.

With the arrival of the police, the Bloods soon resumed their old way of life. They hunted buffalo for food and robes; they sent war parties out to raid their enemies; and the chiefs and warrior societies regained their authority over their bands.

Although the tragedy of the whiskey-trading period had transformed Red Crow from a reckless warrior into a more moderate chief, he had lost none of his confidence or pride. He accepted the arrival of the Mounted Police with thankfulness, yet he felt neither obligated nor intimidated by them. To him, Colonel Macleod was an honest and trustworthy man whom he was pleased to call his friend, but now that the police had driven away the whiskey traders, he saw no need to be involved with them. As long as the Bloods had the buffalo, his people wanted to be the masters of their own land.

As Red Crow resumed his role of chief in a whiskey-free camp, his days became happier and less complex. True, the rift with his relatives, Sheep Old Man and Revenge Walker, was never fully healed and the personal grief of family tragedies left its mark, but in other respects life returned to normal. As chief, he heard the petty grievances and quarrels which were brought before him and offered his advice. On more serious matters, such as theft or violations of morality, he acted as magistrate, knowing that his decisions would be swiftly carried out. In order to be an effective chief, he had to make wise but firm decisions, yet always be available to provide counselling to those in need. Like most chiefs, he was considered to be the "father of his people."[12]

A missionary, observing Red Crow in the role of chief, described him as a leader who had to be "stern in giving his decrees, wise and sympathetic in counsel, dignified in his dealings and impartial in his judgments — a judge on the bench and a father at the lodge-fires of his people. At the campfire he is stern and dignified, at the lodge-fire sympathetic and humble."[13]

In his personal life, Red Crow had a growing family by the time the Mounted Police arrived. Adopted sons Crop Eared Wolf and Black Face Chief were both grown men, while daughters Shaggy Hair Woman and Crow Woman were almost ready for marriage. Chief Moon was fifteen and Ground Diving Woman was six. Just before Red Crow's wife Water Bird was murdered, she had given birth to a son, Not an Owl, later christened Willie. After his mother died, he was taken by her grieving relatives and raised by them, and not until he was older did he return to his father's lodge. As a result Red Crow never was as close to him as to his other boys, Crop Eared Wolf, Black Face Chief, and Chief Moon.[14]

By the summer of 1875, Red Crow and the other chiefs were concerned about the continued presence of the Mounted Police. It was not that they disliked them, for the opposite was true. They had come to respect the red-coated troopers, but at the same time they were appalled by the effects these men were having on their hunting grounds.

Even during the whiskey days, the Blackfoot tribes had been able to keep most of the unwelcome strangers out of their land. Cree and half-breed hunting parties ventured in at their own risk, and a liberal number of whiskey traders died when their actions became too offensive. But with the arrival of the police, the Crees, half-breeds, and white men were streaming into the country unchecked. Some of the half-breeds, whom the Bloods despised, even established permanent settlements at Fort Macleod and at the newly-built posts of Fort Calgary and Fort Walsh.

As was the custom when a problem arose that needed to be considered by the three tribes, a general council was called. Held in the autumn of 1875, the meeting was attended by Red Crow, Medicine Calf, Father of Many Children, Rainy Chief, Many Spotted Horses, Bull Collar, and Bull Turns Around, from the Bloods; Crowfoot, Old Sun, Eagle, and Low Horn, from the Blackfoot; and Sitting on an Eagle Tail, Walking Forward, and Stakkas, from the Peigans. A French-Canadian homosexual living with the Blackfoot prepared a petition for the lieutenant-governor of the North-West Territory as a result of their deliberation.

The council reminded the government that Colonel Macleod had promised them that "the White Men will not take the Indians lands without a Council of Her Majesty's Indian Commissioner and the respective Indian Chiefs."[15] Yet, they complained, white men already were coming into their territory to build houses wherever they pleased and the Americans in particular were establishing a major settlement on the Oldman River near Fort Macleod.

"We are perfectly willing that the Mounted Police and the Missionary remains in our country," continued the petition, "for we are indebted to them for important services."[16] On the other hand, they wanted the American traders removed and the Hudson's Bay Company invited to replace them.

Another major grievance was that "the Halfbreed and Cris [Crees] Indians hunted Buffalo summer and winter in the center of the hunting grounds of the Blackfeet nation . . ."[17] They asked, therefore, that the Blackfoot have an opportunity to meet with an Indian Commissioner at the Hand Hills during the summer of 1876 "for putting a rule to the invasion of our country, till our treaty be made with the Government."[18]

Although the council was held in 1875, the actual document was not delivered until the spring of the following year, by which time steps already were being taken by the government to negotiate a treaty with the Crees, Ojibwas, and Assiniboines north and east of the Blackfoot hunting grounds. Although none of the Blackfoot attended that treaty, the Catholic missionary Constantine Scollen expressed some concerns on their behalf. These in turn were transmitted to the minister of the interior, David Mills, who assumed that the Blackfoot "have for years past been anxiously expecting to be treated with, and have been much disappointed at the delay of negotiations."[19]

But Red Crow and the other chiefs were not anxious to negotiate a treaty.

Rather, as expressed in their petition, they wanted to speak to a high-ranking official to find a way of controlling the incursions of the Crees, half-breeds, and settlers. They were seeking a solution to an immediate problem, not a permanent land agreement. In fact, as Father Scollen explained later, "They have an awful dread of the future. They think that the Police are in the country not only to keep out whiskey traders, but also to protect white people against them, and that this country will be gradually taken from them without any ceremony."[20] Scollen himself believed that a treaty should be made, but he was careful not to put those words into the mouths of the Blackfoot. The closest he would come was to say that the "Blackfeet themselves are expecting to have a mutual understanding with the Government . . ."[21]

During the first two years the Mounted Police were in their territory, the Bloods had made a remarkable recovery. They were now well clothed, able to purchase repeating rifles and trade goods, and had acquired several hundred head of horses through barter and raiding. But the wealth was being realized at a great cost, for during the spring of 1876 alone, almost 60,000 buffalo robes were sold to traders along the Belly and Oldman rivers.

Red Crow and the other chiefs knew that only a part of this massive slaughter came from the Blackfoot tribes. Rather, the Cree half-breeds were accused of slaughtering thousands of buffalo for their robes alone, leaving the carcasses to rot on the prairies. While the Blackfoot also took advantage of the robe trade, they were more likely to lay in large stores of dried meat, both for food and for later sales.

"The Indians look with no favorable eye on these Red River half-breeds," commented a Fort Macleod resident. "They say that their medicine is bad for the buffalo, and I think that they are pretty nearly right."[22]

Angry at the repeated invasions by their enemies and the massive buffalo slaughter, a delegation of Blood and Blackfoot chiefs went to see Colonel Macleod, who had been appointed the new commissioner of the police. They told him that if his men were not in the country, the Blackfoot would destroy the half-breed hunters; they also reminded the officer that he had promised that steps would be taken to preserve the buffalo.[23] As yet, nothing had been done. Macleod sympathized with the chiefs, but was powerless to act, for proposed regulations to control the buffalo herds — which he had been notified would be passed — had never been carried out.

"Before our arrival here," Macleod noted sadly, "the acknowledged hunting ground of the Blackfoot extended from Red Deer River south by Cypress Hills to the Boundary Line and west to the Rocky Mountains. He was at war with the Crees, Halfbreeds, Sioux, Assiniboines and others who were continually endeavouring to press in upon his country. Now that we have come into his country he finds that from all sides his old enemies, who he dare not attack, are under our protection pressing in upon him. A great number, notably the half-breeds whom he considers his worst enemies, are armed with the breech-loader which they procure at Fort Garry, and he has to compete with those who are armed with a better rifle than his."[24]

When all of the factors were taken into consideration, the Blackfoot were not anxious for a treaty, but rather, for some immediate solution to their problem. In addition, the Bloods and Peigans had both been involved in the 1855 treaty with the Americans and saw how it had been violated time after time and how two subsequent treaties had been made to whittle down the size of the reservation. Three of the Blood chiefs, Medicine Calf, Father of Many Children, and Many Spotted Horses, had participated in the original treaty negotiations. Some also had been present in 1865, at the second American treaty, when Little Dog, head chief of the Peigans, had agreed to surrender part of his hunting grounds. "The land belongs to us," he had told the commissioners, "we were raised upon it; we are glad to give a portion to the United States; for we got something for it."[25]

Yet Medicine Calf had seen what had happened to the promises of extra annuities. "The Americans gave at first large bags of flour, sugar, and many blankets," he explained. "The next year it was only half the quantity, and the following years it grew less and less, and now they give only a handful of flour."[26]

In November 1876, Red Crow, Medicine Calf, and nine other Blood chiefs went again to see Colonel Macleod about the invasion by the half-breeds. "There is indeed a great deal of irritation amongst them," Macleod commented afterwards, "and it is not to be wondered at, for I am informed that there is a regular cordon of Half-breeds and Crees extending from Belly River, all the way up [to the] Bow, interposing between the buffalo and the part of the country they usually winter in."[27] In reply to their grievances, all that Macleod could do was to promise to write to Ottawa, at the same time urging the chiefs not to take matters into their own hands.

Although the subject of a treaty had never officially been broached to the Bloods, Medicine Calf brought it up during his visit to the fort.

"I told him ..." said Macleod, "I was not instructed by the Government to say anything about it, but that I believed it was the intention of the Govmt. to treat with them next year.

"He said that he had at first been averse to making any treaty, but that he had changed his mind, and would use all his influence towards getting his followers to consent to it. He is a very fierce, intelligent fellow and I was glad to hear him express himself as he did, as I had been told that he would do all he could to thwart the making of a treaty — or as they express it themselves 'giving their land for nothing.' "[28]

Medicine Calf clearly had the American treaty in mind when he spoke to Macleod. The Peigan chief Little Dog had indeed "given their land for nothing" in 1865 when he had agreed to reduce the size of his reservation in Montana; Medicine Calf had no intention of making the same mistake and would help to negotiate the best deal he could.

Of the leading chiefs of the Blackfoot nation, Crowfoot was the most prominent of those who had not suffered through the inequities of the American treaties. He was the most trusting while some of the others, at best, were skeptical.

Red Crow was not as openly friendly to the whites as Crowfoot, yet he had developed a considerable fondness for Colonel Macleod and the Mounted Police. He had been treated fairly by them and was impressed with Macleod's honesty and frankness. If the policeman wanted to sit down and discuss their problems, he would be happy to see the Bloods take part.

A nephew of Colonel Macleod, who was well acquainted with the Blood chief, commented that "Red Crow had given much more consistent support to the Police on the negotiations leading up to the Treaty than any other chief, even the renowned Crowfoot . . ."[29]

In the summer of 1877, Colonel Macleod and the Honourable David Laird, Lieutenant-Governor of the North-West Territories, were appointed commissioners to negotiate the treaty with the Blackfoot nation and the Stoneys. The original choice of a meeting place was Fort Macleod, which was central to all the tribes, but when Crowfoot insisted that the meeting take place at Blackfoot Crossing on the Bow River, away from any white man's fort, the commissioners reluctantly agreed.

"This will cause great dissatisfaction among the Bloods and North Peigans," observed the Fort Benton Record, "and an outbreak is feared at the place where the treaty is to be held. If hostilities should occur, the Indians will have everything their own way, as they will probably be over ten thousand strong while the whites will hardly number half as many hundreds. . . . Probably the only condition upon which these Indians will treat is that the Police must agree to keep the half-breeds, Crees, Assiniboines, Pend d'Oreilles and Nez Perces out of the Territory, which would be impossible for the Police to accomplish with their present meagre force."[30]

In the weeks following the announcement, Medicine Calf was the only Blood chief who made it clear that he would attend the negotiations. The others were either opposed or non-committal. Red Crow, because he was younger than the others and because of his leadership of the Fish Eaters band, was a key figure in any bid to gain the cooperation of the Bloods. At that time, Father of Many Children was so aged and infirm that the Bloods fondly called him "grandfather;"[31] Many Spotted Horses was old and blind,[32] dying seven years later; and even the outspoken Medicine Calf was seventy-three years of age. This meant that Red Crow, at forty-seven, was by far the youngest of the leading chiefs.

Red Crow's position was simple; he favored the meeting, but he was so angered by the change of location that he was prepared to boycott the whole proceedings. "We did not at first want to make treaty," he explained in later years.[33] Then as the date drew near, white men kept speaking to him, trying to induce him to attend. Yet by early September, when many of the Bloods and Peigans were off to the fall hunt, nothing had been decided; Father of Many Children had taken his followers into Montana, while a band of North Peigans under Big Swan ranged as far south of the line as the Judith River.[34]

Meanwhile, plans went ahead for the negotiations, which were to commence on September 17, 1877. The Hudson's Bay Company sent down a special supply of trade goods to cash in on the expected treaty payments, while like-minded Americans came up from Montana. The traders and missionaries attending the negotiations obviously did not share the Montana press's concern about a possible outbreak, as wives and children were brought to the historic event. Yet they were cautious as well. When the Reverend John McDougall arrived, he advised Laird and Macleod to move across the river from the main camps "should the Blackfoot prove unfriendly."[35] The two commissioners declined.

The son of the Hudson's Bay trader, Richard Hardisty, reflected the concern some felt about the negotiations. "My father and John McDougall," he said, "were aware of the fact that many of the war chiefs were opposed to the treaty. The young bucks were with them in opposition. Word had come to them that U.S.A. was not living up to treaties made with their brothers across the line. There was no doubt of Crowfoot's sincerity and friendship. He was, however, not a war chief."[36]

The concern was not about an uprising, for the relations between the Mounted Police and Indians were on a friendly footing. Rather, there was the fear that the opposition to the treaty would be too great and would be expressed either by demands which the commissioners could not accept or by walking out of the negotiations. Either way, the treaty was not a foregone conclusion.

10

/ The Blackfoot Treaty /

On the broad flat south of the river, tepees were scattered along the entire area, while hundreds of horses grazed on the hillside. The Bow River, its clear water flowing fresh from the Rocky Mountains, snaked through the valley, rippling over the gravelly ridge which marked the river crossing. On the north, and slightly upstream, the Stoney Indians, traditional enemies of the Blackfoot, were camped with their missionary friends, while the Hudson's Bay trading tents were pitched nearby.

The autumn had been mild and many of the cottonwood trees along the river still bore leaves of yellow and brown; the prairie slopes had taken on the dull brown hue which becomes a part of their mantle after the first flush of spring.

When David Laird arrived on the scene September 16 the Mounted Police had already pitched their camp to the east of the Blackfoot, but on the same bottom. Although hundreds of tepees were scattered along the flat and close to the cottonwoods at the bend of the river, almost all of them belonged to the Blackfoot tribe; only a few from the Bloods, Peigans, and Sarcees were in evidence. Bull Head of the Sarcees and Sitting on an Eagle Tail, chief of the North Peigans, were there, but many of their followers were still hunting on the prairies. The only Blood leaders present were Medicine Calf and Rainy Chief, the first there to negotiate and the second because he normally hunted in the area and had been friendly to the whites ever since the first missionaries had come to his camp.

Before the commissioners had left Fort Macleod, they had dispatched messengers to all the camps to remind the Indians of the time and place. But Laird realized that the Bloods were not happy. In fact, a delegation with Red Crow at its head had met with him in Fort Macleod, demanding that a separate meeting to be held with them at the fort rather than at Blackfoot Crossing. Laird replied that after a treaty was made, they could receive their annuities wherever they wished, but for the initial negotiations he wanted all the tribes together.[1]

The proceedings had been scheduled to get underway on Monday morning, September 17, but when it was obvious that the main part of the Blood tribe was absent, the commissioner called a delay of two days.

In the intervening period, the officials waited anxiously for Red Crow and the other chiefs. From time to time, there was gunfire from the top of the valley as a small party announced its arrival, but the Bloods were nowhere to be seen. Instead of serious negotiations during the two days, the camp echoed with "the howling of countless dogs and constant drumming in different tents, night and day. There was always either a dance in progress, some medicine being made, incantations over the sick, or for successful hunts or war expeditions."[2]

On September 19, Laird and Macleod decided they could wait no longer so, with an honor guard of fifty Policemen marching beside them and the band playing, they sounded the cannons to announce that the proceedings were ready to begin.

Laird was aware that the Blackfoot were concerned about the rapid decline of the buffalo and, in an effort to appease them, he explained that a law had just been passed forbidding the killing of calves and protecting the cows in winter and spring. "This will save the buffalo," he promised, "and provide you with food for many years yet, and it shows you that the Queen and her Councillors wish you well."[3] He did not tell them that the law already was proving to be virtually unenforceable.

The commissioners' purpose in being there was to gain the surrender of the vast hunting grounds of the Blackfoot nation and the Stoneys. It was a huge tract of 50,000 square miles, bounded on the north by the Red Deer River, the south by the International Boundary, the east by the Cypress Hills, and the west by the Rocky Mountains. In exchange, Laird was authorized to offer certain benefits, including reserves on the basis of five people per square mile; annual treaty money of twenty-five dollars for chiefs, fifteen dollars for councillors, and five dollars a year for everyone else, with a bonus payment of twelve dollars for the first year; cattle for those who wanted to ranch; implements for those who wanted to farm; and an assortment of incidentals like ammunition money, medals, flags, uniforms, and a Winchester rifle for each chief.

The leaders had all Tuesday night to consider the terms and on Wednesday, when the meeting resumed, Medicine Calf was there to begin serious negotiations. He was the only leader who had taken part in the 1855 treaty with the Americans and he had come with three goals in mind — to secure the Bloods' hunting ground from enemy tribes; to receive compensation from those whites who had come into the area before the treaty; and to be sure that they weren't being tricked into "giving their land for nothing."[4]

To make his position perfectly clear, Medicine Calf launched his proposal by stating that "The Great Spirit, and not the Great Mother, gave us this land."[5] In other words, he recognized that their hunting ground belonged to them until such time as they surrendered it to the Crown.

After praising the Mounted Police for putting a stop to the whiskey trade, the Blood chief said (in the words of the interpreter), "The Great Mother sent you to this country, and we hope she will be good to us for many years. I hope and expect to get plenty."

At this point, Medicine Calf was trying to open two-way negotiations and went on record as expecting a favorable settlement. After outlining the way the Bloods had been swindled by the Americans, he put forth his proposal: "We want to get fifty dollars for the Chiefs and thirty dollars each for all the others, men, women, and children, and we want the same every year for the future. We want to be paid for all the timber that the Police and whites have used since they first came to our country . . . I hope, Great Father, that you will give us all this that we ask."

Even when Crowfoot jumped up and exclaimed: "Great Father, what do you think now, what do you say to that?" Governor Laird, incredibly, did not seem to understand that Medicine Calf was trying to bargain. Even when Sitting on an Eagle Tail commented on the help they had received from the Mounted Police and added: "I expect to get the same from our Great Mother," he did not realize that the others were supporting the Blood chief.

Instead, Laird treated the proposal in an offhand manner. "I fear [Medicine Calf] is asking too much," he scoffed. "He has told us of the great good the Police have done for him and his tribe and throughout the country by driving away the whiskey traders, and now he wants us to pay the Chiefs fifty dollars and others thirty dollars per head, and to pay him for the timber that has been used. Why, you Indians ought to pay us rather, for sending these traders in fire-water away and giving you security and peace, rather than we pay you for the timber used."

At this point, according to the *Globe*, "the Indians indulged in a general hearty laugh at this proposition," that is, at Laird's foolish suggestion.

During his speech, Medicine Calf also brought forward the main concern of his tribe, that their hunting grounds be protected from enemy tribes. This was the main concern of the Bloods and the primary reason for Medicine Calf being present. Yet the request was rejected out of hand.

"[Medicine Calf] wants us to prevent the Crees and Half-breeds from coming in and killing the buffalo. They too are the Queen's children, as well as the Blackfeet and Crees. We have done all we can do in preventing the slaying of the young buffalo, and this law will preserve the buffalo for many years."[6]

That day, only the Stoney chief Bearspaw spoke in favor of the treaty, but he was from an enemy tribe which took no part in the discussions in the Blackfoot camps.

After the meeting, the evening was a turbulent one in the Blood and Blackfoot lodges. Medicine Calf was angry about the curt refusal of his requests, a feeling that was shared by a number of chiefs from the other tribes. At one point during the evening, some of the leaders threatened to leave for the plains and, according to a policeman, "it looked as if all chance of making a treaty would have to be abandoned."[7] Governor Laird, too, heard about the violent arguments his remarks had created, observing that "there was a rumor that the Indians in their own Councils could not agree, that a small party was opposed to making a treaty."[8]

During the evening of confrontation and discussion, Crowfoot proved to be an able arbitrator. Although some of the chiefs, like Medicine Calf, were there only to resolve the short-range problems, Crowfoot realized that his people would soon need the protection and help of the Queen if they were to survive after the buffalo were gone.

At the same time, other factors were at work to sway the chiefs towards signing the treaty. Not only were the police and traders constantly advising the Indians about the importance of signing, but word quickly spread through the camps that twelve dollars would be paid to every man, woman, and child at the conclusion of the treaty. From that point on, many Indians became anxious to get the money so they could spend it at the traders' tents. Leaders like Blackfoot chief Eagle Calf yielded quickly to these pressures and urged the others to accept the terms; the rest of the chiefs also realized that they would have to respond to the wishes of their followers. And, on the fourth day after negotiations began, the people were becoming impatient.

That evening, after sunset, the news was carried through the camps that the Bloods were coming! Red Crow was at the head of his Fish

Eaters band, while the aged Father of Many Children was being born along on a travois with the Buffalo Followers a half day behind!

The messengers had found the Bloods camped almost on the International Boundary and had persuaded the chiefs to attend. Like other leaders, Father of Many Children attached no particular significance to the events at Blackfoot Crossing, for he had attended many treaties in his lifetime — treaties between tribes, treaties with traders, treaties with the Americans. With Red Crow, he had agreed to take his people northward but even when he attended the grand council during his final days, to him it was just another gathering. Father of Many Children, a once-dynamic warrior and now respected patriarch, was also the keeper of the winter counts. He was the man who each year selected the most important event, so it would be remembered in the calendar of years. To him, 1876 was the year "when there were plenty of buffalo;" 1877 was "when we had a bad spring;" and 1878 was a "mild winter."[9] The great Blackfoot treaty — so important to the whites that it captured the front pages of the daily newspapers,[10] so significant that it became a date to be remembered in Canadian history — *was not even worthy of recording* by one of the leading chiefs who participated in it!

Red Crow, the proud and independent warrior chief, also attached no great importance to the treaty. He was almost ready to boycott it when the government perfunctorily reacted to Crowfoot's demands by moving the site farther north. He was further angered when Laird refused to treat with the Bloods separately at Fort Macleod.

Red Crow could afford to react this way, not because he was willing to sacrifice the needs of his people out of spite or pique, but because neither he nor most of the other chiefs believed the treaty was significant. Normally Red Crow was a man of vision and foresight who could plan a raid, organize a hunt, or even consider the ramifications of a pact with an enemy tribe. But this treaty was another matter for it called upon the chiefs to envision a life without buffalo, without nomadic camps, and without freedom. It was simply beyond their comprehension. To them, the meeting was just another opportunity for the Bloods to demand that their hunting grounds be freed of Crees and half-breeds, and a chance to ask for compensation for land and timber used by the whites. There was no need for Red Crow to be present, for his tribe already was represented by Medicine Calf, considered "one of the first orators of his tribe."[11] As Red Crow understood it, the treaty was simply a promise that in exchange for letting the whites come in, the Queen would "furnish them plenty of food and clothing . . . every time they stood in need of them . . ."[12]

Crowfoot, who had spent more time with the whites and who was openly friendly to trader Richard Hardisty, missionary Albert Lacombe, and Commissioner James F. Macleod, was the only man to realize that this meeting was something more than a promise of food and clothing. While not even he could have had a clear understanding of surrendering their land, he knew that the decisions were important to his tribe.

So on the evening when the Bloods arrived, Crowfoot immediately went into session with Red Crow and the other leaders. Besides learning of the terms of the treaty, Red Crow also was told how Medicine Calf had been rebuffed and how the people were anxious to share in the presents which were waiting for them. The main point which Red Crow understood was that Colonel Macleod was one of the commissioners and that he favored the treaty. The chief's only yardstick to measure a treaty he didn't understand was to measure the men who offered it. One was Laird, whom they called *Spitah*, the tall one, and the other was Colonel Macleod, *Stamixotokan*. And both spoke for the Great Mother, who had sent the Red Coats to chase away the whiskey traders. On the basis of these two men and on Crowfoot's favorable attitude towards the negotiations, Red Crow was inclined to accept the terms. They were of no great importance anyway.

On the next day, September 21, Crowfoot made his famous speech in which he accepted the treaty on behalf of all the tribes who had empowered him to speak.[13] Medicine Calf, who had also been pressured by his followers to accept, even if the terms weren't as generous as he hoped, said resignedly: "I must say what all the people say, and I agree with what they say. I cannot make new laws. I will sign."[14]

Red Crow summed up his feelings briefly and succinctly, placing his confidence in the man, rather than the document. "Three years ago," he said, "when the police first came to the country, I met and shook hands with Stamixotokon (Colonel Macleod) at Belly River. Since that time he made me many promises. He kept them all — not one of them was ever broken. Everything that the police have done has been good. I entirely trust Stamixotokon, and will leave everything to him. I will sign with Crowfoot."[15]

While Red Crow may not have understood the white man's talk about reserves and land surrenders, he did know about politics and power. For years, he and his uncle before him had elevated the Fish

Eaters to a position of dominance in the tribe, counteracting the historic leadership of the Buffalo Followers and the rising influence of the Lone Fighters and Many Tumors. So when it came time to choose the government-recognized chiefs of the tribe, Red Crow at once became the politician and strategist.

He learned that a decision had been made to divide the Bloods into two main groups — the northern segment which traded with the Hudson's Bay Company and the southern which traded with the Americans — with a head chief for each. The division was purely artificial, for by 1877 practically none of the Bloods traded in the north.

There were four leading chiefs of the Blood tribe: Red Crow of the Fish Eaters, Father of Many Children of the Buffalo Followers, Medicine Calf of the Many Tumors, and Many Spotted Horses of the Lone Fighters. The two logical men to act as head chiefs were Red Crow and Father of Many Children — and this recommendation was made to the commissioners. However, the latter chief declined, on account of his age and his health. At this point, the head chieftainship should have been offered to Father of Many Children's son, Hind Bull, but this was not done.[16]

Because of their hunting areas, neither Medicine Calf nor Many Spotted Horses could qualify as head chief of the "North Bloods", so Red Crow recommended that his old comrade Rainy Chief be given the position. At that time, Rainy Chief was sixty-eight years old and leader of the Hair Shirts band, a tiny offshoot of the Fish Eaters. So when his suggestion was accepted, Red Crow had effectively neutralized the influence of the Buffalo Followers — without likely realizing what an impact this would have on their future reservation life. Red Crow, always the aggressive leader, had taken power when the opportunity arose; this was the way when a man was born to a family of chiefs.

He further consolidated his position when the treaty money was distributed. Each chief was asked to identify the members of his band, so their names could be written on the paysheets and their money distributed.

The Buffalo Followers came forward in small groups, each being recognized as a separate band — Father of Many Children with 118 followers; Bull Back Fat with 210 followers; war chief White Calf with 107 followers; Morning Writing with 93; and Eagle Shoe with 74. Altogether they had 602 people but they were under five chiefs.

The Many Tumors split into two groups, with Medicine Calf leading 165, and Weasel Bull, 86. The Lone Fighters divided into three, with Many Spotted Horses having 41 followers, Bull Turns Around, 69, and Wolf Collar, 116. The Black Elks, a small separate band, had 132 members under Eagle Head.

Red Crow, on the other hand, did not allow his band to become fractionalized. He appeared at the head of 304 followers, while his fellow head chief, Rainy Chief, had 51. Then, after the payments had been made, Red Crow pointed out that there were a number of men who should sign the treaty, but who had no bands. Obligingly, the commissioners agreed, so the chief selected three Fish Eaters — One Spot, White Striped Dog, and Moon — as well as Rainy Chief's son White Antelope, to be appointed chiefs.[17]

In a deft series of moves, Red Crow ended up with one more chieftainship than the Buffalo Followers and gave the appearance of having the largest band, when in fact the Buffalo Followers together would have had twice as large a group had they remained under one chief. As it was, Red Crow seemed to have a band which was the biggest in the tribe. With those statistics on the paysheets, Red Crow's position as the primary head chief was henceforth unquestioned by government authorities.

On the other hand, when the matter arose of choosing a reserve, Red Crow revealed that he had no clear grasp of the land aspects of the treaty. The idea of the Bloods living on a small parcel of prairie land — on the basis of five people per square mile — was utterly foreign to him. Since time immemorial, the Bloods had wandered from place to place, always pursuing the buffalo, going wherever the rumbling herds had roamed. In the heat of summer the Indians drifted onto the bare plains near the Sweetgrass Hills, camping by turgid prairie streams; in winter the blizzards drove them into the valleys of the Belly, Oldman, and Highwood rivers, where their skin tepees huddled against the cold and drifting snow. When their tepee poles were worn, they travelled to the Rockies, watching the soaring eagle or listening to the noisy raven, as lodgepole pines were cut down in the quiet dampness of the mountain forest.

Always to the west of them was Chief Mountain, that distinctive peak which protruded from the Backbone of the World, while out on the plains the Belly Buttes were a familiar landmark that showed the Bloods they were at home.

All of this was Red Crow's land. What did an X on a piece of paper have to do with the prairies, the mountains, and the skies? The piece of paper would let the white man in, but in the minds of most Blackfoot, there were only a few white men in the world and most of them were already in their hunting grounds.

What was a reserve? How could any Indian stay in one place without moving? How would he hunt the buffalo, which the commissioners said the Queen was going to preserve? Reserves were not realities; they were the strange dreams of the white man. The realities to Red Crow were the buffalo herds drifting across a brown rolling prairie. They were the hills and rocks and mountains, which *Napi* had created when the world began. None of these things belonged to the Indian; while he lived there, he used them, and when he died his spirit went to the Sand Hills. All of the things around them belonged to the sun god, and as Medicine Calf had told the commissioners, "the Great Spirit, and not the Great Mother gave us this land."[18]

So when Colonel Macleod asked Red Crow where he wanted his reserve, the Blood chief wasn't interested. As a result, he had no objection when he learned that Crowfoot was anxious to keep the Blackfoot, Bloods, and Sarcees together. As Red Crow explained many years later, "White men spoke and told us to say where we wanted the Reserve. . . . The Government said they would be good to us. We took what the Government offered us."[19]

The suggestion for a reserve, made by Macleod upon Crowfoot's recommendation, was a miserable four-mile-wide strip of arid land along the north side of the Bow and South Saskatchewan rivers stretching all the way from Blackfoot Crossing to the shadow of the Cypress Hills. At one time it may have provided useful campsites for buffalo hunters, but otherwise it contained some of the most desolate and unproductive land in the whole treaty area. It was many miles from Red Crow's hunting grounds, and not even Rainy Chief ventured there during the winter. In short, it was a useless piece of land accepted by a chief who didn't know what was happening but was placing his blind faith in the commissioners.

Macleod himself was aware of the responsibility the chiefs had placed upon him. There was no question of his honesty when he stated: "You say that I have always kept my promises. As surely as my past promises have been kept, so surely shall those made up by the Commissioners be carried out in the future. If they were broken I would be ashamed to meet you or look you in the face; but every promise will be solemnly fulfilled as certainly as the sun now shines down upon us from the heavens."[20]

The treaty was signed, not after serious negotiations, nor with any spirit of compromise. Governor Laird had come to the session with the treaty in his pocket. The Indians, too, had come with their demands in readiness. When they parted company, the commissioners had a document which said the Blackfoot had surrendered their lands. The chiefs, on the other hand, believed that they had been promised protection for the buffalo herds and treaty money for allowing the white man to come into their hunting grounds. Yet neither side really understood what they had given away. To Laird, buffalo preservation and firewood compensation were minor considerations, not to be taken seriously. To the chiefs, the selling of land and the allotment of reserves was beyond their comprehension.

For Red Crow and the others, the signing of Treaty Number Seven — the Blackfoot treaty — had been a simple act of faith.

11

/ Last Days Of Freedom /

The immediate reaction of the Bloods and Blackfoot to the treaty was one of elation. The people were pleased to receive their annuity money, and by the time they left Blackfoot Crossing, many had new blankets, new guns, and more horses. A month later a Mounted Policeman commented:

"Since the treaty the Indians appear more contented and, if possible, more friendly than ever. No red-coat can pass them either in the village or on the prairie without receiving the kindly grasp of their hand . . ."[1]

Then the doubts began to creep in.

The Blackfoot lived close to nature, close to a world dominated by good and bad spirits where nothing happened by chance. Good luck was a sign that the spirits were happy; bad luck proved that something had been done to offend them. For the whole nation, and the Bloods in particular, the signs were all bad.

Within the first year, three Blood chiefs who had signed the treaty — Rainy Chief, Weasel Bull, and Heavily Whipped — died, almost as though they were punished for dealing with the white man. Then it became obvious that nothing was being done to stop the slaughter of buffalo. The first big promise which Laird had made to them was being broken — just as the Americans had broken their word after the 1855 treaty.

Besides, not only were the Crees and half-breeds pressing them, but the Sioux and Nez Perce, recently arrived in Canada from their battles with the American army, were killing buffalo east of the Cypress Hills.

To add to the misery, the winter of 1877-78 was an open one, with practically no snow. American hide hunters, unwilling to see the main herds drift northward across the border and out of their reach, set the prairies ablaze until they were a blackened ruin. The buffalo, finding no forage, either stayed in Montana Territory or concentrated in a fifty-by-seventy-five mile area of unburned land in Canada north of the Cypress Hills.

The Bloods, of course, had been accustomed to wandering back and forth across the Internatonal Boundary at will, but after the arrival of the Mounted Police, they had stayed in Canada whenever possible. The two frontiers had become virtual opposites — the north quiet and peaceful and the American side infested with whiskey traders and Indian-hating whites.

Following the buffalo, Red Crow took his band northwest of Cypress Hills to an area that was rapidly filling with Indians seeking the last herds on Canadian soil. Close to Red Crow were the Blackfoot under Crowfoot, while south near Pakowki Lake were the Crees under Big Bear. Only forty miles away, on the other side of the hills, were Sitting Bull's Teton Sioux, with other camps of Yanktons and Santees nearby. Farther east on Frenchman's Creek were the Oglalas, Brules, and San Arcs, including a large camp under Crazy Horse. South, along the Milk River, were the Gros Ventres and Assiniboines. Even some camps of Cheyennes from far to the south and Kootenays from across the mountains were hunting in the confined area.[2]

The Sioux, unwanted refugees from their victory over Custer, were anxious to avoid any conflict which might compromise their precarious political position. Accordingly, messengers were sent to the other tribes, seeking treaties of peace. Offerings of tobacco were dispatched to the Crows and Gros Ventres in Montana, to Crowfoot and his Blackfoot, and to the Sarcees. The latter tribe, in turn, sent emissaries to the Peigans and Bloods, who had always considered the Sioux to be · among their bitterest enemies.

By the spring of 1878, most of the tribes had agreed that it was more important to hunt buffalo than to make war. The Bloods, on the other hand, remained consistent in their attitude towards the Sioux. While most of Red Crow's raids as a young man had been directed against the Crow, he also despised Sitting Bull's parted-haired intruders. "The Bloods have not smoked with the Sioux yet," a Montana newspaper observed in May 1878, "but want to fight them."[3]

Interestingly enough, when Red Crow was named head chief of the tribe, he had become a political leader who was expected to maintain peace — a responsibility which he now took seriously. On the other hand, Medicine Calf had more and more taken on the status of the leading war chief. Yet in dealing with the Sioux, their roles were reversed. While Red Crow arrogantly wanted no treaties with the

Sioux, Medicine Calf preferred to remain peaceful unless they acted first. During the spring, for example, a number of warriors decided to form an expedition to raid the fugitive camps. When Medicine Calf heard about it, he chided the leaders, asking them what the Sioux had done.

"They are coming too close to our camps," was the reply.

"Have they done you any harm, that you wish to fight with them?"

"No."

Pausing, Medicine Calf stared at the warriors and said, pointedly, "I fight with my enemies."[4]

The attack did not take place, but neither would Red Crow countenance a peace treaty. Rather, the tribes kept a respectful distance until one winter day, when a small hunting party from Red Crow's camp was attacked by Sioux while busily engaged in butchering a buffalo. The Bloods never had a chance, and when the brief fight was over, five of their party had been killed.[5]

The uneasy peace was shattered, and in the few remaining months that the Bloods and Sioux hunted the diminishing herds, their young warriors were constantly raiding back and forth. At one point, the Bloods even offered their services as scouts to General Miles's American forces to help track down the refugee Sioux who were surrepticiously hunting buffalo south of the line.[6]

Normally, however, Red Crow tried to keep the peace. When a young man from the Fish Eaters band, Jingling Bells, was arrested for theft, he managed to escape from the Fort Macleod guardroom and fled to Montana. As soon as he came back, Red Crow turned him over to the authorities, at the same time asking that his sentence be suspended. In deference to the chief, the young miscreant was given only fourteen days in the guardhouse.

By this time, events were moving rapidly on the western frontier. Although the treaty commissioners had spoken of the buffalo lasting for another ten years, the end was already in sight and the stark realities of what life would be like after the buffalo were gone now faced the political leaders. Soon the Bloods and other tribes would have no food and would need a place to live while the Queen helped them to find a new life.

Red Crow, for the first time, could appreciate what had been said about a reserve. He had shown no interest at the treaty, for the matter did not seem important; now he realized how vital it was to the future of his tribe. Thinking back to the land allotted him on the Bow River, he concluded that it was too far from the friendly valleys of the Oldman and Milk rivers where his people liked to winter. Accordingly, when he met the commissioners at Fort Kipp for the 1878 treaty payments, he told them that he did not want to settle near Crowfoot; instead, he would take his reserve on the Belly River, close to where they were paid. Obligingly, the officials agreed.

His tribe had made a long journey from the Cypress Hills to collect their payments at the former whiskey fort. The country west of the hills had been almost a barren wilderness, for the only animals they saw were a few scattered herds of antelope. The closer they came to the fort, the more graphic were the signs that the buffalo had left their land forever.

The payments came off quietly and Red Crow's old comrade, Rainy Chief, lived just long enough to collect his first annual treaty allotment as a head chief. By the time his spirit left his body, most of the bands were already on their way to the plains, but it was still possible for the government to appoint a successor to the leadership of the North Bloods. Again Red Crow was consulted and once again he chose a candidate who would offer him no competition.

It was a measure of Red Crow's influence that the commissioners accepted his recommendation of a man who was patently unsuited for the role. His name was Running Rabbit and he was the son-in-law of Red Crow's late uncle, Seen From Afar. Not only did Running Rabbit have no connection with the northern part of the Bloods' hunting grounds, but he had not signed the 1877 treaty and at the time of his appointment he had no followers; One Spot's band was transferred to him on the annuity books to make his appointment appear legitimate. Furthermore, Running Rabbit had spent most of his life with the South Peigans in Montana, and for the previous two years he had been listed as an American chief of the Blackfeet Reservation. If Running Rabbit had any affiliation with the Bloods, it was as a Fish Eater, and if he had a leader, it was Red Crow.

Immediately after the payments, the Bloods went back to the buffalo, a few going southeast to the Bear Paw Mountains in Montana, while Red Crow took the rest of his tribe east to the Cypress Hills. He wanted to stay in Canada as long as there were buffalo north of the line.

Unlike the previous year, the winter of 1878-79 was a bitterly cold one, with one blizzard following another. Some of the tribes, the Blackfoot in particular, stayed at their traditional camps far away from the thinning herds; soon they were starving, with no means of travelling through the savage winter storms.

"I have never seen them before in want of food," commented Father Scollen. "For the first time have they really suffered the pangs of hunger, and for the first time in my life have I seen a Blackfoot brave withdraw from his lodge that he might not listen to his crying children when he had not meat to give them."[7]

Red Crow was too impatient to wait for the buffalo to return and too independent to rely on the Mounted Police to feed him. Instead, he went into his winter camp at the mouth of the Red Deer River where he found enough buffalo to live relatively well. But it was obvious that the herds in Canada would no longer be able to support the thousands of Blood, Blackfoot, Sioux, Cree, Assiniboine, half-breed, and other hunters in the area.

Next spring there was no point in going back to the Belly River, which was virtually devoid of game, so Red Crow took his followers to Fort Walsh on the east side of Cypress Hills, where they lived off dried meat from the winter's hunt and rations from the Police until treaty payments in the fall. In the meantime, several bands of Buffalo Followers returned from Montana, bringing back tales of large buffalo herds and hostile ranchers and settlers. But once these Indians had been paid, they had no recourse but to return south, for there was no food to be had. The Canadian government had not yet accepted the fact that all its studied predictions had been wrong. They said the buffalo would last for ten years after treaty but they hadn't survived for even two.

In the autumn of 1879, Red Crow followed the other bands into Montana, settling near the Little Rocky Mountains for the winter. There was no way the whole tribe could be kept together; in fact, even larger bands had split into smaller family units to hunt the remaining herds. And the situation was as bad as he had feared, with whiskey traders, white horse thieves, and belligerent settlers dogging his followers whenever the opportunity arose.

"The songs of the Blood Indians were heard in the Teton valley a few nights ago," said the *Benton Record* wryly. "It is said the whiskey business is again becoming a lucrative traffic in this vicinity."[8] Red Crow's own camp suffered as much as any from the ravages of the human vultures which lurked near the camps. Shortly after they arrived, one of his men was killed by a woodchopper on the Missouri, even though he had done nothing to incur the man's wrath.

Later, a number of white horse thieves ran off twenty-six animals from his herd. Then, when camped on Arrow Creek, another raid by white men resulted in the loss of thirty horses, and during the winter, two more were stolen on Box Elder. In the last theft, two Americans who had known the Bloods in the north came to pay Red Crow a friendly visit and when they left, the horses went with them. Red Crow recognized the men and knew they had a ranch at the mouth of the Marias River, yet his anger turned to disgust when he found he could get no cooperation from U.S. authorities. To them, he was part of an invasion of "foreign" Indians who should be sent back north of the line.

In fact, military patrols were constantly checking reports from outraged Montana ranchers about the wholesale cattle killing they claimed was taking place. In most instances, blame was placed on the northern Indians and active efforts were made to force them to return to Canada. By the spring of 1880, the Mounted Police commanding officer at Fort Walsh reported that "the Indians commenced coming in large numbers from Milk River, on the American side, where they had wintered. In every instance they were starving. Many said they had but little to eat during the greater part of the winter, and would have come to the Fort sooner had they been able."[9]

Yet those who had wintered in Canada at Blackfoot Crossing, Belly River, and Fort Walsh were in more desperate straits. The buffalo had vanished from those regions, and the meagre allowance of beef and flour issued by the Mounted Police was barely enough to enable the Indians to survive.

Red Crow, though a proud and haughty leader, was a realist. During that winter of 1879-80, he had accepted the awful truth: the buffalo herds had been destroyed and the Bloods would need to start a new life. With the impatience of an aggressive man, he was not content to scour the ranges for the last remaining beasts. Rather, he wanted to get on with the strange business of living on a reserve.

He bore no ill will toward the white man for causing the destruction of the buffalo herds. On the contrary, he believed it to be the will of the Creator and stated that "God has taken all the game away."[10]

After the tribe had received its treaty payments at Fort Walsh in midsummer, Red Crow permitted most of his people to set out on the last desperate search for the buffalo, to try to hang on to a fast-disappearing way of life. But, almost matter-of-factly, he chose to go directly to Fort Macleod to finalize the matter of locating his new reserve and of finding out how he would make a living for himself, his family, and his tribe. He was willing to accept rations when he had no way of providing for himself, but he preferred to be his own master, even if the circumstances of his existence had changed.

In September 1880, he arranged for a meeting with the Honourable Edgar Dewdney, the Indian Commissioner, to discuss the matter of a reserve. There he willingly signed a document to give up his rights to the land north on the Bow River, provided "the Government will grant us a Reserve on the Belly River in the neighborhood of the mouth of the Kootenai [Waterton] River."[11]

On September 19, Red Crow, accompanied by the newly-appointed Treaty Seven Indian Agent, Norman T. Macleod, older brother of the Mounted Police commissioner, set out to choose the new reserve. As always, Red Crow knew exactly where he was going and what he wanted. Following the prairie trail towards the abandoned whiskey fort of Slideout, he arrived at nightfall on the banks of the Waterton River, camping on high ground to avoid the mosquitoes. When the others arose early next morning, they found Red Crow sitting on the cutbank, his legs dangling over the side. As they gathered around him, the Blood chief pointed towards the Belly Buttes and said, "That it where I wish to live the rest of my life, and die there."[12]

After breakfast, they hitched up the team and drove across the Waterton to examine the land between the two rivers, and when it started to rain, Macleod pointed out that the soil was heavy gumbo and unsuited for farming. Red Crow, however, was adamant; he wanted to be near the Belly Buttes. Looking across the river, the agent pointed out an alternate site that was even closer to the Buttes.

"I then crossed the Belly River to the south side, and from the mouth of the Kootenai [Waterton] eastwards and extending from the river to the foot of the Belly Buttes there are large level stretches of good clay soil with a large quantity of building and fence timber. .... Red Crow was quite satisfied with the selection of the location."[13]

Until this time, the 800 Bloods who had remained with Red Crow had been camped near Fort Macleod, receiving daily rations. However, with the location of a reserve established, Farm Instructor John MacDougall was sent to build a ration house and to have twenty acres of land broken for spring seeding.

Red Crow was among the first to move his lodge to the Buttes and to begin construction of a log house. Picking a site just downstream from the agency, he cut cottonwood logs from the nearby bottom and had the building up and roofed by the beginning of November. On instructions from the Indian agent, a door and window were made and installed for him. A total of sixty-two families, following their chief's example, also began to erect log shanties.

This action by Red Crow was a reflection of his type of leadership. While the other chiefs — even Medicine Calf and Crowfoot — were clinging desperately to their old ways in the melting pot of buffalo, horse thieves, and whiskey traders in central Montana, Red Crow was already looking ahead. His decisions to settle on his reserve and to build a house were not symbols of his acquiescence to the white man. Just the opposite was true; realizing that the old nomadic life was ending, he was willing to adopt any methods that would give him the self-sufficiency he demanded, not only for himself but for his tribe. Unlike other chiefs, he did not see the end of the buffalo as the death knell for the Indian; rather, he realized that drastic alterations would be required in order to survive.

Just as the warrior used whatever weapons, wisdom, and brute strength he had to defeat an enemy, so did Red Crow see the changing times as an enemy to be faced in the war of survival. And so great was his pride in himself and in his people, that he was willing to accept any means no matter how strange, in order to retain his self-reliance and independent spirit. That it should be the white men's method was of no concern to him, for he was neither cowed nor intimidated by their presence. The thought that he might be considered inferior to them was completely foreign to him.

Most of the Bloods who stayed with Red Crow that winter were either his personal followers or those who were too old or infirm to travel. The only chiefs to remain were three elderly leaders, Father of Many Children, Eagle Head, and White Striped Dog, as well as White Antelope, who was almost blind. During the winter, the new settlers hauled firewood and began to cut poles to be used as railing for their fences in the spring. With daily rations of beef and flour, they were able to subsist in relative comfort, with the monotony of daily life being broken by the visits of a newly-arrived Anglican missionary, Samuel Trivett.

Opening a small school and mission house near Red Crow's camp, Trivett was warmly greeted by the chief and was encouraged to hold regular classes. A year later, the chief even offered his two young sons for baptism under the names of William and Samuel.[14] At that time there was no thought of Red Crow himself becoming a Christian, even though the missionary may have harbored some secret hopes.

When the Anglicans started a school in his camp, Red Crow supported them and often permitted services to be held in his house.

Later, when the Catholics began to dominate his part of the reserve, the chief easily transferred his allegiance to them and sent his children to be educated in their schools.

During his first winter on the reserve, as had been his practise throughout his life, Red Crow based his judgment of the white men upon those who came to his camp. In this respect he was fortunate, for the representative of the Indian Department was John MacDougall, an intelligent frontiersman who had previously been a surveyor and prospector. Similarly, Trivett proved to be a selfless and devoted missionary, while most of the Mounted Police were friendly and respectful.

During this period while Red Crow was becoming adjusted to reservation life, the rest of the tribe was down in the Judith Basin, trailing the herds that had been hunted so often that they stampeded at the first sign of danger. But there was still enough food in the camps for everyone, and from time to time there was excitement when the warriors raided the Crows for horses, or when they had a pitched battle with the Assiniboines. It was almost like the old days.

But by April 1881, even the most optimistic chiefs knew the Bloods could not stay in the Judith Basin. While there were still a few buffalo to be found, there were not enough to go around. Moving westward to Fort Benton, the Bloods intended to trade the balance of their buffalo robes for food to last them until Fort Macleod. However, when they arrived at the fort, a nervous army officer would not let them enter the town. Instead, they camped on the nearby hills, out of sight of the military, where they were descended upon by swarms of whiskey traders.

"At all events," noted a Fort Bentonite, "the consequence was, that the Indians could not come to town to buy grub, the traders went to them on the hills around Benton, and in return for the remnant of their buffalo robes, revived their falling spirits with some more Yankee Doodle rot gut."[15]

Nor were the whiskey traders the only ones to harass the now-destitute Bloods. As they crossed the Teton River, white horse thieves ran off fourteen animals belonging to Red Crow's young relative, Fox Head, and in the same area, Big Porcupine lost another ten. Running Wolf's band, which had taken forty horses from the Crows during their stay in the Judith Basin, also lost out to the white man. Just before they left for the north, a posse came into the camp and, acting in an official manner, demanded that the animals be surrendered. Only later did the Bloods learn to their chagrin that the men were horse thieves under the leadership of a man named Jim Morton and that the herd had been taken north and sold at Fort Walsh.[16]

As the Blood buffalo hunters travelled the long, sad journey back to Canada, Red Crow and his followers were on their reserve just beginning their spring work. Another hundred acres of land were being broken under contract while Red Crow enthusiastically put a squad of men to work with hoes to prepare the previous fall's breaking for planting potatoes. Others were busily engaged in driving fenceposts and erecting rails.

In the middle of May, a strange reunion took place. Leaning on their hoes, the one-time warriors looked up from their tiny fields to see a slow, ragged line of people coming towards them. A few were on horseback, but many others were afoot, their worldly belongings pitched over their shoulders as they trudged along. Past the edge of the coulee and along the newly-built rail fences they wound their way, with only the jingling of a few bells on a staff or the yapping of a dog betraying their presence. They were hungry, tired, and sick. The children were dying with measles and scarletina, and the horses were succumbing to scabby mange.

The Indian farmers, although destitute and poorly clad, were rich when compared with the new arrivals. Most of the reservation Bloods still had their horses, which were healthy and sleek after a mild winter, and the daily rations had been enough to keep starvation from the camps.

There was subdued happiness as friends greeted friends and news spread about events which had taken place on the plains during the winter months. A treaty chief, Little Drum, of the Sarcees, had died. . . . The Blackfoot under Crowfoot were still across the line and being hard pressed by the military. . . . The whites had been stealing more horses than the Bloods. . . . Running Rabbit, their new head chief, was stopping in Montana to collect his annuities from the Americans before coming to the reserve. . . .

The Blood hunters had suffered on the plains during the winter, but their losses had been light. They had left the Judith Basin while they still had food and horses to travel and, except for the whiskey traders and disease, their main hardship had been a severe rationing of food. But it was good to be home.

"On the 24th," reported Agent Macleod, "we drove to the Blood Reservation where we found the seeding about finished and the Instructor working under very great difficulties, in consequence of the large numbers of Indians who have lately arrived from across the Line. His numbers increased in the course of a few weeks from 800 to over 3,300 and coming at this Season when the Indians we had settled were busy with their planting, it had disturbed and unsettled the whole body — the new comers insisting to camp along side of their friends among the houses already built, and in some cases sharing their lands with them."[17]

Within a few weeks, most of the fences had been pulled down by the newcomers to use for firewood or had been knocked down by scabby horses rubbing against them, while many of the seed potatoes had been dug up and eaten. Such was the respect the tribe had for Red Crow, however, that both his fences and his garden remained intact.

Around him, scattered indiscriminately in the fields and among the cottonwood groves, the Bloods suddenly found themselves in a strange and alien world. It was true that the clear waters of the Belly River still flowed by their tattered lodges, and Chief Mountain still stood as a solid sentinel on the western horizon. The hawk still hovered in the clear prairie sky and the brown prairie grass rippled in the breeze. It was the same as it had been for centuries, but it was different.

The buffalo were gone.

The buffalo truly had been their staff of life. It had given meat for food, skin for lodges and clothing, bones for tools, horns for ladles, the paunch for containers, teeth for necklaces, hair for stuffing saddle pads, and the hoofs for rattles. Even the tail had been used to sprinkle water on hot stones for the sweat lodge.

But the buffalo was more than just a means of supplying their material needs; it was the basis for much of their religion. In order to sponsor a Sun Dance, the holy woman had to offer dried strips of buffalo tongue as the sacrament. The *Motokix*, the women's society, based its rituals upon the movement of the buffalo. The most revered object on the altar of a holy man was his *iniskim*, the buffalo stone, which embodied the spirit of the buffalo.

The buffalo was the very foundaton of their existence. It was at the heart of their religion, their mythology, their daily lives, their annual migrations, their food, and their shelter.

The old people in particular could not understand where the millions of buffalo had gone. They knew the animal had been a gift of the Sun spirit, so they assumed that the Bloods had offended him and that the Great Spirit had opened a hole in the earth and driven all his animals into it. For many years after that tragic winter of 1880-81, the older Indians waited and prayed for the buffalo to return.

Even Red Crow shared this belief, commenting years later that "God has taken all the game away."[18] But he was too pragmatic, too practical, to wait for the shaggy beast to come back. Without the buffalo, the Bloods needed a new source of livelihood, and the only viable alternatives were those being offered by the white man. If the Bloods were to survive, they had to change the entire pattern of their lives. And this, Red Crow was ready to do.

12

/ A New Life /

When Red Crow settled on the reserve in 1880, he was a fifty-year-old man with a young family. Although he had taken his first two wives when he was in his twenties and had adopted Crop Eared Wolf as his son, his early years had been so devoted to war that there had been no time to become a family man. His first son to reach manhood, Chief Moon, was not born until Red Crow was twenty-nine.

But after he became leader of the Fish Eaters, he settled readily into the family routine. His forays on the warpath had made him rich in horses, with the result that he needed three or four wives in his household. These women tanned hides, fed the young men who were hired as herders, and provided help to others in the camp as was befitting a chief's wife.

By 1880, Red Crow had several living children born of at least five different wives. Besides Chief Moon, the only other boy to reach manhood was Not An Owl, born in 1874, and later christened Willie Red Crow. Two other boys, given the names Joseph and Noah by missionaries, died before reaching their teenaged years, one in 1882 and the other in 1889. Three others were adopted — Crop Eared Wolf, Black Face Chief, and Frank Red Crow. In addition, a deaf Blackfoot named Two Chiefs, baptized David Scollen, came to Red Crow's lodge when he left school and looked after the chief's horse herd.

The oldest girl to reach maturity was Shaggy Hair Woman, born in 1858. She married No Chief and became one of the holy women of the tribe. Another daughter was Ground Diving Woman, born in 1868, who first wed John MacDougall and then Jack Wagner before moving to Montana. A third was Crow Woman, who married Many Mules. There was also a daughter christened Jane who died in 1886; her mother, Pretty Woman, separated from Red Crow at that time and returned to her people in Montana. Similarly, one of the chief's other wives, Many Fingers, died in 1893 and her mother, Beaver Woman, took the three surviving daughters to the Blackfeet Reservation in the

United States. None reached adulthood. Another member of the Red Crow household was Waiting Woman, a young relative raised by the chief until she married Longtime Squirrel in 1891.[1]

Red Crow's wives in 1880 included Spear Woman, The Shield, Many Fingers, Pretty Woman, Longtime Pipe Woman — by whom he had no children — and Lazy Woman, a Stoney Indian who had been abandoned by her husband when that tribe was returning from Montana in 1880. Alone and in enemy territory, she had been taken in by Red Crow and remained a member of his household for about two years before returning to her own people.

But of all Red Crow's wives, his favorite was Singing Before, who was also the youngest. After the killing of his first wife, Water Bird, during the whiskey days, Singing Before had become his "sits beside him" woman who accompanied him on visits to other tribes and was considered to be the mistress of the household.

As a husband and father, Red Crow was a stern disciplinarian who expected to be obeyed. Sometimes this caused dissent within the household and if a wife was unwilling to follow the role assigned to her, she had no recourse but to return to her parents or family. Red Crow was similarly severe with his children, expecting his boys to become warriors and leaders, just as he had been. That Willie, his youngest son, did not measure up to his expectations was always a great disappointment to him. Similarly, his daughter Ground Diving Woman had been a rebellious child and eventually left the country when, as an adult, she proved to be too strong-willed for her chieftain father.

Yet Red Crow was not a tyrant; if his family followed his advice and direction, he could be a patient and loving man. He often had a merry twinkle in his eye and his lodge echoed with laughter as he joined in the good-hearted merriment of some incident or story. And he could also be considerate and understanding when the occasion arose. This was demonstrated when Singing Before, who was childless, became a mother through a chain of unusual circumstances.

A Blackfoot girl named Short Woman had been living with a white trader in Fort Benton, but when she became pregnant he had abandoned her. By that time, most of the Bloods and Blackfoot were hunting in the Judith Basin, so the girl was destitute and helpless in a white man's town. Taking pity on her, a freighter named Joe Beebe, who was married to a Blood woman, offered to take her north on an ox-drawn wagon and when they reached the Blood Reserve she took refuge in Red Crow's camp. There she gave birth to twin boys during the winter of 1880-81. The girl realized that she did not have enough milk to keep both twins alive so, as was the custom, she took the youngest of the two, wrapped him carefully, and went out into the deep snow and bitter cold to place him in the trees to die.

Singing Before heard of the incident and, rushing to Red Crow, she begged him to adopt the child. When he agreed, she rescued the baby from its frozen nest and took it as her own. The chief found two women who had recently lost children who could provide milk and, between them and hot broth, the baby was given enough food to survive. Named *Astrokomiw*, or Shot Close, he was later christened Frank and immediately became a favorite of the chief.

It was a strange characteristic of Red Crow that during his lifetime, his two most beloved children were Crop Eared Wolf and Shot Close, both of whom were adopted. While he had a comfortable relationship with Chief Moon and his other offspring, he poured his love and affection on the two boys whose lives he had saved.

Although there was periodic dissension within the Red Crow family, peace usually reigned in the household. The wives collected the weekly rations and saw that there was always a pot of beef simmering on the fire. Besides his log cabin, Red Crow continued to use his tepee to provide accommodation for his large family. When visiting the camp in September of 1885, a missionary observed that Red Crow was living in a tepee "which was pitched in the midst of a village consisting of huts & tents where about 1200 Indians were living. His tent was about 20 feet in diameter. There were ten Indians present including the chief's five wives. . . ."[2]

During his lifetime, Red Crow owned a number of tepees which bore religious designs. These painted tepees originated through dreams or war experiences and the designs were transferred from one owner to another through solemn ceremonies. The chief's best-known design was the Middle Painted Lodge, which consisted of a wide red band around the middle of the tepee, with otters painted on it. He also owned a war lodge, known as the Gambling Painted Tepee, which he had obtained from his uncle, Seen From Afar; it bore pictograph figures depicting the war experiences of both Red Crow and his uncle. A third was the Yellow Painted Tepee, which bore a blue symbol of the morning star on its upper surface.[3]

Because he was from such a large and closely knit family, Red Crow had a constant stream of people into his lodge — sometimes fellow chiefs to discuss problems, and often visiting Indians from other reserves, but usually relatives and fellow warriors were his most frequent company. With his family he was friendly, open, and talkative; story-telling and gossip were often interspersed with jokes and laughter. With guests he was more reserved, and when white men came to his home, he was solemn and dignified.

His favorite visitors were his companions of the warpath, some of whom had become chiefs of their own bands. Hours were spent recalling the events of their raids, humorous sidelights bringing gales of laughter from their lips. Like the time Red Crow was pursuing a young Cree who defecated all over his saddle just before he was killed. Or when one warrior went to scalp a half-breed and was disgusted to discover he was bald! Or the time when some Blackfoot stole their own tribe's horses, thinking they belonged to the Crows. These were the stories which were told and retold, the narrator being careful never to depart from the facts. The veracity of a leader was often measured by his complete honesty in relating the events of the past.

Besides his direct relatives, Red Crow was also close to those related by marriage. Sleeps on Top, a brother-in-law, became a close companion, as did a younger son-in-law, Many Mules. As he grew older, Red Crow enjoyed hunting with them, particularly when the deer came back to the Belly Buttes after the starvation years had passed.

On other occasions, Red Crow liked to visit the Peigans in Montana, where he had a number of relatives. Not only had some of Seen From Afar's girls remained there, but his own daughter later settled there. Similarly, Red Crow had old friends at the Blackfoot Reserve, although the distance across surrendered land made travelling in that direction infrequent. More often, such trips were taken if there were stolen horses to be recovered or disputes to be settled. In those instances, Red Crow and the Blackfoot chief Crowfoot worked well together.

At home, Red Crow's cabin often served as a council chamber, as fellow chiefs came to discuss their problems, or families came to have disputes resolved. At that point, Red Crow became the magistrate of the reserve, his judgment automatically having the weight of an official edict. If it was not carried out, he had the right to order one of the warrior societies to see that it was done. Sometimes these family disputes were resolved with the aid of the farm instructor, John MacDougall, with whom Red Crow worked very closely. He admired the man — the senior government official on the reserve — and was pleased when MacDougall later married the chief's daughter.

Two people who did not come to visit Red Crow were the chief's brother and sister, Sheep Old Man and Revenge Walker. The former still resented Red Crow for assuming leadership of the Fish Eaters band and was even more alienated when he became head chief of the tribe. Sheep Old Man believed he should have been a leader, and in 1880 he was continuing to agitate among his followers to be appointed a band chief.

Revenge Walker, on the other hand, had withdrawn from tribal politics after she married D. W. Davis. She had four children by him and lived in Fort Macleod until the pressures of an expanding white society split the couple up. During the early 1880s, Revenge Walker returned to the reserve with her youngest child, while Davis took a white wife and the other children stayed in Fort Macleod and Lethbridge. Once back on the reserve, Revenge Walker remained aloof from Red Crow; she married a man named Falling Over a Bank and devoted her remaining days to her husband and son.

One aspect of his nomadic life which Red Crow continued to support after the Bloods went to their reserve was native religion. From the days of his boyhood, when he received his spiritual powers from a gopher, Red Crow was a faithful follower of his tribe's religious practices. He owned medicine pipes and bundles, received and transferred memberships in secret societies, and possessed such sacred objects as the trailing feathered headdress and weasel-tailed shirt.

When the chief took his first long trip on a railroad train, his youngest wife, Singing Before, vowed to sponsor a Sun Dance if he returned safely. After his successful journey, she joined with another woman, Holy Feather On Head, and together they put on the sacred ritual. Similarly, when the leadership of the *Motokix*, the women's society, came vacant in 1897, she became the head of that powerful women's secret society. During the same decade, one of Red Crow's daughters, Shaggy Hair Woman, also sponsored a Sun Dance.[4]

In each case, Red Crow's support was necessary to pay for the transfer ceremonies, as well as to sponsor a massive giveaway of horses, blankets, and other gifts. That he did so willingly is an indication of his lifelong support of his native religion. Even though Christian missionaries tried for two decades to gain his conversion, with one even claiming success, there can be no doubt that Red Crow remained true to his own religion to the end.

While the Peigans and Blackfoot settled dejectedly on their lands after their return to Canada in the spring of 1881, the Bloods were not so willing to give up their old ways. A few stopped with relatives in

Montana, receiving rations from the American government, while others continued to hunt along the foothills.

Farther south, a number of young warriors, angered by white men who had run off their horses during the winter, also stayed behind to recoup their losses. Late in May, when most of the Bloods were straggling into the camps on the Belly River, a war party was on the Musselshell River, scouting the ranches for horses. After finding a suitable herd on a ranch reputed to be owned by a white man who had been stealing from the Indians, they made a night raid and were well on the trail toward Canada by dawn.

The rancher, with two other "Indian fighters," set out immediately in pursuit of the raiders. When they discovered that the trail led to Canada and the Blood Reserve, they went to Fort Macleod to file a complaint with the Mounted Police. There, the commanding officer assigned Inspector Francis Dickens to the task of recovering the missing stock.

There were few policemen less suited to the frontier than Dickens. The son of novelist Sir Charles Dickens, he was insensitive to those around him — particularly the Indians — and was accused of showing poor judgment. He was later obliged to resign from the Force after he abandoned his position during the Riel Rebellion of 1885.

Making no effort to check out the veracity of the Montanans' story — in spite of the fact that there were men living near the fort who were aware of the trio's reputation — Dickens selected Sergeant F. W. Spicer, a policeman who spoke Blackfoot fluently, and Constable Callaghan to accompany the ranchers and him to the Blood Reserve. Arriving while the Indians were still scattered along the river, fresh from their exodus from the United States, he sought out Red Crow and demanded the return of the stolen horses. The chief, realizing that the old controls had broken down during transition and that the young warriors were not at the moment accountable to their chiefs, refused to aid the officious Mountie. He also told the officer angrily that many Blood horses had been stolen by whites during the winter and that nothing had been done to recover them.

With Spicer as his guide, Inspector Dickens and the three Montana ranchers started a search on their own, riding through the camps where they succeeded in recovering fourteen of the missing animals. While they were waiting near the agency building for another cayuse which an Indian had promised to bring in, Many Spotted Horses came forward and shouted to the young warriors not to return any horses. His speech set the camp astir, with angry rumblings becoming violent

Portrait of Red Crow, taken by Winnipeg photographer Fred Steele in 1895. (Glenbow Archives, NA-56-1)

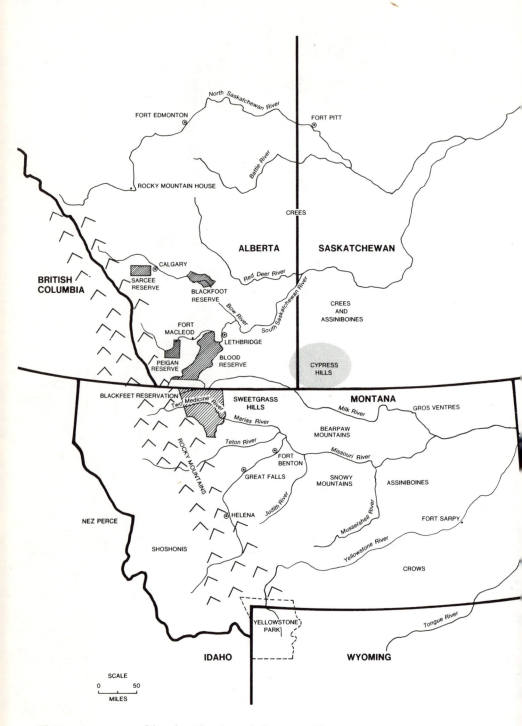

The territory ranged by the Bloods and their neighbors.

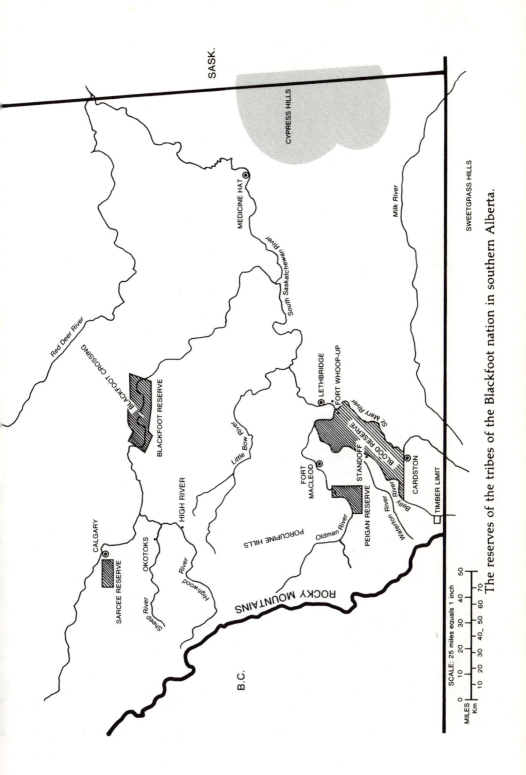

The reserves of the tribes of the Blackfoot nation in southern Alberta.

Bull Back Fat, the great leader of the Blood tribe, was painted by George Catlin in 1832. Later, Bull Back Fat's leadership was successfully challenged by Red Crow's uncle, Seen From Afar. (U.S. National Museum)

Red Crow's aunt, Medicine Snake, is seen here with her husband, Alexander Culbertson, of the American Fur Company, and their son Joe. This photo was taken about 1863. (Montana Historical Society)

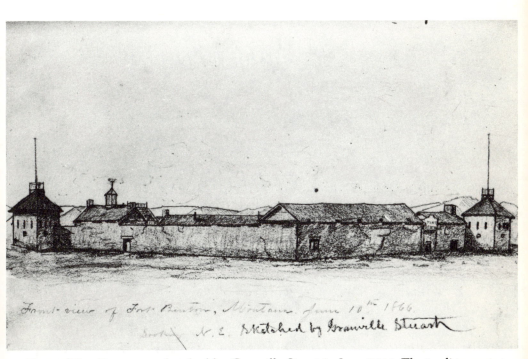

Front view of Fort Benton, Montana June 10th 1866.
Sketched by Granville Stuart

View of Fort Benton, as sketched by Granville Stuart in June 1866. The trading post, located on the Missouri River, was a focal point for the Bloods, and onetime home of Red Crow's aunt, Mrs. Alexander Culbertson. (Montana Historical Society)

Seen From Afar, who was Red Crow's uncle, was a leading chief of the Blood tribe. He is seen here in a sketch by Gustavus Sohon made at the 1855 treaty with the Americans. Seen From Afar died in the smallpox epidemic of 1869. (Glenbow Archives, NA-360-16)

Bad Head, or Father of Many Children, was the patriarch chief of the Buffalo Followers band at the time Treaty Number Seven was signed. Because of his age, he refused to accept a head chieftainship. He was painted by an itinerent artist, D.B.R., in 1876. (Glenbow Archives, NA-344-2)

Many Spotted Horses was a leading Blood chief who signed a treaty with the Americans in 1855 and with the Canadian government in 1877. As leader of the Lone Fighters band, he tended to support Red Crow's opponents in council matters. The above sketch was made by Gustavus Sohon at the 1855 treaty. (Glenbow Archives, NA-360-14)

Medicine Calf was one of the most able chiefs of the Blood tribe. Having experienced the disappointments of the 1855 treaty with the Americans, he tried to negotiate a better deal with the Canadian government in 1877. He was sketched by Gustavus Sohon at the American treaty. (Glenbow Archives, NA-360-17)

This tepee, bearing designs showing the war exploits of native leaders, was originally owned by Seen From Afar and was later acquired by Red Crow. It was photographed in 1892. (Glenbow Archives, NA-668-7)

View of the Blood Sun Dance, below the slopes of the Belly Buttes. Photo by S. A. Smyth of Calgary in July 1893. (Glenbow Archives, NA-237-1)

One of the first missionaries among the Bloods was Rev. Samuel Trivett, 3rd left rear, seen here at his Anglican mission in 1885. (Glenbow Archives, NA-443-4)

Blood Indian agency near Slideout, 1890. (Glenbow Archives, NA-725-1)

Lt. Col. James F. Macleod, assistant commissioner of the North-West Mounted Police when they arrived in the west in 1874, was a man of outstanding ability. Through his efforts, peaceful relations were established with the Indians. Red Crow considered him a friend. (Glenbow Archives, NA-354-1)

Sir Cecil E. Denny, an ex-Mounted Policeman, was an efficient Indian agent, but tried to undermine the authority of Red Crow. (Glenbow Archives, NA-1096-1)

William B. Pocklington was one of the more progressive and amiable Indian agents on the Blood Reserve. An ex-Mounted Policeman, he respected the leadership of Red Crow. (Glenbow Archives, NA-659-62)

James Wilson, Indian agent on the Blood Reserve, locked horns with Red Crow when the government official tried to suppress the Sun Dance. (Glenbow Archives, NA-3238-1)

The leading chiefs of the Blackfoot nation were photographed during a trip to Regina in 1884. Left to right, back: Jean L'Heureux, interpreter; Red Crow, head chief of the Bloods; and Sgt. W. Piercy, NWMP. Front: Crowfoot, head chief of the Blackfoot; Sitting on an Eagle Tail, head chief of the Peigans; and Three Bulls, Crowfoot's brother. (Glenbow Archives, NA-13-1)

Chiefs from the Blackfoot nation were photographed in Regina in 1886, just before leaving on their eastern Canadian tour. Left to right, standing: One Spot, minor Blood chief; Red Crow, head chief; Dave Mills, interpreter; and E. R. Cowan. Seated: Indian agent William B. Pocklington. (Glenbow Archives, NA-769-6)

The Blackfoot delegation was photographed at the city hall in Ottawa in October 1886. In the front row, 3rd left, is Mayor McDougall, while next to him are North Axe, head chief of the Peigans; Three Bulls, minor Blackfoot chief; Crowfoot, head chief of the Blackfoot; Red Crow, head chief of the Bloods; and One Spot, minor Blood chief. Standing at right is Father Albert Lacombe. (Glenbow Archives, NA-1542-1)

Blackfoot Old Woman attempted to gain the title of head chief of the Lower Camp, but was thwarted by Red Crow. (Glenbow Archives, NA-100-1)

Red Crow, in 1892. Photographed by R. N. Wilson, a trader at Standoff. (Glenbow Archives, NA-668-52)

demonstrations when an Indian named Flying Chief claimed that one of the Montana ranchers was actually a horse thief who had stolen Bull Back Fat's horses during the winter.

Medicine Calf was looked upon as the leading war chief at this time and whenever the tribe was in danger, he automatically took control of the camps from Red Crow, who was considered the political or peace chief. But on this occasion, the aging Medicine Calf was nowhere to be seen so another minor chief of the tribe, White Calf, took command. When apprised of the situation, he ordered his followers to seize the white trespassers and to prevent them from taking the horses.

"It was impossible at the time to get a word in," reported Dickens, "so I started in front of the Indians towards the corral, and shouted to the party to mount their horses and to be ready to start in order to avoid disturbance."[5]

At that moment Sergeant Spicer, who had stayed behind, called out to the Bloods and told them that he wanted to speak with them. The diversion delayed the intended attack and during the few moments of uncertainty, the policeman rode into the crowd and began speaking to White Calf and the others about the possible consequences of their actions. Dickens took this opportunity to round up his party of ranchers and horses, and as soon as Spicer parted from the sullen Bloods, they started on a rapid journey to Fort Macleod.

Medicine Calf lived for another three years after this altercation, but from that moment on, White Calf was recognized as the new war chief of the tribe. A great warrior, fearless, and a magnificent orator, he was the only leader of the Buffalo Followers who could at last challenge the supremacy of Red Crow and the Fish Eaters.

He had signed Treaty Number Seven as leader of the Marrows band, which was an offshoot of the Buffalo Followers. A close relative of Father of Many Children, he was a tall muscular man who impressed everyone with his strength and forcefulness. As observed by a missionary: "White Calf, the war chief of the Blood Indians, is a typical Indian, hating the language, customs and religion of the white man. As he sees the gradual decrease of his people, and their dependence upon the Government for support since the departure of the buffalo, and the encroachments and haughty spirit of the white men, remembering the freedom of the old hunting days and the valor of the young men, and seeing them transformed into a band of peaceful farmers, he mourns the loss of the martial days."[6]

The trouble in the spring of 1881 gave White Calf the opportunity he needed. His decisive and successful attempt to drive the Montanans off the reserve was in sharp contrast to Red Crow's inaction and won many dissident young warriors to his side. And it was only his first salvo in a battle to gain a leadership role in the affairs of the tribe.

During the next few weeks, some of the Bloods began to settle into the new routine, but when reports were spread that buffalo had been seen near the Sweetgrass Hills, many of them were ready to ride. As soon as the treaty payments had been made in August, One Spot announced his intention of going south.

"We are going after the buffalo," he proclaimed. "The whites must be stronger than we are to turn us back and if that happens, then we will camp along the boundary line and steal every horse and drive off every head of stock that crosses until the whites allow us in the country which belongs to us."[7]

Reports were circulated that 500 Bloods would be going to Montana, but in the end only a few scattered parties set out for the south and the east. And when they straggled back empty-handed and starving, the great buffalo hunt was abandoned. Yet many who left the reserve were more anxious to find enemy horses than buffalo. One war party from the Fish Eaters camp intercepted a raiding party of Piapot's Crees who were on their way to take horses from the South Peigans. In the running battle which followed, one Cree was killed and a young relative of Red Crow's was badly wounded.

"The Bloods are well armed and the Crees are not," reported a Mounted Policeman. "I wish it was the other way, as the Bloods are getting very saucy at Fort Macleod."[8]

The results of such raids were to keep the Bloods in an unsettled state throughout the summer and fall of 1881. The crops had been virtually destroyed by the new arrivals in the spring, and by the time they had spread out along the river, it was too late for them to consider farming for that year. In addition, the government had promised to supply tools for farming and for building houses but when these were not forthcoming, the Bloods were content to pass the time hunting, visiting, and trying to adjust to reservation life.

During the summer, the Many Children band under Running Wolf had been the butt of considerable humor for having permitted white men to victimize them out of their horses during their last days in Montana. Fretting over the incident, one of the warriors of that band, Packs His Tail, organized a war party of seven young Bloods to gain revenge. The fact that the horses had been taken by white men meant that a raid against any rancher would be just compensation. According to tribal custom, there was no need to seek out the actual perpetrator of the deed.

Upon reaching the Yellowstone River in Montana early in October, the warriors spied a large herd of Indian cayuses and horses at the ranch of Albert Harrison and ran off forty-seven of them. Travelling rapidly northward, they crossed the Judith Basin and went to the Marias River, where they believed they were safe. At that point the party split, some remaining at a hunting camp on the river and the rest proceeding across the Canadian line to the reserve.

When Harrison discovered his loss, he immediately formed a posse which was in hot pursuit only hours behind the raiders. However an autumn snowstorm near the Judith River wiped out all traces of the raiders, so the posse rode into Fort Benton to get help from Sheriff John Healy. Giving them a letter of introduction to the Mounted Police, Healy made for the Blood camp on the Marias where he seized thirteen horses and arrested a Blood named Bad Bull.

Realizing that he had no evidence to convict the prisoner, Healy meted out his own punishment by bringing a barber into the jail cells and cutting off most of the Indian's hair. In a few minutes he was "the most bald headed Indian in Montana. His own scalping knife never did work half so quickly."[9]

Meanwhile, Harrison and his party proceeded to Fort Macleod, where they presented their letter of introduction. In it, Sheriff Healy outlined the problem and then issued a warning to the police. "Should this missive prove futile," he wrote, "serious consequences are liable to follow, as the people of Montana have tired of being harassed by the marauding hordes of the north, and will wreak vengence upon all war parties caught this side of the line. . . ."[10]

Upon receipt of the complaint, the police inspector contacted Red Crow and other leading chiefs. Harrison, unlike the unsavory Montanans who had been to the camp in May, was a respected rancher and head of the local stockmen's association. He explained that he did not want to take legal action against the Bloods, but rather that he simply wanted his horses returned.

Responding to the request, Red Crow rounded up sixteen horses and two colts as well as bringing the news that some of the other animals had been taken to the foothills to trade with the Kootenay Indians, while still others were in Blood hunting camps on the Little Bow River and Lee's Creek. Within the next few days, three more horses were recovered, and Packs His Tail and his seven friends were arrested.

In the quick trial which followed, all eight were found guilty of bringing stolen horses into Canada, but were let off with a warning. Evidence was also presented to prove that Bad Bull, who had been humiliated by Sheriff Healy, had played no part in the raid.

Red Crow was worried about the veiled threats in Healy's letter, for a few years earlier the sheriff had been a co-owner of Fort Whoop-Up, the most notorious post during the tragic whiskey-trading years. Red Crow knew that the warning was not an idle one and that the indignities heaped upon Bad Bull were obviously intended as a lesson to the tribe.

Although he neither respected nor feared the Montanans, he realized that many of his more audacious young warriors could be lynched if they ventured on raids south of the line — at least during these troubled times. Accordingly, he contacted the chief of the nearby Peigan Reserve and they agreed to send their camp criers out to announce that no more raids into Montana would be permitted; warrior societies were instructed to set up night guards to patrol the camps so as to intercept anyone trying to go south.

"These chiefs say they are bound to put an end to this horse stealing business," announced the *Benton Record*, "and will return as soon as they can get them together, the horses already taken. They have voluntarily surrendered about twenty-five head. Five head of shod horses were recently picked up in the brush by Bloods. They evidently belonged to some party of white men who had been set afoot. The horses were promptly sent to the government farm, to await claimants."[11]

But the Bloods were too independent and the young men too wild to give up raiding entirely. Although Montana was temporarily forbidden territory, nothing had been said about the Cree and Assiniboine camps farther east near the Cypress Hills. This area was in Canada and was rich in horses. At onset of the winter of 1881-82, a Mounted Policeman reported that a mixed Blood and Blackfoot camp was at the mouth of the Bow River and that "Parties of Bloods have been seen hanging round [Fort Walsh] at night, by Crees, and have even been into the lodges."[12]

But just as the snows of winter put an end to the sounds of wind whispering through the prairie grass, so did the weather quiet the talk of battle. Warriors, whether Blood or Cree, were content to huddle in their cabins and lodges, accepting government rations of beef and flour and killing a few deer in the wooded valleys. They might still talk of raiding their enemies, but they would wait until spring when the grass was green and the captured horses could graze on their way home.

In the meantime, Red Crow could look upon this first year on the reserve with some satisfaction. While rumors of hunger and disillusionment were filtering down from the Blackfoot Reserve, the Bloods were relatively contented. Rations were issued on time, the white employees treated the Indians with respect, and the food, while not always of the best quality, was sufficient to keep starvation away.

The epidemics of measles and scarletina had run their course and, with the onset of winter, fewer women went to mourn for their children whose bodies were buried in the trees along the river. Even the mange which had deciminated the horse herd seemed to vanish with the cold.

As the tribe settled in for the winter, the chiefs regained the authority with had been lost to the warrior societies on the plains. At the same time Red Crow realized that much of the authority now lay with the government agents. They controlled the Indians' food and thus controlled their lives. But Red Crow also observed that no attempts were made to interfere with the Indians' daily routine as long as it did not violate the white man's law. With the farm instructor as a friend, Red Crow was able to maintain his leadership without sacrificing either his principles or his feeling of independence.

Similarly, his influence was such that when an interpreter was required by the Indian Department, the agent chose David Mills, a half-Blood half-Black who had previously been criticized because "he favoured Red Crows camp more than the rest."[13]

Red Crow's role was further strengthened during the winter when the farcical situation of Running Rabbit's leadership finally ended. Although ostensibly a head chief of equal rank with Red Crow, Running Rabbit was a man without a following who considered the Blackfeet Reservation in Montana his real home. Thus when trouble arose with customs officials during the winter, Running Rabbit resigned and handed in his treaty medal, scarlet coat, and Union Jack, declaring that he intended to spend the rest of his life across the line. No immediate move was made to find a successor — in spite of requests from the Buffalo Followers — so Red Crow temporarily became the only head chief of the tribe. As each month passed, both the Bloods and Indian Department officials tended to accept him as the sole leader and even if another chief were elected, he would have had difficulty in being accepted as Red Crow's equal.

Red Crow, on the other hand, worked hard to carry out his

responsibilities. In February 1882, for example, he heard that two Montana traders had camped on the Milk River Ridge and were coming onto the reserve at night to sell whiskey. When he found that the rumor was true he sought out the pedlars and even accepted a drink from them while they were busy trading. Then, instead of returning home, he rode to Fort Macleod to report to Superintendent L. N. F. Crozier that the whiskey traders were at work. As evidence, he produced a small glass bottle filled with a brownish liquid; instead of drinking the whiskey, he had held it in his mouth and later spat it into the container. The hospital steward checked it and pronounced it to be diluted alcohol. A patrol was dispatched from the fort and a short time later Louis Conn and William Davis were arrested for trying to bring forty gallons of whiskey onto the reserve. Each man was given a $300 fine or six months in jail.[14]

While Red Crow was learning to adjust to the new life, other events were taking place which would ultimately challenge his leadership. Since he had first come to the reserve, his only contacts with the Indian Department had been through Norman T. Macleod, the Indian agent, and with John MacDougall. Regardless of the fact that the Indian agent was a brother of Colonel Macleod, the Mounted Police accused him of obstructing them in their duties, and such a feeling of antagonism developed that the commissioner of the NWMP recommended that the police be given direct responsibility for the Blackfoot tribes.[15] In the spring of 1882, when a scandal erupted in Macleod's office over the falsification of invoices by a clerk, the Indian agent was finally removed.

His replacement was Cecil Denny, a former inspector of the Mounted Police who had worked closely with Indians since his arrival in the West in 1874. Denny, as soon as he took office, dismissed several of Macleod's appointees, including MacDougall. Not only that, he threw his full support behind the Mounted Police in their efforts to keep the Indians on their reserves and concluded that the chiefs did not cooperate as fully as they might. Although he showed no direct antagonism towards Red Crow, it was obvious by his actions that he disagreed with the chief's broad powers and set out to undermine or circumvent them.

His first action was to seek out the warrior societies, realizing that they were nominally under the control of the head chief, yet were a truculent body which needed little encouragement to act independently. At Denny's direction, the warriors were appointed "to act as police for the purpose of assisting me in getting back stolen horses, and also

helping in a great many ways on the reserve."[16] The leader of the
warrior society was Heavy Shield, a son of Red Crow's rival, Many
Spotted Horses, so he and his followers were pleased to cooperate in
return for extra rations.

During the two years which Denny spent as Indian agent, relations
between him and Red Crow were at best cool and distant. Mac-
Dougall's replacement as farm instructor, W. C. McCord, on the other
hand, recognized the necessity of maintaining the chief's cooperation.
On one occasion he reported: "Red Crow assisted us in rationing and
does very well to keep the peace," and on another, "Held a court to day
and tried some queer cases, but had Red Crow to assist me."[17]

With the arrival of spring in 1882, Denny made full use of the
Mounted Police and the warrior societies to keep the Bloods from
making their intended raids upon the Crees in the Cypress Hills. At
first he was successful, but with unexpected results, for the Crees took
the Bloods' inaction as a sign of weakness. As he reported in May:
"The Bloods have been a little uneasy owing to parties of Crees having
been round their Reserve and stealing some of their horses. I had some
trouble to prevent them going down to Cypress Hills to make a raid on
the Crees, but I think they have now given up this idea."[18]

He was wrong.

A couple of days later, the Crees ran off forty horses belonging to
Running Crane, a prominent member of White Calf's band. When the
first raids had occurred in the spring, White Calf had gone to the
Indian Agent for action, but had been convinced that the police would
recover the stolen animals. Now, with a theft taking place in his own
camp, he angrily led a delegation of warriors to see Denny,
complaining that the Bloods "had not gone to war, and now the Crees
took them for children and stole their horses just as they pleased."[19]

Realizing that the expedition would set out, with or without his
permission, Denny prepared a letter of introduction for White Calf to
take to Superintendent James M. Walsh, the officer in command of
Fort Walsh in the Cypress Hills. In it, he said that the bearer knew the
stolen horses were in the Cree camps "and is bound to go down to get
them, although I have advised him otherwise. . . . He is after a good
many horses taken this spring, and goes down with tobacco to make
peace with the Crees."[20]

Armed with this letter, White Calf believed he was in a position to
lead a war party with the full sanction of the Indian agent. As this was
a war situation, Red Crow as political chief had no voice, yet White
Calf's forceful actions in outmanoeuvring the Indian agent could not

help but be compared with Red Crow's efforts in discouraging Montana-bound war parties and encouraging farming. For the first time since they came to the reserve, the young Bloods could rally around a leader who seemed to be doing something more than eating government rations.

Denny had expected White Calf to take a dozen young men with him to Fort Walsh where a treaty could be negotiated. Instead, the war chief organized a massive revenge party of 200 Bloods, all armed with repeating rifles and ready for battle. Arriving in the Cypress Hills a week later, they went directly to Fort Walsh, where the letter was presented to the commander. Realizing that such a large force could never enter a Cree camp peacefully, the police asked White Calf to choose six warriors who might form a treaty party. Then, with the war chief at their head and a Mounted Police escort beside them, the Bloods went to Piapot's camp where they succeeded in recovering three of the missing horses.

The Crees greeted the Bloods sullenly and when White Calf offered tobacco as a sign of peace, Piapot threw it in the fire. Angry and insulted, White Calf stalked from the camp and returned to Fort Walsh. That night his party attacked a small Cree encampment near the fort, venting their rage upon the hapless party, shooting one man eight times, stabbing him three times, and tearing the scalp from his dead body. When they returned to their reserve, the Bloods put on a gigantic scalp dance and vowed to avenge any more raids which might take place on their camps.

White Calf was tremendously popular because of the successful raid, yet he gained the ill will of Agent Denny, who was criticized for letting the Indians leave their reserve. Earlier, Denny may have considered backing White Calf as a means of undermining Red Crow, but he had no wish to create another obstruction in his efforts to control the reserve. His goals were to stop horse stealing, keep the Bloods at home, and introduce farming. He did not believe that many of the chiefs supported him, so his intention was to work directly with young men who showed a propensity for farming and to use the warrior societies to maintain law and order. Red Crow had a place in his plans only insofar as he supported Denny's policies.

Interestingly enough, Denny was sympathetic to the plight of the Indian and was often in trouble with the bureaucrats for his unorthodox ways of conducting business. He cut red tape whenever possible, eliminated practices which unnecessarily antagonized the Indians, and ran his office in a casual and offhand manner. He was down-to-earth and friendly with the chiefs, gambled and drank with his companions, and on more than one occasion he had a Metis girl sharing his bed.

But, like so many people of that period, he fully believed that the only way the Indians would progress was by abandoning their old ways and accepting the white man's ethics and values. As he stated in later years, ". . . the younger generation, to whom the old wild life was unknown, were to prove that the provisions made for their benefit by the Government — the shepherding of them on the reserves, the schools they were required to attend, the instructors sent among them to teach them farming and stock-raising — had been wise provisions."[21]

At the same time, he was sure that most of the old nomadic chiefs would never accept such changes and that it was necessary for him to place the power in the hands of more pliable leaders.

Knowing that there was a vacant head chieftainship, Denny kept a close watch on his wards, looking for a leader who would suit his purpose. At that time, the only men who wielded much power were Red Crow and White Calf, with lesser chiefs like Medicine Calf, Bad Head, and Many Spotted Horses being too old and too intractable for serious consideration. In the fall of 1882, Denny had government permission to hold an election for head chief at the treaty payments, and with an obvious reference to Red Crow, he stated: "I am going to make a change among them. Many of the old chiefs I find encourage the young men to go out horse stealing, and I intend to get a head chief elected . . . who will help us, and who is really a chief among the young men."[22]

However, when the treaty payment time came, Denny decided to postpone the election "on account of jealousy among the Indians."[23] The rising popularity of White Calf probably made him realize that any hand-picked candidate of his would be defeated. But by the autumn of 1883, Denny had at last found the man he wanted. Unable to discover a leader who would follow his wishes, he chose Calf Tail, a nonentity from the Buffalo Followers camp. Although he had no following and no proven leadership abilities, he and his brother Bull Horn were related to the aged Bad Head, and either could conceivably inherit the leadership of the Buffalo Followers band when the old chief passed away. As an added advantage, Calf Tail was married to a sister of White Calf, the redoubtable war chief. Fully conversant with tribal politics, Denny surmised that Calf Tail could consolidate the anti-Red

Crow factions and provide the Indian agent with the control over the young men that he needed to carry out his policies.

Denny was confident that he could influence the outcome of an election. "I think that a vote of the whole will elect an Indian called Calf Tail," he reported, "who has shown himself a very good man, and one who has been of great aid to me in taking stolen horses from Indians."[24]

White Calf was furious when he learned that his brother-in-law was a candidate for the head chieftainship. Although the war chief wielded a great influence in the tribe and unofficially was accepted as its second leader, he realized he was no match for any man hand-picked by the agent. Direct appeals to Calf Tail to withdraw proved fruitless and even the argument that he was being groomed as a puppet to counteract Red Crow fell on deaf ears. When the election was held on September 27, Calf Tail and White Calf were the only candidates. Denny called a council of the entire tribe, and when the votes were counted, Calf Tail had won.

Denny was elated. "The election was a good one," he exclaimed, "he being really the only chief among the Band. I am very glad of the selection as he is by far the best man."[25]

A new band had to be established for Calf Tail and a number of Indians, recognizing the favored position of the leader, flocked to his side. Notable among them was Sheep Old Man, Red Crow's estranged brother, who had actively supported Calf Tail for the candidacy and, in the minds of some, hoped eventually to assume that position himself. Evidence that the new chief would receive preferential treatment came soon after the election. As Denny stated, "I should be glad if the government would give the new Blood chief a present of a wagon as he is poor, but has great influence among them for good or bad. He is much more of a chief than Red Crow, and has five times the influence."[26]

What happened next is part of tribal lore.

When the results of the election were announced, White Calf angrily confronted his brother-in-law and cursed him. He said he was unfit to be a chief, that he had turned his back on his own people, and that he would be dead before winter. Two months later, on November 27, Calf Tail died "from the disease prevalent among the Blood Indians."[27]

There was no doubt in the minds of the Bloods that he had been killed by the war chief's curse. And so, with perverse humor, the newly-formed band was named the Orphans, because their "father" had died so soon after it was formed. Even when Calf Tail's brother Bull Horn was unofficially chosen over Sheep Old Man to become chief of the band, the name remained. As for Sheep Old Man, his abortive attempt to take control of the Orphans was his last political move in a fruitless life-long battle to compete with his more successful brother.

There was no way that Agent Denny could fill the head chieftainship until the next annual treaty payments, but by that time he had resigned and left the area. Red Crow, without being directly involved, had seen his leadership attacked, threatened, and in the end emerge unscathed. If anything, it had been strengthened by Denny's support of poor Calf Tail. Without that support, White Calf's election would have been a virtual certainty and Red Crow's leadership would have been shared with one of the most intelligent and capable leaders in the tribe.

13

/ Unsettled Conditions /

Throughout Cecil Denny's two-year campaign to wrest control of the reserve from Red Crow, the head chief had remained confident, complacent, and friendly to the agent. Although Denny had directed the rationing system and had the support of the Mounted Police, it was impossible for him to be involved in the day-to-day affairs of the reserve. Red Crow continued to hold council with his minor chiefs, to settle disputes, and to take action for the welfare of his people.

Often his authority was exercised by example, rather than by edict. When he erected fences and planted potatoes, turnips, and wheat, he indicated that he favored the introduction of farming; the fact that he did not actively encourage others to farm may have rankled the Indian agent but to Red Crow such action was unnecessary. Similarly, he encouraged the young men in his family to stay at home, but he seldom prevented his followers from going to war, and only then when it was in the best interests of the tribe. As in the nomadic days, Red Crow led the Bloods by consensus and by his own actions.

As a political leader, he made no effort to negotiate a peace treaty with the Crees, partly because he disliked the tribe more violently than any of his other enemies and also because his people were angry at the Crees for their frequent forays since the Bloods had settled on their reserve. Even if a peace treaty had been made, the young warriors could have broken it.

In the summer of 1883, the chief himself was a victim when a Cree war party under a warrior named Eagle Child ran off eighty Blood horses of which thirty belonged to Red Crow; one in particular was a fine sorrel race horse. The raiders were followed eastward towards the Cypress Hills, but the trail was lost. A few days later, Red Crow and five warriors went to Fort Buford, in Montana, hoping that the horses might be on the American side of the line, but they were never recovered. So notable and audacious was the raid that it was recorded in the Blood calendars as the year "When Red Crow was robbed."[1]

While not prepared to make peace with his enemies, Red Crow

made several efforts to keep the young warriors at home and to recover missing horses. In May 1883, he helped a number of Gros Ventres to search the reserve for missing horses and, when they were unsuccessful, he accompanied them to the Blackfoot Reserve. There, after a meeting with Crowfoot, the stolen animals were found and returned to their owners.

Later in the same month, Red Crow stopped some young Bloods who were starting south to join a war party of Peigans in Montana. At that time the Peigans were being accused by ranchers of killing livestock, and uneasy relations existed between Indians and whites in that territory. To let the untried fledglings join the troubles across the line was exposing them to needless danger.

Although the skirmishes with enemy tribes had an unsettling effect upon the Bloods in 1882-83, other events were occupying Red Crow's attention. Within his own family, one of his sons died in infancy during the summer of 1882 at a time when Agent Denny reported that "a good many children died."[2] A few months later, the chief adopted the abandoned twin child which his wife had rescued from the woods; he named him Shot Close and made him a favorite in his lodge.

While ostensibly Red Crow had settled on the bottom lands at the Belly River, he had not given up his wandering. Besides his journeys to Blackfoot Crossing and to Montana in search of missing horses, he sought a few buffalo reported along the Milk River Ridge and made regular hunting expeditions to the Sweetgrass Hills.

During this period, while the Blackfoot and Peigans were unsettled and complaining about starvation on their reserves, the Bloods were in relatively good condition. While hunger and suffering did exist and the mortality rate was unreasonably high, many of the Bloods supplemented their rations with deer and antelope, often killing the animals in coulees right on the reserve. Besides this, in 1882 they harvested several tons of potatoes and turnips from their little gardens, with thirty-five tons being stored in three root houses built by the Indian Department. Men like Red Crow, however, kept their harvest in their own root houses and, in spite of the fact that the government temporarily reduced their flour ration from a half pound a day to a quarter pound, there was enough food to prevent actual starvation.

Those who suffered most were the very young and very old. Influenza, whooping cough, and pneumonia were among the respiratory ailments which carried away many children, while the tiny, windowless cottonwood cabins were littered with the disease-ridden refuse of a people who had been accustomed to moving from place to place. A newly-appointed Mounted Police constable noticed the situation on his first visit to Red Crow's camp.

"Seen from a distance, it was beautiful, with its background of green cottonwoods and grey buckbrush, the river winding and sparkling in the sunshine, and the mountains towering behind. Blue whisps of smoke curled upward from the open tops of the tepees scattered about in picturesque disorder, while a few old squaws pottered around attending to the chores of the camp — gathering firewood, fetching water from the river, etc. The beauty of the distance ceased abruptly as actual contact with the camp was made, for rags and decaying bones and refuse of every description littered the ground in all directions and poisoned the atmosphere."[3]

The elderly suffered too, from each sickness which swept the reserve as well as from blindness and eye diseases caused from living in smoky lodges and from abject poverty. Agent Denny was saddened by the sight of old women "being literally in rags." "They fight," he said, "over the old cotton flour sacks, of which they make dresses."[4]

However, there was little that Red Crow could do. He had no ready supplies of clothing, and rationing was the prerogative of the agent. While the amounts of beef and flour were not generous, they were enough to prevent actual starvation.

Another problem which arose during Denny's tenure was the setting of the reserve's boundaries. In 1880, when Red Crow had gone to the Belly Buttes with Agent Macleod, he had selected the land on the south side of Belly River for his tribe. In the following year, a delegation of Bloods met the Marquis of Lorne, the governor-general of Canada, during his tour of the West and asked that the reserve be broadened to include Standoff bottom, between the Belly and Waterton Rivers. Whatever answer the vice-regal visitor gave, the Bloods took it as an indication of approval, and many of them began to build cabins and pitch their lodges in that river bottom.

When Agent Denny was appointed, he told the Bloods that they could not claim Standoff bottom and that their reserve was still on the south side of the Belly, "17 miles down and 17 miles up" from the Agency.[5]

In that year, Agent Denny reported that the Bloods had a population of 3,542 and, on the basis of the treaty provision of five persons per square mile, they qualified for a reserve 708.4 square miles in size. The area along the Belly accounted for only a small fraction of that total.

Accordingly, in the summer of 1882, John C. Nelson, a surveyor appointed by the Indian Department, arrived to lay out the reserve and to set aside a timber limit in the mountains. As Red Crow had chosen the land for his reserve south of the Belly, Nelson took that river as his north and west boundary and the St. Mary River as his east boundary. Proceeding towards their sources, he drew an east-west line between the two rivers at the point where he believed the land entitlement ended. It encompassed some 650 square miles — considerably below the requirement to meet the Indian Department's official population count. Not only that, but in 1883, Nelson was called back to resurvey the southern line and to reduce the size of the reserve to 547.5 square miles.

The actual size of the reserve was of no concern to Red Crow, as he asked for all the land between the two rivers as far as the Rocky Mountains. Artificial survey lines across the prairies meant nothing to him and so he took no interest in the work of Nelson and his party. In fact, at the time of the survey, he was down at Fort Buford in Montana trying to recover his stolen horses.

On July 2, 1883, the leading chiefs of the tribe gathered at the Agency to sign a new treaty to give up their rights to the former lands allocated on the South Saskatchewan and to officially accept the new ones. Representing the government were Lieutenant-Governor Edgar Dewdney and their old friend Colonel James F. Macleod. This time there was no charade of discussing new terms; the government simply informed the Bloods that they must legally surrender the old reserve promised in the 1877 treaty and the new one surveyed by Nelson would be theirs. In the treaty, the new reserve was described as: "Commencing on the north bank of the St. Mary's River ... thence extending down the said bank of the said river to its junction with the Belly River; thence extending up the south bank of the latter river to a point thereon in north latitude forty-nine degrees, twelve minutes and sixteen seconds ... and thence easterly along in a straight line to the place of beginning."[6] Excepted from the area was a small parcel of land around old Fort Whoop-Up and a ranch near Standoff owned by Dave Cochrane.

The document was interpreted by Dave Mills, with a second interpreter being brought in by Red Crow, an educated Blood named Joe Healy.

The order in which the Bloods signed the treaty was politically significant. The first, of course, was Red Crow. He was followed by Father of Many Children; even though six years had passed since the old chief had been carried on a travois to the original treaty negotiatons, he was still looked upon as the main leader of the Buffalo Followers. By this time he was "a very old man, practically blind, with one squaw nearly as old and helpless as himself." He passed away the following year.[7]

White Calf, the ambitious war chief, was absent, as was his predecessor, Medicine Calf. But the rest of the council was there — the old leaders like Many Spotted Horses and the younger men such as One Spot, Bull Shield, and Blackfoot Old Woman. The latter sub-chief was taking an increasingly dominant role in tribal affairs as his own leader, Eagle Head, withdrew from the perplexing problems of reserve life.

As far as Red Crow and the others were concerned, the treaty merely confirmed the agreement made between the chief and Lieutenant-Governor Dewdney in 1880. Only in later years did the actual boundary designations become significant. Likely they were interpreted correctly at the time, just as Jerry Potts claimed to have told Red Crow about the boundaries after the 1882 survey. But an east-west line at 49 degrees, 12 minutes, 16 seconds — what did it mean to a chief who measured boundaries by rivers, lakes, and mountains?

As Red Crow understood it, he had received all the land between the two rivers to the Rocky Mountains. Even the two plots of land farmed by Dave Akers and Dave Cochrane within those boundaries were seen as incursions on Indian territory.

Regardless of its size, their new home was a magnificent land, the largest Indian reserve in Canada. From the rugged slopes of the Belly Buttes, Red Crow could look out across the rolling plains to the west and see the Belly River snaking through the foothills until it became lost in the Rocky Mountains. To the east, he could see the grass-covered slopes of the Buttes give way to the flat plains, interrupted here and there by shallow coulees or isolated ridges. Most prominent of these was Wild Turnip Hill, a landmark at the north end of the reserve where Many Spotted Horses had killed a Kootenay buffalo hunter and had marked the spot with piles of stones.

Along the Belly River itself, Red Crow could see the numerous river bottoms, some quite large, which offered protection from the bitterness of winter. Gnarled cottonwoods and stunted willows crowded together near the banks, as though reaching towards the water for life. And back from the river, the banks rose steeply a hundred feet or more up to the tableland above. This created the kind of pleasant, tree-dotted bottomland which Red Crow had used for camping places all his life. It was a haven from the harshness of the elements, just as the new reserve was becoming a haven from the outside world. As more and more white men came into the region, the reserve was the only place which offered some semblance of the old life. Red Crow could relax beside his tepee and see all the things which were familiar to him — the trees, the mountains and rivers. Yet even this scene was not unspoiled, for intruding upon it were the cottonwood cabins and tiny gardens — grim reminders that the buffalo were gone and a new and uncertain future faced the tribe.

But to Red Crow, these indications of changing conditions were simply evidence that there was another enemy to beat. If the white man could do it, so could he.

The 1880s were the years when the tribe needed help, but Canada had just slumped into a recession, and the Department of Indian Affairs launched an economy drive in 1883 which ultimately affected Red Crow and every other Indian in the West. After making a quick tour of the prairies, Ottawa mandarin Lawrence Vankoughnet, deputy superintendent general of Indian Affairs, concluded that his department had too many employees, spent too much on rations, and supported too many Indians. With the single-mindedness of an ambitious bureaucrat, he set out to make some drastic changes. The fact that many Indians were just settling on their reserves and the country was virtually devoid of game was of little consequence to an administrator whose measurements were balance sheets and budget figures.

On the Blood Reserve, Agent Denny reacted to the austerity by closely examining the paysheets and concluding that many of those enrolled as Bloods actually were from the Blackfeet Reservation in Montana. Similarly, he was convinced that many families were being overpaid, that they claimed to have more children than was really the case.

When the time came to make treaty payments in the fall, Denny continued to ignore Red Crow, but called on Interpreter Mills to sit beside him at the pay table. "Through his thorough knowledge of the Bloods," said the Agent, "he has been mainly the means of saving the Government several thousands of dollars ... it was almost entirely through his actions that a reduction of one thousand souls was made."[8]

Before the payments, the Bloods were being paid and rationed for 3,542 persons; when Denny closed his books, there were only 2,589. On none of the other reserves in Treaty Seven did such a drastic cut take place; the Blackfoot were reduced by only 97, while the Peigans and Sarcees actually showed an increase in their enrollment.

The result was not simply a loss of the annual five-dollar treaty money for 1,000 persons. Rather, the annuity lists were the basis for the rations received by each family for the rest of the year. If a family's ticket indicated eight people, the daily rations were eight pounds of beef and four of flour. On the other hand, if the number was cut in half, so was the amount of food.

Red Crow's own ticket remained unchanged. In 1882, he was being paid for seven women, four boys, and five girls, and in 1883 he was reduced by one when a son died, but increased by one with the adoption of Shot Close. But there were some families in his own band which were reduced by four or five persons and others that were eliminated completely. Even when Running Rabbit, former head chief, tried to return and receive rations, he was refused.

Red Crow listened to the pleas of those who had been reduced to a starvation level, but as long as Denny was the agent, any appeal would be fruitless. All the chief could do was to discuss the problems with Interpreter Mills who was almost as powerless in trying to influence the agent. It was a sad experience for a proud leader to see his followers go hungry, yet he knew the power lay in the hands of the white man as long as the Bloods depended on them for food.

By Denny's one stroke of administrative efficiency — whether justified or not — the total food consumption of the Blood tribe was reduced by nearly 3½ tons of beef and two tons of flour per week. The results were predictable, as a noticeable upswing occurred in the incidence of cattle killing, with the nearby Cochrane Ranch being the heaviest loser. The South-Western Stock Association even accused the Bloods of training their dogs to run cattle down; regardless of how ridiculous the claim may have been, it was a reflection of the cattlemen's concern for the loss of their stock.

To add to the misery, the winter of 1883-84 was a bitter one which made it hard for the Bloods to hunt wild game. At one point the farm instructor complained that "a large Band of cattle, several thousand, has passed down the river bank & numbers of them has died. I have a time of it keeping the Indians from taking the animals out there, & they will take them & may eat some of them, in spite of all I can say. They will steal them at night if they cannot otherwise, as the cattle are dieing almost on the Reserve."[9]

The second phase of Vankoughnet's economy drive occurred the day after Christmas, when Agent Denny received a telegram ordering him to dismiss all of his clerks, teamsters, storekeepers, and laborers. On the Blood Reserve, this meant firing five men, or more than half his staff, leaving only a farm instructor, interpreter, and ration issuers.

Then, to save yet more money, Vankoughnet made the decision to issue bacon instead of beef for one day out of every seven, commencing January 1, 1884. The Bloods, like other Plains Indians, were a meat-eating people who had considered the buffalo to be the only real food and everything else inferior. They did not eat fish, seldom ate fowl, and could live on a diet consisting solely of fresh meat. To them, bacon was not real food; when shown a live pig, one of the chiefs refused to believe that it was the same animal which supplied such meat. And when bacon had been issued to them during the American treaty of 1855, they had thrown it away in disgust. Now, with a reduced paylist, a smaller staff of white employees, and starvation becoming a spectre to haunt every camp, the Bloods were told to take bacon instead of beef.

"The Indians does not like it," Instructor McCord said, "but I do not mind much what they like . . . they will get in the way of using it with their potatoes."[10]

He was wrong. The reactions of Red Crow, Eagle Tail of the Peigans, and Crowfoot of the Blackfoot were instantaneous. Red Crow and Crowfoot demanded to see Governor Dewdney while Eagle Tail contacted Agent Denny, protesting that already his tribe "are starving and many are dying from some sickness that is among them."[11]

The chiefs may also have heard that Vankoughnet planned to reduce the amount of beef and flour issued to the Indians. When Agent Denny received his instructions in mid-January, he complained to Dewdney that "the ration in this treaty is now as low as is safe to issue and should I reduce it further I cannot answer for the consequences. Please notify me if this reduction must be made."[12] When Dewdney replied that he was not authorized to countermand Vankoughnet's instructions, Denny submitted his resignation, stating that the reductions of staff and the new policies made it impossible for him to carry out his duties. He was replaced by the sub-agent from Blackfoot Crossing, an ex-Mounted Policeman named William Pocklington.

At the same time, Crowfoot with a delegation of twenty-six men came south from Blackfoot Crossing to confer with Red Crow and his council. Arrangements already had been made with Dewdney to meet them on the Blood Reserve in order to ratify a new treaty dealing with the locations of reserves, so the two chiefs planned to use the occasion for a joint protest of the rationing situation.

This placed Dewdney in an awkward position, for he did not agree with Vankoughnet's austerity program and had complained to the prime minister about the transfer of authority from his office to Ottawa. Now, with Denny having resigned, he had no alternative but to mollify the uneasy leaders.

Arriving on the Blood Reserve on January 19 with his clerk, William McGirr, Dewdney held two meetings with Red Crow, Crowfoot, and the other chiefs, primarily to discuss the ratification of the 1883 treaty but also to deal with the vexing matter of rations. According to Instructor McCord, "the arrangement was settled satisfactorily . . . between the commissioner & the Indians."[13] He did not state what the arrangement was, but the issuing of bacon ceased, at least for the time being, and the rations were not reduced. On the lieutenant-governor's return to Regina, he reported that the Bloods were "perfectly quiet and contented."[14]

Apparently satisfied with the outcome of the discussions, Crowfoot returned north and Red Crow left the day after the meeting amid cold and stormy weather to go hunting in the Sweetgrass Hills. When he came back three weeks later, a chinook wind was blowing and the two storms — one political and the other natural — seemed to be over.

At the same time, there was another storm gathering on the northern horizon, in the camps of the Crees in the Battleford area. Disillusioned with the rations and their treatment by the government, leaders like Big Bear and Little Pine sought to unite the tribes in the hopes of gaining the favorable attention of the Ottawa authorities. Instead, their organizing efforts were met with suspicion and hostility by a government which suspected that the Indians were planning an uprising.

The first effort of the Crees to contact the Blackfoot tribes was made by Big Bear during the summer of 1883, when he sent presents of tobacco to Crowfoot, asking for a meeting in the Cypress Hills. In December, a courier from Big Bear invited all the Bloods, Peigans, and Blackfoot to meet with the dissidents at Blackfoot Crossing during the summer of 1884 in order to make peace and to stop the operations of the Canadian Pacific Railway. However, when the Blood Indian agent learned of the messenger's purpose, he announced that no such meeting would be permitted.

Red Crow had no intention of going, for he still hated the Crees as much as he had during his warring youth. He neither trusted them nor did he make them welcome in his lodge. And while he, too, was having problems with reduced rations and other effects of Vankoughnet's austerity drive, he would never look for a solution among the northern Crees.

Yet the western unrest continued to grow. In the spring of 1884, Louis Riel was persuaded to return from Montana to the Saskatchewan country to take up the cause of the Indians and half-breeds. One of the messengers sent out to spread the news was arrested on the Blackfoot Reserve, but not before a violent confrontation had taken place between Crowfoot and the Mounted Police.

Concened about the unsettling rumors on the Blackfoot reserves, Governor Dewdney invited Red Crow, Crowfoot, and Eagle Tail to visit him in Regina and to continue on to see the city of Winnipeg. In that way, he hoped to offset "the influence brought to bear upon the Indians of Treaty 7 with a view of prevailing upon them to join in a general stand against the government."[15] Where Eagle Tail and Red Crow were concerned, he need not have worried. Even while the chiefs were at Blackfoot Crossing waiting for the train, the Peigans and Bloods were preparing to greet any Crees with guns and war whoops. "The Indians are a little excited at present," said the Peigan farm instructor, "by a rumor that the Crees are on their way South on a horse stealing expedition and consequently their horses are driven into camp every night and the best of them picketed to be in readiness for a chase."[16]

While Crowfoot listened to the appeals of Cree and half-breed messengers, Red Crow's attitude remained unaltered. In 1880 he had accepted the fact that the Bloods would need to make new lives for themselves and, regardless of any misgivings he might have had about individual white men, he realized that they offered the only viable means of self-sufficiency. And, as a politician, he preferred to negotiate openly with the government rather than to join any intrigues with his age-old enemies.

The trip to Regina and Winnipeg was an enlightening experience. None of the chiefs had ever travelled beyond his own hunting grounds, except on war expeditions, and none had ever visited settlements larger than Fort Macleod and Calgary. In their minds — an attitude shared by most Indians — there were very few white people in the world and most of them already were in Blackfoot territory. Yet when they arrived in Winnipeg, they saw a massive community of brick, stone, and frame buildings with a population of more than 15,000 persons.

There they met journalist George H. Ham, who took them to a confectionary where Red Crow was given his first dish of ice cream. Delighted, he called the dish "sweet snow" and said during the next blizzard he would tell his wives to gather in a plentiful supply for him.

When Ham took the chief to the theatre that night, they were walking along the sidewalk when the electric street lights were turned on. "Gazing up at them," said Ham, "he put his hands over his mouth and exclaimed, 'Oh my, oh my, oh my, the white man is wonderful! See! he has plucked a lot of little stars from the skies and put them on poles to light the village with. He is wonderful.' "[17]

Later, when they saw the play *Around the World in Eighty Days*, the chiefs were excited by the sequence where the Indians attacked the Deadwood stage. "All called out encouragingly in the Indian tongue to their fellow reds on the boards, and they became greatly excited and their unceasing activities of person and guttural whoops attracted more attention to the group than did the actors."[18]

They visited the nearby Stony Mountain Penitentiary to see some of their tribesmen incarcerated there and could not help but observe how the white man had the facilities and weapons to annihilate every Indian on the plains.

And there was another sight at the penitentiary which impressed Red Crow even more. The warden, Sam Benson, had a small herd of buffalo which he had domesticated; when the chief saw them, he said in disbelief: "If civilizaton can domesticate the buffalo, it is a lesson to us which we will not soon forget."[19]

Although the knowledge of the white man's power neither frightened nor intimidated the chief, it did surprise him. On the other hand, Crowfoot was visibly shaken by the experience, for he had come to believe that the Cree and half-breed cause might succeed. Now, that idea was tempered by the visible example of the white man's strength.

The trip gave Red Crow and the others a chance to air some of their grievances to Governor Dewdney. Since the onset of the financial cutbacks, they had been suffering from a lack of food and were uneasy about the future.

The main grievance was the issuing of bacon on the three reserves. Crowfoot was the first to raise the matter and after some discussion he emphasized "that they did not wish bacon to be served out to them in warm weather" but Dewdney assured them it would only be given "in the Spring of the year while the cattle are poor."[20] He said that instructions would be sent to issue bacon once a week during the spring months.

Although Red Crow had not been a confidant of Agent Denny

during his two-year tenure, he had admired the forthright way he had conducted business. The new agent, the chief complained, possessed much less authority than Denny and asked that this power be extended to him. Although unaware of the political infighting going on between Dewdney and Vankoughnet, he had pinpointed one of the main problems in the West since much of the decision-making had been transferred to Ottawa. Dewdney made no comment, but dutifully — and probably with some satisfaction — communicated the complaint to the prime minister.

Red Crow was pleased by the way he had been treated in Regina and Winnipeg, but when he disembarked from the train at Blackfoot Crossing, he was angry to discover that attempts already had been made to issue bacon, even though it was mid-summer, and the matter had become an explosive situation. Even while he and the other chiefs were discussing the problem with Dewdney, the agents had been instructed to give the hated food on all three reserves. And to make matters worse, the farm instructors on the Blood Reserve misunderstood the directive and announced that bacon would be given out twice a week, rather than once.

When Instructor McCord opened the doors of the ration house to make his first issue of bacon, he expected to find the usual assortment of young and old women in shawls and blankets, ready to pick up their food. Instead, he was met by a formidable group of Bloods from the warrior society, all painted and in full regalia. Their leader, Heavy Shield, loudly proclaimed that none of the women would be permitted to take the bacon and Red Crow had left instructions before his departure to accept only fresh beef.

The next day, Agent Pocklington went out to the reserve to meet the chiefs and members of the warrior society. They reiterated their demands, claiming that at the signing of Treaty Seven they had been promised that their rations would be in fresh meat only. The agent in turn claimed that Red Crow had agreed to accept bacon once a week and that the council was acting against his wishes. Surprised, the chiefs finally agreed to take the bacon, not wishing to upset any arrangement Red Crow might have made with Dewdney.

It was at this time that an irate Red Crow arrived at Blackfoot Crossing and immediately sent a messenger racing to Pocklington, demanding that he not issue any bacon as no agreement had been reached. Similarly, Crowfoot refused to allow it on the Blackfoot Reserve and Eagle Tail sent the same instructions to the Peigans.

When the next day came for giving out rations, the Blood warrior society and war chief White Calf were at the agency door, insisting that no bacon be issued, at least until Red Crow returned. In face of such stern opposition, Pocklington had no choice but to back down. He learned later that the same situation had occurred on the other reserves, with Crowfoot insisting that Dewdney was writing to Ottawa to get permission to give up the idea of issuing bacon. When Red Crow returned, the demonstrations continued until at last a telegram arrived saying that the plan to issue bacon had been suspended.

The decision had been influenced by the inflexible stand of Red Crow and the other chiefs and the fear that their demonstrations might get out of hand. Dewdney knew that the trip to Regina and Winnipeg had impressed the chiefs, so he did not want his good work upset by further heavy-handed bumbling from Ottawa. He needed all the support he could muster, for during the remainder of the year Cree messengers continued to seek the support of Crowfoot in their campaign against the government. Even Little Pine, a leading chief from the Battleford country, personally visited the Blackfoot, encouraging them to come north in 1885 to help the Crees. When he went back home, he reported that a large force of Blackfoot supporters could be expected in the spring.

Red Crow, however, had no such dealings with the northern Indians. Likely they already knew that he had no sympathy for their cause and considered them his real enemies, not the white men. Instead, Red Crow spent the summer and fall hunting, farming, and battling with the Indian agent about food supplies and the location of a new ration house. When the first Indians had settled in 1880, temporary buildings had been erected east of Standoff but in the spring of 1884, work had started on a new Indian agency headquarters at Slideout, some twelve miles downstream. Red Crow was already located near the original agency, so it meant that he had a fifteen-mile ride every time he wanted to see the agent, and his wives had a thirty-mile round trip to collect rations two or three times a week.

When he came back from Regina, Red Crow demanded that the agency be kept at its old location, but by that time the buildings were almost finished. Then, when treaty time came in the fall, he refused to take his band to the agency, but insisted that they be paid in a little Anglican schoolhouse in his village. Usually a quiet and even-tempered man, Red Crow was "in a very surly humour"[21] when Pocklington met him, and even after the agent agreed to the chief's demands, he noted that "On the first day there was a very unpleasant feeling among the

Indians such as I had never seen before. They were very quiet, and I am of the opinion that the least thing would have caused a row."[22]

When it was apparent that the Indian agency was moving to Slideout, Red Crow asked that rations be issued from both the old buildings and the new. The agent agreed in principle but the shortage of staff due to the economy drive would not permit it.

During this period, any Indian who seriously undertook farming was important in the eyes of the agent. The government still held the view that the tribe could become self-sufficient if they all became farmers, and each new piece of land was considered evidence that their program was succeeding. By 1884, Red Crow and his son Crop Eared Wolf shared the largest farm on the reserve with 58½ acres planted to potatoes and grain. Next was the Many Tumors band which jointly farmed fifty-five acres of wheat, potatoes, turnips, and carrots, while the Many Children planted twenty-three acres, Blackfoot Old Woman eighteen acres, and Bull Back Fat, eight acres. In most instances, the land was farmed in tiny individual plots by members of each band; Red Crow, on the other hand, operated a single farm, directing the operations through members of his family and maintaining an active personal interest in all phases of work. With his own root house, he was able to provide extra food for his band in the cold weather.

During the winter of 1884-85, while Canadian officials worried about the rapidly escalating hostilities in the Saskatchewan country, Red Crow was completely unconcerned. In February, he observed that three young Bloods left for the Cypress Hills to steal horses from the Crees, and in March another four men left on the same mission. Rather than joining the Crees, his people still wanted to fight them.

In other years, the departure of war parties would scarcely have raised official eyebrows but on the eve of a threatened rebellion every act of defiance was greeted with fear and concern. Accordingly, when a party returned with seven captured horses, the Mounted Police were already on the lookout for it. One of the Bloods arrested was Oral Talker, a son of war chief White Calf, and while the police were attempting to take him away, the chief interfered and was thrown in the guardroom.

Although White Calf was released on the following day, Red Crow was furious that one of his leading chiefs should have been so treated and, still a warrior at heart, he disagreed with any white man's law which said a warrior capturing enemy horses was a criminal. Leading a delegation of chiefs and warriors, he galloped to Fort Macleod the following day where he met the magistrate, former commissioner

James Macleod. But even though "stirring speeches were made by Mecasto, or Red Crow"[23] the judge insisted that the young man be held for trial or until someone came from Cypress Hills to claim the missing animals.

After the angry delegation left the meeting, White Calf threatened that "if after waiting two weeks, the boy was not released, that they would send their old people away across the line and the younger men would remain and 'turn loose.'"[24] Although the Bloods no longer followed a nomadic life, they still adhered to a tribal law which left the political chief in command during times of peace, but the instant there was danger of attack, the war chief assumed undisputed control. Red Crow knew that if White Calf tried to carry out his threat, he would have no difficulty in amassing a party of young warriors and that as soon as the Mounted Police realized what was happening, the Bloods would be in a virtual state of war. Then, and only then, would White Calf take command and Red Crow be relegated to the role of common man.

Anxious to avoid that possibility and to curb any actions which might result in unnecessary deaths among his followers, the chief watched the events as they unfolded during the next few days. He may even have hoped that the Bloods would not support White Calf because of his purely personal motives in trying to create the confrontation. The local Methodist missionary, who also watched the drama with increasing concern, marvelled at the way it was finally resolved. "Mekasto remained silent," he said, "until the Indians began to move their lodges to another place on the prairie under the direction of the factious chief, and then the peaceful ruler of his people quietly went among them, and addressed a few words of authority and wisdom, and the faction was at an end."[25]

Red Crow had stemmed a possible ugly confrontation just as the West swung into the hectic and bloody months of rebellion. While he obviously wanted peace and was known for his hatred of the Crees, officials would still wonder whether one of the most powerful warrior tribes in Canada could be kept out of the conflict. Or whether its chief could resist the temptation of returning to the war trail.

14

/ Riel Rebellion /

When the Riel Rebellion erupted in late March of 1885, the Metis in the Battleford area, assisted by Crees and Assiniboines, took up arms to vent their rage and frustration at the policies of the Canadian government. Within days, militia forces in Manitoba and eastern Canada were being mobilized and the uncompleted Canadian Pacific Railway readied to move troops into the area. Across the prairies, communities like Edmonton, Calgary, and Prince Albert feared imminent Indian attacks and the whole country was in a state of unrest.

In Fort Macleod, the closest town to the Blood Reserve, a cowboy militia unit dubbed the Rocky Mountain Rangers was formed and two blockhouses constructed to serve as forms of defence. Many ranchers, settlers, and missionaries rushed to town for protection as rumors spread about the possibility of the Blackfoot tribes joining the fray.

The experience of rancher John Craig was typical of the hysteria sweeping the region at the time. Hearing of the rebellion, he decided to take his family to Fort Macleod.

"On the way we got quite a scare. While on our journey we saw horsemen which we took for Indians riding towards us from the prairie on a gallop. The faster I drove the more they quickened their pace, apparently trying to cut us off. Seeing they could intercept us on the trail I halted the team. I had two rifles, a Marlin and a Winchester, and concluded to give them a shot at long range from the Marlin before they got too near. . . . As they galloped nearer, our anxiety was over. Three cowboys, as scouts, had been out over the range and were riding in to intercept us to get the latest news from the North.

"We continued our journey, and met a Concord coach with a number of ladies, officers' wives from the Fort, escorted by Mounted Police, on their way to Calgary as a safer refuge until the danger was over.

". . . The next day I drove the family over to our Stand Off ranch, and found it deserted by our men from fear of the Blood Indians . . .

The next morning we crossed the Belly river and drove down through the Blood camp. We were struck with its unusual appearance. There was not an Indian in sight. A few squaws peered out through the opening of their tepees at us as we passed by. I had been through this agency before frequently, and had always seen Indians and squaws and the youngsters around in considerable numbers, but everything was different now. ... I returned to Macleod, and found the ranchers' families from the surrounding district had come to the Fort for protection."[1]

Another rancher, W. F. Cochrane, expressed the same kind of fear when he decided to stay on his ranch, adjacent to the Blood Reserve. A month earlier, he had had a dispute with Red Crow over the grazing of Cochrane cattle on the reserve. The rancher had broached the matter to the Indian agent while Red Crow was in Regina, and in spite of the fact that the lease had been approved, the chief refused to recognize it until he was approached personally and had discussed it with his council.

Writing to his father within days of the outbreak of fighting, Cochrane observed: "There is some uneasiness about our Indians breaking out. Riel's runners are in the camps and it looked so serious Friday when Dunlop was at Stand Off that I drove into town in the evening and got 4 more rifles and 1500 rounds of ammunition. Dunlop thinks we should not be without them at any time. If the half breeds have any success north we will be pretty sure to get it. There are not more than enough police here to protect Macleod, and we will have to look out for ourselves. ... There are enough Indians to clean us all up here before help came. And it may come to that any time."[2]

Red Crow first heard about the rebellion through wild rumors which were picked up from traders and settlers. As they flashed through the reserve, the stories caused the same kind of hysteria and excitement they were creating among the nearby ranchers and settlers. Warriors decamped from their villages and gathered in excited groups; farms were ignored and abandoned; and each new rumour was magnified and enlarged.

The feelings were a mixture of excitement, fear, and elation. Many of the younger warriors were chaffing under the restrictions of the reservation system and would have been happy to join in any battle, just as their ancestors had done. Others feared that the rebellion might escalate into an Indian-white war which would bring the Mounted Police and soldiers galloping down on the Blood camps, just as Colonel Baker's American troops had massacred the Peigans fifteen years earlier.

But to most, it was an thrilling break in the monotonous routine, an excuse to toss away the hoe and plough and relive some of the excitement of the past when, as a warlike nomadic people, they had ruled the plains.

Red Crow was more pragmatic. Upon receipt of the first rumors, he went directly to the Indian agent and asked him what was going on. Pocklington, realizing that the unfounded stories were causing considerable unrest, told the chief all he knew. That Riel's forces had engaged the Mounted Police at Duck Lake; that Fort Carlton had been abandoned and destroyed by fire; that the village of Battleford had been pillaged by Crees under Crowfoot's adopted son Poundmaker; and that Big Bear's followers had killed the inhabitants of Frog Lake. At the same time, he told the chief that thousands of troops were being mobilized in Winnipeg and farther east, and the West would soon be flooded with soldiers to put down the insurrection.

From the onset of the rebellion, there was no doubt about Red Crow's stand. The Crees and half-breeds had been his enemies since his youthful days on the warpath, and he saw no reason to change his views. On the other hand, although he had had minor disagreements with government officials, he bore no general hatred for the white man. Indians on other reserves may have come to consider the whites their masters and oppressors; as such they despised them for their superiority, their callousness, and their low regard for the Indian. Red Crow, however, had never lost the pride he held in his tribe and in himself. He did not consider himself inferior to white men, therefore he had no reason to hate them. He may have been enraged by low rations, the bacon issue, and other irritants, but he saw them in their proper perspective. While he may not have had any love for the officials, neither did he dislike them as a whole.

Cecil Denny had tried unsuccessfully to usurp Red Crow's authority, yet the chief had admired him for his dynamic leadership. On the other hand, Colonel Macleod was an old friend who had persuaded Red Crow to accept the treaty, but in later years he seemed to side more with the whites than the Indians. In short, he saw each man as an individual, with all his strengths and weaknesses.

The Crees were a different matter. As a Blood chief, Red Crow looked down upon them as inveterate foes, to be stamped out the way a man would crush an insect under his moccasin. For years the Crees had harrassed his camps and in turn the Bloods had raided their horse herds and killed them at every opportunity. Red Crow had even killed and scalped one of their women.

So a war between Indian and white did not automatically place Red Crow with the Indians; to him, it was a fight between Crees and whites — and that made all the difference in the world.

Within the tribe, however, the situation was not so clear-cut. Most of the minor chiefs shared Red Crow's dislike of the northern Indians, but a few Bloods had married into that tribe or had established friendships with them. And several young men were ready to join with anyone who gave them a chance to kill someone. Perhaps this would be the opportunity to establish a war record as their fathers had done, to give them coups to count and stories to tell around the campfire.

So attitudes on the reserve ranged from those who wanted to join the Crees to those who wanted to kill them, from those who saw the white man as an ally to those who saw him as their foe. The majority, however, agreed with their chief.

On April 7, Agent Pocklington and Superintendent John Cotton of the Mounted Police went to the Blood Reserve to meet with the council. There, Red Crow made it clear that his tribe would not join the rebels and, on the contrary, if the Mounted Police "would give the word they would be ready at any time to fight the Crees."[3] This intelligence was passed on to Governor Dewdney, who in turn wired the prime minister that the Bloods were quiet "but wanted to fight Crees."[4]

Red Crow realized that the rebellion had placed him in a good bargaining position, so he raised many of the problems which had concerned the tribe. By the time the initial meeting was over, Pocklington had agreed to double the flour ration to half a pound a day, to increase the meat ration, to open a new ration house for the upriver Indians, and to speed up negotiations to buy Dave Cochrane's spread. And, sure enough, the latter deal was concluded within three weeks.

Contrary to the wild rumors circulating through Fort Macleod, no Cree or half-breed messengers arrived at the Blood Reserve during the early weeks of the rebellion. White Calf, the war chief, whose son was released at the onset of the rebellion and who had great influence over the young men, was emphatic in his rejection of the Crees; similarly, Bull Shield, leader of the Scabbies band, went to Agent Pocklington and said: "Give us the ammunition and grub and we'll show you how soon we can set the Crees afoot and lick them."[5]

The idea of using Blackfoot warriors against the Crees came from several other sources as well. *The Macleod Gazette* editorialized that "the authorities could not do better than enlist as allies the Blackfeet, Bloods, Peigans and Stonies. The first three of these, at any rate, are the natural and bitter enemies of the Crees, and would hail with enthusiastic joy the prospect of marching against their old enemies."[6] Even the prime minister considered using Blackfoot troops and asked Dewdney, "Could a body of Blackfeet under white command be trusted?"[7] However, concerns were expressed that once off their reserve, the Indians would be hard to control and might be mistaken for rebels.

As the fighting moved into its early weeks, the advantage was with the Metis and Crees, and messengers from the rebel camps tried hard to convince Crowfoot to support them. The Blackfoot chief was sorely tempted and, to gauge the feelings of his fellow chiefs in the nation, he sent gifts of tobacco to the Bloods and Peigans, inviting them to join the rebels.[8] Red Crow not only refused to smoke, but he pointedly sent the tobacco back with the messenger who had brought it. Eagle Tail also rejected the offer.

A short time later, the arrival in Fort Macleod of a company of the Winnipeg Light Infantry, and later two companies of the ninth Quebec Battalion, was more the source of wonderment than of fear. As skilled equestrian warriors, the Bloods could not understand why the government would send infantry onto the prairies. Missionary John Maclean recalled how Bull Shield viewed them:

"He laughed at the idea of little men on foot being able to do anything upon the prairie if the Indians should go to war. Requesting me to act the part of a sentinel, he went through a series of native military tactics to show me that the Indians could kill every man placed on guard and never be discovered. Crouching on the ground with a knife in his teeth, and his whole body covered with a blanket, he sprang unsuspectingly upon me, as I walked to and fro.

" 'I would not shoot my gun, for that would alarm the enemy,' said he, 'and I would lie near at hand without any fear, until I was close enough to strike him dead.' The white men seemed foolish in his eyes to send such a contingent to protect anyone."[9]

Although most of the Bloods favored fighting the Crees, a few remained sympathetic towards them. Shortly after the outbreak of the rebellion, two prominent Bloods named Black Eagle and Young Pine went to Red Crow to urge him to join the Cree cause. Young Pine was a good friend of a Cree leader named Lone Man and was convinced that the rebels would win.[10] Red Crow, however, flatly refused them. Instead, he cautioned his people "to stay quietly at home, and look after their fields and listen to what he told them."[11]

Red Crow had always been sought out by visitors to the Blood

Reserve, but now he found that more attention than usual was being lavished upon him, as one official after another wanted to be assured of the tribe's loyalty. Besides frequent visits from Agent Pocklington, Red Crow saw Superintendent Cotton on many occasions and even was visited by his former agent, Cecil Denny, who was on special assignment for Governor Dewdney. Another visitor was Father Albert Lacombe, who labored among the Blackfoot.

Most officials left Red Crow's lodge unreservedly accepting his repeated assurance that the Bloods wanted no part of a Cree insurrection. Yet there were exceptions. Superintendent Cotton, who was in charge of the Macleod district during the rebellion showed clear signs of panic and suspected that the Bloods were merely waiting for the successful outcome of the fighting before joining the rebellion. He even telegraphed a wild rumor to Ottawa, stating that the Bloods "have been sent tobacco from Riel and Northern Crees, if they smoke the tobacco they will send their women to South Peigans and join Half-Breeds and Crees. They have been holding secret Council the last three nights . . ."[12] Similarly, Father Lacombe seemed to be particularly worried about the Bloods, and after he visited their reserve he told the people in Fort Macleod he was "not any too well satisfied with the attitude of those Indians. Father Lacombe is of opinion that more troops should be sent here at once, if for nothing else, to show these Indians how well prepared for them Canada is."[13] Later, he suggested to the prime minister that the Bloods, Blackfoot, Peigans, and Crees should all be lumped on a single reserve with a large fort constructed to guard them.

Red Crow had told the authorities that the rebellion was a northern matter which did not concern his tribe, and in spite of the fears of Cotton and Lacombe, none of the Bloods set out either to attack the whites or to join the Crees. On the other hand, when a message came that a South Peigan Indian had been killed by Gros Ventres in Montana, a war party of twenty Bloods immediately set out for the south. Red Crow and One Spot tried to keep them at home, but they slipped away in twos and threes during the night.

It was evidence that nothing had changed.

From the beginning of the rebellion to the end, Red Crow remained steadfastly opposed to his old enemies, the Crees. He was delighted when the agent "told him of Riel's capture and of Colonel Otter's victory of the Crees . . . and said it would be well to beat the Crees quickly before they took to the bush as they were good fighters under cover."[14] The fact that they and their half-breed friends were finally defeated was the source of grim satisfaction to him. And when it was over, Agent Pocklington summed up the situation: "Too much praise cannot be given Red Crow for his staunch loyalty during the rebellion, as from the first I was not in the least anxious about him and his followers. It is a positive fact that Red Crow had tobacco sent him more than once, urging him to rise, but in every instance he sent the tobacco back, and would not listen to the accompanying messages."[15]

Throughout his career, Red Crow saw life in sharp contrasts of black and white; there were few grey areas. He knew his friends; he knew his enemies. He could remember the past, but lived for the present, and looked to the future. And, throughout it all, he gazed at the world around him with a secure feeling of self-satisfaction and pride. The white man may have gained his hunting grounds, but the world was still Red Crow's.

15

/ Old Life and the New /

In the months following the rebellion, life returned to normal on the Blood Reserve. With the completion of the ration house on Standoff bottom, Red Crow moved upstream and began construction of a new house. Unlike the old one, which was of rough cottonwood trees, the new structure was of pine logs brought down from the mountains. Complete with wooden floor and glass windows, it was one of the best homes on the reserve.

"The Indians are all in lodges, but they have good cabins," said Inspector Alex McGibbon, "and some new ones were being constructed. The whole appearance of the camps had a tidy look about them. This is especially the case in the Upper Camp — Red Crow's."[1]

One of the first effects of opening the new ration house was to divide the tribe into two groups, the Upper (or upriver) Indians, consisting almost entirely of the Fish Eaters, Lone Fighters, and Orphans bands, and the Lower Indians, including the Buffalo Followers, Black Elks, and Many Tumors.

Because a number of minor chiefs, including Medicine Calf and Many Spotted Horses, had died during the preceding months, four new men were elected in June. These were Calf Shirt and Eagle Rib, two young men favored by the agent; Bull Horn, whose replacement of Calf Tail in 1882 was finally confirmed; and Heavy Shield, turbulent leader of the warrior society. In addition, when Father of Many Children had passed away in 1884, his son Wolf Bull was considered by everyone to be his successor.

Ever since White Calf had lost his bid for the head chieftainship in 1882, he had bided his time, waiting for the old leaders to die and gaining the support of the young men. Also, he saw that his unalterable opposition to the Crees and half-breeds during the rebellion had made him a grudging ally of Agent Pocklington.

Shortly after the election of the young men as minor chiefs, White Calf made a move in his quest for leadership. Approaching Pocklington, he asked for permission to officially unite the Buffalo Followers band under a single chief — himself, of course.

"He asked me to let him take the whole of Hind Bull's Band, also Father of Many Children's into his own," said the agent, "that Hind Bull was willing to give up his chieftainship and that Father of Many Children's son Wolf Bull would forego the chance of being made chief in his father's place."[2]

Pocklington flatly rejected the war chief's request and, with a fairly accurate appraisal, stated: "The fact is, being a great talker and no worker, he is jealous of Red Crow having so large a Band, and thinks by having a large Band he would be more thought of by Departmental officials and the public generally. For my part, I think it would be the worst possible thing that could happen, for being very much gifted as a talker, he would use his influence to put bad thoughts into the heads of the young men on the Reserve."[3]

In fact, if White Calf had the concurrence of Hind Bull and Wolf Bull, he *should* have been permitted to unite the band and then, as war chief and leader of the largest band on the reserve, he should have been named a head chief. Under the old tribal system, there had always been two leaders — a political chief and a war chief. And there was no doubt that Red Crow now filled the former position and White Calf the latter.

Yet, as a political chief, Red Crow had no desire to share his leadership with anyone. He was jealous of his position and played an astute political game to retain it. The head chieftainship meant power, and Red Crow liked power. He was wise enough to know that White Calf was his only potential opposition and that with support from the young warriors, he could conceivably shift the power base from the Fish Eaters back to the Buffalo Followers band. And it hadn't been there since Bull Back Fat died in the 1840s.

Red Crow apparently took no active part in persuading Agent Pocklington to reject White Calf, other than advising him "to pay no attention to him as he is crazy."[4] He knew that Pocklington did not want the turbulent war leader any more than Red Crow did.

However, the division of the reserve into the Upper and Lower Indians made Red Crow realize that another potentially dangerous situation had been created. White Calf lived in the Lower Camp where the Indian agent resided, while Red Crow was in the Upper Camp. While he was still the undisputed head chief of the tribe, it was now convenient for the agent to have someone in the other villages to consult with. Rather than letting this responsibility fall to White Calf, who was by far the most influential leader in that camp, Red Crow put forward the name of Blackfoot Old Woman, leader of the Black Elks band. A one-time warrior of renown, he was one of the first men on the reserve to take up farming and was considered to be a good friend of the Indian agent and the missionaries. A minor chief since 1878, he attended the council meetings and was praised by the agent as "one of my mainstays."[5] Yet Red Crow was careful to control the extent of Blackfoot Old Woman's influence, permitting him to speak for the Lower Indians, but never acknowledging that he was anything but a minor chief of his own small band.

The result of this careful manoeuvring was that besides being head chief of the tribe, Red Crow was also the spokesman for the Upper Indians, while the Lower Camp was divided — Blackfoot Old Woman speaking for the farmers and White Calf for the warriors. Again, the division assured the chief's domination of tribal politics.

Yet Red Crow's leadership was not based simply upon political intrigue. He was one of the most respected leaders the Bloods had ever known. Wise, thoughtful, and fair, he listened to countless tribal disputes, settled grievances, and counselled his people to follow those paths which were to their best advantage. And this did not always mean farming and staying peacefully at home.

While he welcomed the Anglican, Catholic, and Methodist missionaries to his reserve, he actively supported the native religious societies. And when his reserve was threatened or harrassed by enemies, or when the honor of the tribe was involved, he made no attempt to stop the young men from going to war.

Late in 1885, another enemy began to lurk near Red Crow's camp — one that he had not seen for more than a decade. It was whiskey. True, a few gallons of brew were slipped across the border from time to time, but not enough to create a problem. However, early in the fall an enterprising trader built a small shack at St. Mary's Lake, on the Montana side of the border, and began to peddle whiskey at two dollars a bottle. Heartened by the man's success, an American army deserter started to sell intoxicants from a camp on the Belly River.

Within a few weeks, some of the old nightmares began to return. In November, an Indian named Running Weasel murdered his wife in a drunken quarrel and shot at some friends who tried to apprehend him. At about the same time, a bunch of drunken Indians broke into the Methodist teacher's house, smashing the windows, breaking the locks, and carrying away all the tools, clothing, and groceries they could find. During this period, missionary Maclean met his first intoxicated

Indian, a chief named Bull Back Fat. "He was riding rapidly," Maclean noted in his diary, "his hair flying loose & he shouting at the top of his voice like an insane man. I held a short conversation with him & from what I saw of his actions I learned how great the danger would be from a drunken camp of Indians."[6]

Reacting immediately to the problem, the North-West Mounted Police contacted a U.S. marshall in Montana, who promptly closed down the St. Mary's operation. At the same time, the police learned that a rancher named Paddy Hasson was heading up a local whiskey ring and, with evidence from cooperative Bloods, the man was apprehended and given a six-month jail sentence.

However, whiskey continued to trickle into the camps and as rumors of the troubles got out to the press, many people began to believe that the Bloods were ready to go on the warpath. In December, when the Methodist schoolteacher returned to the reserve to find his house ransacked, he added fuel to the rumor fires by writing letters about the incident to Toronto newspapers. He claimed that "Our Indians have been in a much more unsettled state this fall than they were either before or during the Rebellion"[7] and claimed that they had forced the police off the reserve at gunpoint.

Excited by the possibility of another outbreak, the eastern newspapers echoed the stories and rumors until at last the *Toronto Mail* sent a reporter, George Ham, to interview Red Crow and the other chiefs. By the time the reporter arrived on the prairies, Red Crow had heard about the rumors. He had already bitterly assailed a half-breed named Sanderson for spreading stories that the Bloods were storing ammunition for a rebellion, and demanded that Governor Dewdney be notified of the lies that were being circulated. As a result, he was pleased to learn that the Eastern correspondent was coming to his camp.

The reporter, too, was impressed with his visit. "Red Crow's house," he wrote, "is a double one, well built of logs, one storey high, and apparently very comfortable. The room to which I was ushered is what is commonly known as the 'living room'. In the centre is a large cooking stove, and there are two walnut bedsteads, one being covered with a clean white counterpane. The walls are 'papered' with cotton, and decorated with several pictures, one of which was the Lord's prayer and the ten commandments illustrated. On a small table was some silverware which belongs to Red Crow's sister [sic], a Mrs. Culbertson, whose husband, a factor in the American Fur Company, died some years ago. Red Crow, a fine looking specimen of humanity, advanced and shook hands with me."[8]

The chief displayed many doubts about the credibility of the reporter, claiming that other white men had come to see him and had gone away to spread lies.

"All my people want to be quiet," Red Crow observed. "The only trouble is that the Government is all the time looking for trouble with us. . . . Take pity on us and write the truth, and get the Great White Mother to hear the good news. White people write down bad news all the time.

"We want to be good friends with the whites as long as we live. A long time ago we had enough war and trouble, and we are tired of fighting. Tell the Great White Mother her red children are getting along all right, and not to fear any trouble with them. All I say is true."[9]

Red Crow went on to complain about the stories spread by the mission teacher and demanded that he be removed from the reserve. He denied that his people had ever confronted the police and laughed at the foolishness of the report. Then, reflecting his philosophy that the Bloods had to farm to become independent and self-sufficient, he added: "Tell them the Bloods are well satisfied and want to work in the spring. The only way to make a living is by working. I have told you all. We love the Blood reserve and don't want anybody to settle on it but ourselves. Don't be afraid there will be trouble in this place; tell the people so. That is all I have to say."[10]

Ham was convinced and by the time he finished his tour of the West, he had exploded all the rumors and wild stories which had been circulating through the land. He realized that whiskey was creating a problem and that horse stealing was still being practiced, but these were only minor irritants, not a cause for rebellion. During the previous summer, for example, the Bloods had gone south to help their Peigan cousins and succeeded in running off a large number of horses from a Gros Ventre camp. This was the kind of incident which the Toronto correspondent could relate as part of the color of the "wild West," completely unrelated to any thought of a general uprising.

To Red Crow, however, the raid marked a serious resumption of hostilities with one of his tribe's southern enemies and gave him new cause for concern. For the remainder of 1885 and into 1886, a number of horse-raiding expeditions set out for the Gros Ventre-Assiniboine camps in Montana. In spite of Red Crow's efforts to stop them, small parties slipped away at night and, travelling through the remote Milk

River country, they easily eluded the police patrols as they made their way to the enemy reservation.

In April 1886 alone, three or four war parties were out in search of the same prey. One of these was a four-man expedition led by Big Snake, and another consisted of three warriors, Packs His Tail, Medicine White Horses, and Eagle Plume; both teams returned with sizable herds of Gros Ventre horses. Their successes were greeted with jubilation by the young Bloods, who performed their victory dances and vowed to go back to their southern enemies again and again until no more horses were left.

After being harrassed for months by the Blood war parties, the exasperated Gros Ventres finally turned to the American military authorities for help and received permission to go north in search of their stock. Armed with letters from the Indian agent and the army officer, a group of nine Gros Ventres arrived at the Blood Reserve and made straight for Red Crow's house. When word flashed through the villages that their enemies were among them, a number of young warriors gathered near the Fish Eaters camp, threatening to shoot them if they dared to venture out alone.

Red Crow ignored the dissident youths and called in fellow chief One Spot to help recover the missing animals. They learned that some horses were on the nearby Peigan Reserve and, with the assistance of Mounted Police scout Jerry Potts, they recovered five head. In the meantime, Red Crow had rounded up another ten from his own reserve and placed them in his corral.

The young warriors were indignant and resentful as they saw the captured horses herded into the chief's corral. Even White Calf was outraged by Red Crow's actions in seizing the booty of his young raiders. That night, the dissidents crept into the Fish Eaters camp, cut the wire on Red Crow's fence, pulled down the rails of his corral, and made off with the herd. Outraged at the audacity of the young men, the chief provided the visitors with ten animals from his own herd, and next morning he grimly escorted the Gros Ventres safely on their journey home.

Red Crow was concerned that the rapidly escalating hostilities with the Gros Ventres could get out of hand, and as political chief he had hoped that a peace treaty might be made. While the visitors were there, he learned that they had been authorized to conclude such a treaty but the youthful raiders in the Blood camp destroyed any hope of negotiation with their ill-timed foray on the horse corral. As political chief of the tribe Red Crow could make as many treaties as he wished, but as long as the Bloods were in a state of virtual war, then White Calf was the only who could stop it. And there was no doubt that the war chief, twice thwarted in his attempts to gain a head chieftainship, would never countenance a treaty. Rather, he was probably pleased with the embarassment caused to Red Crow. The white officials, with their simplistic view of Indian government, could not understand why the Blood chief was suddenly powerless. The idea of dual leadership, one for war and another for peace, was utterly beyond their comprehension.

As a result, there was no treaty and the Blood raids continued unabated. Two or three parties slipped away each month, with retaliatory raids being launched by the Gros Ventres and Assiniboines with similar frequency. Finally in August 1886, a party of Bloods set out for the south and didn't come back. They were not raiders, but a group of two men and four young boys who had gone to recover ten horses stolen from White Elk of the Scabbies band.

Rumors spread through the reserve that the boys had been killed by American cowboys. Then the South Peigans said they were attacked by a mixed party of soldiers and Indians near the Sweetgrass Hills and their scalped bodies left to rot on the prairies.

Calf Shirt, a newly-elected chief and relative of three of the missing boys, immediately organized a revenge party of more than a hundred warriors, promising to set out immediately for the south. When Red Crow learned what was happening, he got his fellow chief to promise not to let a revenge party leave until the true story was discovered. In the meantime, Agent Pocklington was writing to the American authorities to see if they could shed some light on the matter.

The timing couldn't have been worse for Red Crow. Ever since the rebellion, plans had been afoot to take some of the "loyal" chiefs on a tour of eastern Canada. Now, with the possibility of an ugly confrontation in the offing, the chief had to leave. All he could do was extract a promise from Calf Shirt that no action would be taken until he came back.

The trip to the east was Prime Minister Macdonald's idea. Eight months earlier he had broached the suggestion to Dewdney, but the decision was made to postpone any definite plans until the stories of Indian unrest had passed. Macdonald realized that his North-West policies had created political turmoil in eastern Canada, even in Conservative ranks, and the execution of Louis Riel had caused a bitter division between the French and English. An eastern tour would let the rest of Canada see some of the chiefs who had been so important to the government during the rebellion and, at the same time, it would reward the Indians for their loyalty.

The whole tour revolved around Crowfoot, for he had become a romantic symbol of Indian loyalty. A telegram he sent to Macdonald during the rebellion had been widely publicized, as had his other public expressions in support of the Crown. It was ironic that the politicians and public should have lionized the Blackfoot chief in this way, for he was the one leader who most agonized over his eventual decision to remain at peace. Men like Red Crow, Eagle Tail, and Bull Head had never wavered in their hatred of the Crees and in their intention to stay out of the conflict. On the other hand, Crowfoot had been sorely tempted, almost won over to the rebel cause, but in the end he was the one who was praised and glorified for his loyalty.

The decision to take the chiefs east was finally triggered by an invitation from the Brant Memorial Association, asking that Crowfoot be invited to the unveiling of a monument to the great Mohawk chieftain, Joseph Brant, at Brantford, Ontario. The prime minister also agreed to enlarge the party to include Red Crow and his fellow Fish Eater, One Spot; North Axe, newly-elected chief of the Peigans; and Crowfoot's foster brother, Three Bulls. To accompany them was a one-time French Canadian renegade, now a government interpreter, Jean L'Heureux.

As the time approached, Father Lacombe received permission to take Crowfoot and Three Bulls on ahead to visit Montreal and Quebec. Finally, at the beginning of October, Red Crow and One Spot left the dangerous mystery of the missing boys and entrained for the East with young North Axe.

They travelled with Indian agent William Pocklington as far as Regina where they were met at the territorial capital by Jean L'Heureux, who had been sent back from Quebec to pick them up. En route to Ottawa, they learned that Crowfoot had been followed by great crowds wherever he went and that journalists were devoting their front-page columns to the activities of the illustrious chief.

On the day that the Blood and Peigan chiefs reached Ottawa, they joined Crowfoot and Three Bulls for a meeting with the prime minister. Travelling by carriage, they passed through the Byward market, where they saw dozens of farmers selling their produce. Finally, they reached the magnificent stone edifice, Earnscliff, official residence of the prime minister. After being greeted by Lady Macdonald they were taken before the prime minister, and Crowfoot, by now accustomed to the ways of the white man, made a short speech which was interpreted to his hosts and the press.

For One Spot and North Axe, both young men, these experiences were entirely new. They had never travelled on trains before, nor had they ever been out of Blackfoot country. Even L'Heureux, their interpreter, had never been on a train for any great distance prior to the tour. Large cities with streets of stone or brick buildings and thousands of people milling around were new and frightening scenes to the prairie-dwelling leaders.

Although the activities of the chiefs were fully reported by the press, their own interpretations of the events were not recorded. However, after they returned home, One Spot and North Axe told so many tales about their eastern trip, that missionary John Maclean wrote some of them down in a series of stories. One of his informants, likely One Spot, described the visit with John A. Macdonald:

"The head chief was an old man of grave countenance and very tall and dignified. . . . He smiled and told me to sit down that he might have a talk with me. He enquired very kindly and carefully about the welfare of the Blackfoot Indians, and I told him how the white savages were stealing our land, and destroying our people with the white man's water which burned like fire, and that we were becoming poorer every winter. He was much interested in all that I said, and he informed me that he had intended for a long time to pay a visit to our camps to see for himself, as he had been told of the doings of the bad savages, but that he had been very busy, and could not get away."[11]

Although Crowfoot had given the prime minister the name "Brother-in-Law" during his trip west on the newly-built Canadian Pacific Railway a year earlier, the Bloods during their Ottawa visit gave him the name "One Spot." Under this title, Maclean's informant gave another impression of Macdonald, particularly in comparison to Red Crow.

"I was deeply impressed with the ability and wisdom of One Spot," he said, "who is a great friend of the Big Mother. With a single nod of his head or a smile the wise men obeyed him, and he had only to make a request when they would hasten to grant it. He governed them all and they did not know it, and when he scolded them, they fell upon their knees and kissed his hand.

"There was only one chief to whom I would liken him, and that was our own chief, Mikasto [Red Crow], but Mikasto is a greater chief than One Spot and all his wise men."[12]

After the interview, Red Crow and the other chiefs were taken on a tour of downtown Ottawa, and again Maclean paraphrased the Indian impressions of a visit to a major store and a ride in an elevator.

"It was a big stone house, a hundred times larger than our medicine lodge, and there were as many slaves, men and women, who were trading the goods, as in one of our big camps. The trader placed me under the protection of one of his slaves, who was dressed like a chief, and told him to show me through the building. The slave took me from one lodge to another and explained many things to me, until I became bewildered with the variety of the articles, and their number. . . .

"He took me along to a small iron house, which we entered, and the house rose in the air. It was full of holes and I looked to see whether or not there were a lot of men lifting it up, but I did not see any, and the guide told me that all he had to do was to speak to the house, and it would obey him, going up or down as he told it to go. He spoke the magic word which I did not hear and it stopped, so we got out."[13]

The next day was a Sunday, so Father Lacombe took the entire delegation to mass at the Basilica, where he gave a sermon in which he praised the role played by Crowfoot during the rebellion. Later in the day, the visitors were taken to Beechwood cemetery, and in the evening to tour the governor-general's residence at Rideau Hall before going to a lecture at the Ottawa College. As the chiefs entered the college hall there was "a general outburst of applause by the audience. All eyes were fixed upon the chiefs, and they at once became the 'observed of all observers.' "[14] Again, Crowfoot was the man they had come to see, and the chief was called upon to make a speech.

In some ways, it was a repetition of the roles taken during the negotiations for Treaty Seven. Crowfoot had been on the scene first and had understood the ways of the white man, therefore he had been the logical one to speak for the group. And just as white observers concluded in 1877 that Crowfoot had been chief of the entire Blackfoot nation, so did the eastern press assume in 1886 that the other chiefs were subservient to him. "The Great Blackfoot Chief and His First Lieutenant,"[15] "Crowfoot and his chiefs,"[16] "Crowfoot and Comrades,"[17] were common phrases, while on one occasion One Spot was referred to as the "pipebearer of Crowfoot."[18]

Crowfoot had indeed been an impressive figure during his eastern tour. Tall, dignified, and with the ability to make impressive speeches, he fulfilled all the romantic images people had about the prairie Indians. Red Crow, North Axe, and One Spot, on the other hand, were still floundering about in the alien culture. Likely all would have preferred to let Crowfoot retain his position of diplomatic leadership, but it was not to be. Suffering from fatigue and the effects of strange food, the Blackfoot chief decided to return directly to the West, rather then attending the Brantford unveiling.

On October 11, a delegation of four "loyal" Crees joined the Blackfoot in Ottawa and remained their uneasy comrades for the trip to Brantford. Of the four, Starblanket and Big Child were the most important; they commanded the same kind of leadership and respect among the Crees as Crowfoot and Red Crow did in their tribes. The other two were Flying in a Circle and Back Fat.

After a levee at Ottawa's city hall, Crowfoot left for the West with Father Lacombe, while Red Crow, North Axe, and One Spot were taken by L'Heureux to the home of General Frederick Middleton, the man who had commanded the government troops during the Riel Rebellion. Treating them to ginger ale, cigars, and gifts, he informed the chiefs that he would be with the official party at the Brantford unveiling.

Leaving by train the following day, the chiefs passed through Toronto and reached Brantford in the evening. On their arrival, *The Globe* observed, "The Indian chiefs have nearly all their treaty medals hanging by chains from their necks, and four of them [the Crees] have bright scarlet military coats with brass buttons." They were taken directly to one of the finest hotels in the city to prepare for the unveiling on the following day.

When interviewed by the press, Big Child confessed that the Cree delegation slept on the floor of their rooms, remarking that "the bed was much too white and clean for them to soil."[19] Red Crow and his friends, on the other hand, had no hesitation in using the finest things the white man had to offer. Red Crow had owned a regular bed for some time, so the comforts of mattresses and sheets were no stranger to him. Similarly, the taste of ginger ale had been so pleasant that the chiefs urged L'Heureux to find them more. And there were other problems.

"The chiefs were not accustomed to eat at stated times," complained L'Heureux, "and became hungry between meals at the hotel. I was therefore obliged to satisfy their hunger. They were also annoyed at the meals in the regular dining rooms, by being stared at and crowded about. ... As the sudden change in habit and diet together with the use of fruit and iced water in hot weather being liable to disorder them, I was instructed by a medical adviser to give them freely of a tonic to their taste, ginger ale being mentioned as suitable I gave it to them as charged."[20]

The morning of October 13 was cloudy, but by noon when the skies cleared, more than 20,000 people had gathered in Victoria Park for the unveiling of the Brant monument. Promptly at twelve o'clock, the parade set off from the Indian office on Dalhousie Street, with Mohawk Chief William Wage at the lead. Following immediately behind were Red Crow and the other western chiefs, all dressed in their finest regalia. Behind them was the twenty-six-man band made up of Six Nations Indians, six Mohawks in warrior costume, and leaders of the Mohawks, Oneidas, Onondagas, Senecas, Cayugas, and Tuscaroras, with a Chippewa band taking up the rear.

Following the Indian procession came carriages with other guests, such as the lieutenant-governor of Ontario, the mayor of Brantford, and General Middleton, while interspersed among them were other bands and a cavalry escort. Amid the clanging of bells and the shrieking of whistles, the parade wound its way through Dalhousie, George, Colhorne, King, and Nelson streets to Victoria Square, where a platform had been erected in front of the veiled statue.

For the next two hours, Red Crow watched with interest as tribute was paid to the great Mohawk chief. Speaker after speaker extolled the man's virtues, particularly those which resulted in aid to the British Empire. The president of the Brant Memorial Association also linked the past to the present.

"It is very gratifying," he said, "to see present so many of our old friends, the chiefs and warriors of the Six Nations Indians, who have associated with them the distinguished Chief Red Crow and other leading chiefs from the North West. These Indian tribes that you now see before you, are from various parts of America, and are the descendents and living representatives of that great and powerful race that for so many centuries controlled the destinies of the American continent."[21]

At the proper moment, Lieutenant-Governor John B. Robinson came forward and pulled the cord to unveil a tall statue, caste from the melted barrels of British cannon. In Victorian fashion, it showed Brant in buckskin costume and with a long flowing robe. Moments later, the chiefs of the Six Nations pulled other cords and a series of Union Jacks fell away to reveal bronze panels illustrating the life of Brant.

As the Six Nations Indians began a war dance, the western chiefs let loose with the shrill war whoops of the plains. Then came more speeches, a poem written by Pauline Johnson, a speech from Onondaga chief John Buck, and the ceremony was over.

That evening, the festivities continued with a banquet at the Kerby

House, during which Red Crow thanked his hosts "for the kindness they have received"[22] and L'Heureux promised that the chief would give the press an account of his opinion of Ontario. The food laid before the chiefs was unlike the boiled beef, bannock, and tea which was their standard fare back home. Some of the items on the evening's six-course menu were oyster soup, veal with Indian corn, macaroni and cheese, wild partridge, mutton, plum pudding, blanc mange, and trifle pudding.

In the speeches which followed the banquet, Red Crow received the greatest inspiration of his trip. After the lieutenant-governor and other dignitaries had spoken, Six Nations Chief A. G. Smith arose and, in perfect English, made an impressive address which at times had the audience laughing and at other times applauding. "The Chief made one of the best speeches of the evening," commented a reporter, "much to the surprise of the American visitors."[23] That an Indian should excel in the white man's tongue and surpass even the oratory of their greatest chief was a lesson Red Crow would not soon forget.

The clouds which had been hovering over Brantford finally unleashed their torrents of rain which swept through the city that night, but the next morning the fascinating tour continued. The chiefs were taken by carriage two miles out of town to the grave of Joseph Brant, within the shadow of a small Indian church. From there the chiefs went to the Mohawk Institution where ninety Indian boys and girls were attending school. The students were all assembled in a schoolroom and sang "Tell Me, Ye Winged Winds" as a greeting to the western guests.

Glad to be back among Indians, the chiefs were openly surprised and pleased with what they saw. At the time of the visit, two girls were just leaving to teach school while two boys had graduated and found employment, one as a carpenter and the other as a blacksmith. "The Crees were much interested in a knitting machine," observed a reporter, "and both Crees and Blackfeet wondered at the exhibition of work done by the pupils, some of which was being done while they were there. Each of the chiefs was presented with a pair of mittens made by the pupils under Miss Osborn's charge, and Red Crow was so delighted with them that he wore his on the way home."[24]

During the rest of the day, despite rain and high winds, the chiefs were taken through the buildings and business establishments of Brantford. In the evening, they went to Stratford's opera house where they were provided box seats for the entertainment. Performed primarily by young Indians, the program included choruses, duets, and demonstrations of Mohawk rituals, including the snake dance, which had a scalping scene which "was true to the life, or rather death, to be more literal."[25] To Red Crow, whose shirt was decorated with the scalps of his enemies, the scene must have seemed like a strange one to depict to a white audience.

On October 15, the western delegation was loaded into six carriages again, this time for a ten-mile journey to the Six Nations Reserve. Arriving at the council house at Ohsweken, the visitors were invited to a special council meeting where interpreters stood ready to translate into Blackfoot, Cree, Iroquois, and English. After a speech of welcome by Chief John Buck, the firekeeper, the western chiefs were gathered into a semicircle and the Iroquois leaders walked by in single file, shaking hands with each of them. They were followed by the dozens of men, women, and children. As they passed, each said *Sako*, or "good day" to their visitors from the West.

Red Crow then addressed the Iroquois chiefs. He said he "wished to express freely his gratitude for the kindness of the Six Nations, including the hand shakes of the chiefs, warriors, women, and children. He would store in his heart their handshakes. His heart was so full of gratitude that he forgot to-day the long journey behind the iron horse which he had made to the land of the rising sun. He would report to his council of their kindness, and of the wonderful things he had seen while among them and while passing through."[26]

North Axe, One Spot, and the Cree chiefs spoke in a similar vein, Back Fat adding that "He was thankful that he had met red and white men together, and that here the red men were equal to the white men."[27] He said he had been opposed to schools on his reserve, but after what he had seen at the Mohawk Institution he had changed his views and intended sending his own children to school.

But the surprises for Red Crow weren't over yet. For two days he had seen Indian entertainment, Indian schools, and Indians assuming their places in white society. Now he and the others were taken to a shingle and planing mill which was owned and operated by the Iroquois. The chiefs were "lost in wonder at some of the machinery, especially a jig-saw and moulder."[28] It seemed to Red Crow that there was no limit to what Indians could accomplish, once they had the education.

On Saturday, the formal functions ended when Red Crow and the others were given bronze medals by the Brant Memorial Association. As the chiefs left for their hotel, a street vendor stopped their carriage and, in a friendly impulsive gesture, presented each man with a bag of peanuts. By the time the western visitors pulled away, a good-natured, smiling crowd had flocked around them to get a look at the exotic visitors. A day later, Red Crow, North Axe, and One Spot boarded the train bound for Ottawa, where they had meetings with the Honourable John Carling, minister of agriculture, and Mackenzie Bowell, minister of customs and later prime minister of Canada. As a reporter noted: "Red Crow expressed the thankfulness of the chiefs for the great kindness shown them wherever they had gone. He told the ministers that he, the chiefs and the young men were loyal to the Great Mother and the Government, and could always be depended upon. He could not speak the white man's language, but he felt much in his heart. He would tell his people of how warmly he had been taken by the hand and welcomed."[29]

On October 18, the chiefs set out for the West, but their journey wasn't over. Arriving in Winnipeg, they were taken to Clifton House and remained in the prairie city over the weekend.

Now that they were back in the West, the chiefs were anxious to get home. For more than two weeks they had been subjected to long hours of travel, unusual food, and strange but friendly faces. Many of the sights were beyond their comprehension and from time to time they asked L'Heureux to buy them things like a small steamboat, a baby carriage, a piano, electric light, and a live monkey. Finally, the trio of wanderers left the hub city and reached Lethbridge, their final stop before setting out for the Blood Reserve.

What did they do in the last white man's town on their itinerary? They got drunk. Roaring, gloriously drunk. They cast aside all the stoicism of the previous days, wiping out all the tensions and strangeness of the white man's world, and relaxed within sight of the familiar Rocky Mountains. It was a fitting end to a journey which Red Crow compared to a war expedition. He had gone into an unknown land, faced many dangers, seen supernatural happenings, and had returned unharmed. And because of the significance of the warlike event, he took a new name, Sitting White Buffalo.

Many people speculated what effects the tour had on the chiefs. A Brantford newspaper editorialized that "the primary object has been that of affording these still practically wild tribes of the plains an insight into the power and civilization of their white brethren, and of the development of kindred races of such advanced tribes as the Six Nations."[30] Jean L'Heureux was sure the object had been achieved. "By the unanimous opinion of the Press both here and in the U. States and by private letters by eminent men that I have received since the arrival at the Crossing, with the effect on the Indians themselves that I am now witnessing, everything assures me that the trip was a complete success and that the intentions of the Government were entirely well satisfied."[31]

North Axe responded to the journey by sending his own son all the way to Brantford to be educated at the Mohawk Institution. He had seen the effects which education had had on the Iroquois and hoped to achieve the same results for his reserve. One Spot, according to Agent Pocklington, "is the most delighted of any. His visit I am satisfied will be very beneficial as he probably has more influence over the young men than many of the others. One Spot never believed me when I told him about the white people out numbering the Indians by thousands. He tells me now that he was a fool."[32]

As for Red Crow, he was convinced that education could answer the problems of the future. While he had no school-aged children in 1886, he supported the Anglicans, Methodists, and Roman Catholics in their efforts to provide schools, and in later years he sent his favorite adopted child, Shot Close, to be educated in an industrial school.

Red Crow had always firmly believed that he and his people were inferior to no one, whether Indian or white. In Brantford, his beliefs were confirmed, as he saw Indians growing crops, operating a factory, and being educated so well that they could equal the white man in his own society. And if the Iroquois could do it, so could the Bloods. All they needed was the education.

From that time onward, if Red Crow ever became discouraged by the heavy-handed actions of the bureaucrats, he had only to think back to Chief A. G. Smith's speech at the evening banquet, or to the children singing "Tell Me, Ye Winged Winds." With a proper education, he knew his people would also find their rightful place in the new society.

16

/ Another Treaty /

During Red Crow's absence from his reserve, the powder keg had exploded.

Not only had the deaths of the six boys been confirmed, but there was irrefutable evidence that the deed had been committed by Gros Ventres. The earlier rumors of cowboys or soldiers being responsible were now dispelled. Six boys were dead. There was Hog Shirt, leader of the party; Spy Glasses, a son of minor chief Strangling Wolf; Yellow Snake and Small Gut, nephews of minor chief Calf Shirt; Dog Running Back, a brother of Calf Shirt; and Little Kettle, a son of Blackfoot minor chief Bull Elk. Hog Shirt and Dog Running Back were the only adults and the only ones with guns; the others were teenagers.

The tragic tale had filtered back from Montana. After White Elk's horses had been stolen from the Blood Reserve, the six young men had gone to the American army post at Fort Assiniboine, where they had contacted Otter Robe, war chief of the Gros Ventres. The leader said he was unable to help them and advised the military commmander to supply the boys with rations and that he would escort them on their way home.

After the chief had left them on the road, the Bloods were nearing the Sweetgrass Hills when their trail was seen by two American soldiers and a Gros Ventre scout who were out on patrol. They followed it along the east slope of the hills but abandoned it when they saw the trail heading north towards Canada.

At this point, the story became cloudy, but it was said that a Gros Ventre named Crazy Bull, hearing that the Bloods had been to the fort, organized a war party of twenty-three men who galloped off in search of the youthful horse hunters. Encountering the military patrol, they were tipped off by the Indian scout about the location of the trail, and a short time later they surprised the Bloods who were camped on Dead Horse Coulee, just inside Canadian territory. After a short battle, all six Bloods were killed and their scalps triumphantly carried back to the

American reservation. And there were well-founded rumors that Otter Robe himself had been a member of the attacking party.

In spite of Calf Shirt's earlier promise that he would keep the peace until Red Crow returned, he had been unable to restrain some of the young Blood warriors when confirmation was received about the killings. Although a mass revenge expedition had not been formed, two or three small parties of raiders had slipped away. The majority of Bloods, however, were "waiting Red Crow's return, when they will be guided by him as to what action they will take. Some want to go to war while others wish to go in a large party and make peace."[1] To add to the unrest, a number of Blackfoot had come down from the north to avenge the killing of Bull Elk's son.

In Brantford, Red Crow had seen a statue unveiled which showed an Indian holding a symbolic tomahawk. On the stage, actors had depicted a mock scalping scene. Now, days later, Red Crow was thrust back into the realities of his own world. Somewhere within the shadows of the Sweetgrass Hills, six bodies lay mutilated and unburied. Farther south, six scalplocks were drying on willow hoops after having been displayed in a victorious war dance.

Plans were made for an immediate search of the Milk River area for the bodies of the slain boys, but autumn blizzards swept across the plains just after Red Crow returned and nothing could be done until early December. In the meantime, the Bloods waited. Two of Calf Shirt's grief-stricken wives called on missionary John Maclean, begging him to find out what had happened to the missing boys. Their husband had decided not to do anything until the bodies had been found.

In the meantime, warriors like Eagle Child, Young Pine, Prairie Chicken Old Man, Morning Owl, and Eagle Plume had set out in small parties to raid the neighboring tribe. As each party slipped away, fears were expressed that they might be killed.

A search of the Milk River country was made early in December, after a chinook had melted the snows, but no signs of the bodies could be found. During the passing weeks, the heavy air of foreboding and expectancy hung over the reserve. Life went on as usual, but everyone seemed to be marking time, waiting for the inevitable news. A few women held out hopes that somehow the boys might still be alive, but even that faint hope grew dimmer as the new year of 1887 was upon them.

Then it happened.

In mid-January, Big Wolf had been on a hunting expedition to the Sweetgrass Hills when he discovered the gruesome remains of the ill-fated party. "He informed me," wrote Pocklington, "that there had evidently been a fight and that at least one of the attacking party had been wounded, as he found an American Infantry jacket with a bullet hole through the sleeve & one through the back near the collar. The bodies as found by him were entirely without any flesh but the clothing was all there, also a large butcher knife which he recognized as belonging to Small Gut. The knife he brought with him and showed me last night."[2]

Although Red Crow tried to calm the excited Bloods it was obvious that Calf Shirt, the most prominent leader to be affected personally by the killings, would ultimately decide what action to take. If he chose to form a revenge party, he had the prestige and war record to do so; Red Crow would be powerless to stop him. And Calf Shirt intended to have his revenge. He announced that "He would be satisfied with three Gros Ventres scalps, as three of his relatives had been killed by them, [but] the Bloods would want six scalps."[3]

No one — missionary Maclean, agent Pocklington, or Red Crow himself — doubted that the retaliatory raid would take place. All that prevented it were the wintery storms, but when spring arrived, the Bloods predicted that a revenge party of 400 men would set out. And in spite of the weather, for the Bloods did not traditionally go on the warpath in winter, two or three parties, totalling forty-two Indians, announced that they would defy their chiefs and raid the Gros Ventres' horse herds immediately. One party of twelve went beyond the point of boasting but was stopped before it could leave the camp.

In March, as the snows started to melt, more Bloods said they planned to attack the Gros Ventres. Finally, when four war parties, totalling about fifty men, slipped away on March 10, Red Crow concluded that there was no way he could control his warriors through conciliatory means. Accordingly, the chief and his adopted son, Crop Eared Wolf, announced their plan to Agent Pocklington.

"Red Crow and the others," said the agent, "are of opinion the only way to settle this trouble between the Bloods and Gros Ventres is to go over with a party of Bloods and make peace with them. He says that this is the only thing that will stop the young men from going to war."[4] Pocklington concurred and asked officials in Regina and Ottawa if diplomatic channels could be opened to provide for such a pact.

In the meantime, Red Crow worked diligently to prevent the situation from getting completely out of hand. Calf Shirt agreed to wait until they heard from Ottawa, but many of the young men had become openly defiant. In an attempt to convince them of their folly, Red Crow called general council meetings at the Upper and Lower camps, urging the young men to be there. Crowfoot, who also was concerned about the Blackfoot who were waiting on the Blood Reserve for the onset of spring, came to help check a bloody confrontation. Both men showed the effects of their eastern trip, for they not only advised the warriors to give up the idea of revenge but told them "to quit going to war and try to learn the white man's mode of earning a living."[5] About half the gathering agreed to the idea of a peace treaty, while the others wanted to kill some Gros Ventres first. And, to emphasize their point, three small war parties left right after the council, intending to raid their enemies. When Red Crow learned what had happened, he immediately set out in pursuit, and after a fifty-mile ride he caught two of the groups on the Milk River and forced them to turn back. The third party, consisting of eight men under the leadership of Low Man, eluded him and continued south.

A week later, on April 13, seven of the Blood party returned triumphantly with sixteen Gros Ventre horses. The eighth man had been shot and badly wounded; when he could travel no further a war lodge had been built for him and he was left behind on the Milk River until a relief expedition could go for him. With the news, the ripple of excitement on the Blood reserve became a tidal wave. The wounding of another Blood added fuel to the fires of revenge and caused many warriors to abandon the idea of a peace treaty. Some had to be forcibly restrained by their chiefs and even Red Crow began to wonder whether a major war could be avoided. Later, when the wounded man was brought back to the reserve, tempers cooled slightly, but within days another war party had gone, one of the co-leaders being Red Crow's own grandson, Big Rib.[6] They picked up twelve horses and when they were intercepted by Mounted Police, several shots were fired by both sides, although no one was injured. The war party then made raids on a ranch and a Cree camp near Medicine Hat, finally returning triumphantly to their reserve.

With the hostilities escalating, Red Crow knew that he would have to make a peace treaty with the Gros Ventres immediately. In April and May alone, one man had been wounded, the police and Bloods — who were normally on good terms — were shooting at each other, and dozens of Bloods were ready for war.

What else could go wrong?

On the night of May 22, a war party of Gros Ventres crept into the Fish Eaters camp and stole forty horses, all belonging to Red Crow and his family.

As soon as the loss was discovered, the angry chief led a pursuing party which picked up the trail and followed it as far as St. Mary River. From there, Red Crow sent his son-in-law, Many Mules, back to tell the agent what had happened while the chief and his warriors continued to follow the trail to the Milk River. Had the raiders been caught, there is no doubt that a bloody battle would have occurred and any thought of peace would have been shattered. But the Gros Ventres had too much of a head start and Red Crow had to abandon the chase.

Back in camp, the chief realized that a treaty was now essential for a personal reason. Not only did he want to stop the intertribal raiding, but if he was ever to get his horses back, it would only be with government help. A treaty was not only a political requirement, it was an economic necessity.

The attack also triggered the Canadian government into action and by early June the negotiations had been completed between the American Department of War, the Department of the Interior, and Canada's North-West Mounted Police to negotiate the treaty. On the Blood Reserve, the crisis situation calmed down after the horse raid, for everyone knew that Red Crow now had a personal stake in the dispute, and such was the respect that he held in the tribe that raiding virtually ceased.

On June 3, the treaty expedition finally set out for the United States. It consisted of Red Crow, his son-in-law Many Mules, One Spot, Running Sun, Inspector Gilbert E. Sanders and two Mounted Police constables, Indian Agent Pocklington, interpreter Jerry Potts, and two teamsters.

Their first stop was a melancholy one at the place where the young warriors had died.

"We went up on to the high land," said Pocklington, "and the buttes on which the six Bloods were killed. We made a diligent search for the remains, found a legging belonging to Small Gut & some hair; in one of the pits two Indians were killed, none of their remains being left. Another place on top of the butte, good size boulders had been piled. This was evidently the place where Hog Shirt was killed as the Indians identified some scraps of clothing. There was also a small piece of the blade bone of the shoulder of a fully grown man. The ground where the bodies fell was much discolored. About 400 yards from the butte was discovered the skull of a young man, I should say about 20 years of age. There was no doubt the fight was a hot one while it lasted from the number of empty cartridge shells we found near the pits."[7]

At the border, the party was met by an American cavalry escort and on June 8 they reached Fort Assiniboine. There Red Crow was pleased to learn that thirty-five of his horses had been recovered and that six Assiniboines were languishing in jail. On the following day, the expedition continued on another twenty-six miles to Fort Belknap, the headquarters for the Gros Ventres and Assiniboines, who shared a common reservation.

Although the head chiefs of the two tribes, Lame Bull of the Gros Ventres and Little Chief of the Assiniboines, were friendly, the general attitude of the tribes was hostile. The young warriors were upset that some of their men were in the guardhouse, while others obviously had no wish to see a treaty concluded. However, when the negotiations began, all the leaders were there. Even Otter Robe, who had precipitated the killings, hovered in the background.

The Canadian and American Indian agents opened the proceedings by urging the tribes to accept a treaty, but before the chiefs could speak, a young Gros Ventre named Black Crow jumped to his feet.

"I want the 21 horses back from the Bloods," he spat. "The Bloods have come after their horses and have got them. I have a good heart. When the Bloods steal our horses we want them back. There are some of our horses on the Blood Reserve. We want them back!"[8]

Ignoring the outburst, Lame Bull agreed to accept a peace treaty between the two tribes. "I know we are going to make a good treaty," he said. "All the young men obey me now. I can sleep well; now my horses will be safe and we can leave them on the prairie. We won't carry arms on the prairie now. I am glad to see Red Crow come over and see us. Our country is quiet; what I say is true. If I lose any horses now I will not be afraid to go straight to the Blood camp for them. When we make a treaty we will visit our friends."[9]

Pleased that the Gros Ventres had accepted their offer, Red Crow arose to speak.

"Now we have made a treaty with the Gros Ventres and Assiniboines we want all the Chiefs to try and make it lasting. This was my country once. We used to hunt the prairies with the Gros Ventres and Assiniboines and I like visiting them. I have come over to see them, to make a treaty, and what I say I mean. I know there is lots of trouble and I have come over to stop it. I hope you will stop your young men going to war. I will do the same when I get home. I am glad I have got my horses back; I feel good. We have made a treaty and we will smoke the pipe at last. It is good for us to meet as brothers and not be afraid. I would like to have a visit from the Assiniboines and Gros Ventres and the Bloods to visit them. Now the Indians must stop fighting with one another. I will not say we do not steal horses; all Indians steal horses and the whites are just as bad."[10]

Red Crow assumed that Lame Bull's acceptance meant that both the Gros Ventres and Assiniboines were agreeable, but as the discussions continued, it was obvious that the Assiniboines were less than enthusiastic.

"Twelve years ago," said Little Chief, "we were asked by the President to make a treaty. Where were the Agent and Red Crow then? We made friends once and thought it was lasting. I want to know what they mean about peace. I thought they had it long ago, but the Bloods have been bothering us all along. Now they have no horses to lose. Four of our young men stole some horses, but gave them up when they got to the Reserve. They are now in jail. I hope the Agents will get them out."[11]

The Assiniboine chief was supported by another member of his tribe, The Male, who asked: "Where were the chiefs in Heaven and on earth they did not make that Treaty lasting? We all used to travel on the prairie together; all of a sudden the Bloods became unfriendly."[12]

Yet as the speeches continued, it was apparent that the Assiniboines intended joining with the Gros Ventres in signing the treaty. They simply wanted to make it clear that the blame lay with the Bloods, not with them, for the reopening of hostilities. At the conclusion of the council, the chiefs were shaking hands when suddenly Otter Robe, who had remained sullen and quiet, began to shout at the Blood delegation. He demanded that Red Crow return all the horses that the Bloods had stolen and made several more inflammatory remarks before being stopped by the captain of the Indian police, who called him a dog and told him to shut his mouth as he was not wanted. Otter Robe then turned savagely on his own people and accused them of following their Indian agent "like so many calves after their mother."[13]

That evening a dance and feast were held in honor of the visitors and of the successful negotiation of the treaty. As a parting gesture, Red Crow asked that the Assiniboine prisoners be released "as it would show a disposition to let bygones be bygones on the part of the Bloods."[14]

Like most treaties between Indian tribes, the pact did not last very long. The Bloods were the first to break it in the spring of 1888, when Flat Head Bull and Lightning Killing took nine horses from the Gros Ventres. A few weeks later, the Americans retaliated by taking thirty-one horses from the Bloods. Within days of the raid, several small Blood war parties were on their way south to renew hostilities.

Red Crow was furious about the violations, particularly by his own people, and promised to arrest anyone coming back with stolen horses. And true to his word, he picked up six horses early in June and helped arrest four of the raiders. One of those he turned in was his own son, Black Face Chief, and another was his close relative, Many Fingers. When the trial was held, only three men were convicted and sentenced to three months in jail. The others, including Black Face Chief and Many Fingers, were acquitted. The firm stand taken by the chief cooled the spirits of the young warriors for the rest of the year, but as soon as the grass was green in the spring of 1889, other war parties were on their way south.

In all fairness, the first raiding party of that season did not intend to raid the Gros Ventres, whose treaty they recognized, but instead went farther south and picked up a few horses from the Crows. However, when they were pursued, they swung into eastern Montana and ran into a band of Assiniboines. In a running battle, one of the Montana Indians was killed.

There were six in the Canadian party, Prairie Chicken Old Man, Calf Robe, Young Pine, Crazy Crow, Scout, and a Peigan, White Calf. When the first raider returned to the Bloods, Red Crow immediately seized him and took him to Fort Macleod. This man, Young Pine, recounted the events and then said, defensively, "The Gros Ventres killed six Bloods. I thought you would be glad that we had killed them. The Gros Ventres started the trouble. They stole Red Crow's horses and gave you lots of trouble to get them back. You know it is our custom to take revenge. The Indians are all glad at our killing the Indian for the six killed by them."[15]

This incident virtually ended the hostilities between the Bloods and their American enemies. By 1891, a few friendly visits were beginning to occur, with even the intractable Otter Robe sending an invitation for his Blood father to come south. Although some minor horse raids may have taken place from time to time, the 1889 raid was the last one involving a loss of life and the scalp of the Assiniboine was the final one taken by the Blood tribe.

Red Crow had been a great warrior in his day, but he had realized in 1886 that the days of fighting were over. He had seen in Brantford what the Indians could accomplish, and he had no patience with those who tried to live in the past. At one time there had been a need for war — even during the first years on the reserve — but that time was past.

So from the moment he shook hands with the Gros Ventre and Assiniboine chiefs, Red Crow became an advocate of peace. Not because he hated war. Not because he was afraid of his enemies. To him, war had simply outlived its usefulness.

He knew there were other ways for young men to gain prestige. There was a myriad of secret societies to be joined, medicine bundles to be bought, and horses to be bred. Red Crow had no intention of casting aside his heritage, for native religion remained an integral part of his life. One of his medicine pipes even helped to save the life of a fellow chief's child.

Several years earlier, Red Crow had purchased one of the most important pipes on the reserve and in 1888, when Blackfoot Old Woman's six-year-old son contracted tuberculosis, the man made a vow to have the pipe transferred to him. Red Crow was agreeable and, after an exchange of fifteen horses in a solemn ceremony, Blackfoot Old Woman took the pipe with all its supernatural powers.

"The boy is rapidly recovering," remarked missionary Maclean wonderingly, "& the cure is attributed to the holy influence of the pipe."[16]

Similarly, in 1892, Red Crow transferred his favorite tepee design to his adopted son, Crop Eared Wolf. Known as the Middle Painted Lodge, its design dated back to the beginnings of Blackfoot religion, when the first medicine bundle was given to the tribe by the beaver spirit.

Religion was always a part of Red Crow's life. War was the only element that he abandoned.

17

/ The Boundary Conflict /

Red Crow had been down in Montana when his reserve was surveyed in 1883, but he hadn't been worried, for he asked for all the land between the Belly and St. Mary rivers to the Rocky Mountains. During the next few years, the matter was all but forgotten as the empty prairies around the reserve were occupied only by large herds of cattle on grazing leases.

But in May 1887, Red Crow learned that a party of about forty white men, women, and children had come to the southern part of his reserve and had pitched their tents near the St. Mary River. Calling for an English-speaking Blood named Joe Healy to go along as his interpreter, the chief summoned about two dozen leaders to find out what the intruders wanted.

When they arrived at the site, Red Crow observed that the whites had camped in the valley of Lee's Creek, where they were intending to settle. They proved to be a group of Mormons from Utah under the leadership of Charles Ora Card and, as one of the Mormons later recalled:

"They advised us that we were on their land. President Card had assured himself that we were not, and showed the Indians a stake which he told them was on the southern boundary of the Blood Reservation. The quarter section the town was laid out on, adjoined the reservation."[1]

Neither Red Crow nor Card would concede that the other was right, so at last the chief said that he would ask Agent Pocklington to resolve the question. However, as the survey had taken place before Pocklington's time, the agent had to write to the Indian Commissioner for direction. In reply, a copy of Nelson's 1883 report was forwarded to the Blood agent with the information that the Mormons were not on reserve land.

Pocklington, realizing the implications of the situation, observed that "Red Crow has always claimed the whole of the lands lying between the Belly & St. Marys river from their junction at old Fort Kipp clear back to the mountains."[2] He told the chief that he already had more land than he was entitled to, but believed that the line would have to be resurveyed so that the chiefs could see for themselves where the southern boundary was situated.

This was the first salvo in a long battle between the Bloods and the government over the size of the reserve. It was a battle which Red Crow lost, yet it carried on from one head chief to another long after he had passed away. The problem was a complicated one so often encountered when two cultures have entirely different concepts of an agreement. On one hand, the Bloods could comprehend only the natural boundaries of rivers, lakes and mountains. That was why they always considered the Internatonal Boundary to be a magical line. They could not understand how there could be an imaginary barrier on the open prairies beyond which the Mounted Police could not ride south, or the American cavalry north.

The government, on the other hand, had its well-established concepts of land ownership and surveying which they assumed everyone would understand. But even then, government had no firm policy regarding which population figures were to be used when a reserve was surveyed. Under the treaty, the Bloods were promised a square mile for every five people. But upon which population — the one in 1877 when the treaty was signed? Or the one in 1882 when the reserve was surveyed? Or in 1883, when it was resurveyed? The population figures varied widely among those three dates.

Red Crow, however, was not concerned about population. To him, the southern boundary was the Rocky Mountains, even if it caused his reserve to extend into the United States. And that meant that the Mormons were trespassing on his reserve.

In February 1888, Red Crow, together with several other chiefs and the agent, held a meeting with Inspector Percy R. Neale, the Mounted Police commander at Fort Macleod, hoping that he would take up the case. The chief also asked Colonel Macleod to attend the meeting, and was angry when informed that the judge was too busy to be with them. However, he presented his argument to the police in attendance.

"God made the mountains for us and put the timber there," said Red Crow, "and we said at that time that we wanted the country where the mountains and the timber were. The Government said they would be good to us. We took what the Government offered us."[3]

White Calf, the war chief of the Bloods, was quick to support the head chief. "You are treating our little children badly," he said angrily.

"The whites are cutting the reserve off and we know nothing of it. We claim between the two rivers up to the mountains."[4]

One after another the chiefs arose to voice their complaints. When Bull Horn claimed that "the Surveyors ran the lines without telling the Indians where they were going to put them,"[5] Pocklington turned to Interpreter Mills and asked him if this was true. Instead of answering, Mills put the question to Red Crow and then said, diplomatically, "Red Crow says I never told him where to mark out the reserve."[6]

However, it was obvious that the meeting was an inconclusive one, and after Pocklington told them that their reserve boundaries were correct, Red Crow got up disgustedly, turned to his fellow chiefs and said, "Let us go home."[7]

Realizing that the argument could never be settled until Red Crow actually saw the boundary line, Pocklington recommended that surveyor John Nelson be asked to return to relocate the old survey mounds. When he came in August 1888, a party made up of Red Crow, Blackfoot Old Woman, White Calf, Agent Pocklington, and Interpreter Dave Mills joined him at the southern boundary. There, Pocklington explained how the size of the reserve had been determined, and then warned them that "the area of land allotted them is in excess of what their number called for according to the stipulations of the original treaty at the Blackfoot Crossing."[8] Perhaps it was not his intention, but the agent's oft-repeated statement could have been interpreted as a threat: don't demand more or you may end up with less.

Nelson located the first survey post at the southeast corner of the reserve, not far from the new Mormon village of Cardston. Then, as they followed the survey line west, the original survey mounds were found at one-mile intervals, some hidden in the long grass, others damaged by cattle. But all except one were located and rebuilt.

As they passed the Mormon settlement, White Calf complained that the whites had been cutting trees on the reserve. Nelson immediately summoned Card, who apologized for the trespass and promptly paid for the wood that had been taken. Other than that, the Mormons kept a discrete distance during the entire resurvey. There had been no open hostility shown to the settlers, only a deep resentment and a feeling that they were stealing Indian lands.

After the southern line had been examined, the party travelled westward to the mountains, where Nelson showed the chiefs the boundaries of the timber limit which had been established in 1883. It provided 6½ square miles of heavily timbered land which could supply the reserve with building logs and fence posts.

According to both Nelson and Pocklington, Red Crow accepted the evidence which was offered to him. Nelson said that "Red Crow was now asked if he was satisfied, and he answered in the affirmative."[9] Pocklington went even farther, claiming that "Red Crow said he now knew where his Reserve ran and was satisfied."[10] And perhaps they were right, for although the rest of the tribe did not really accept the southern line, the matter never again became an issue during Red Crow's lifetime. In fact, a year before his death, the chief objected to fencing the southern border, claiming that "the mounds are sufficient to mark the boundary. He says Mr. Nelson explained [them] to him when he ran the line, that the older Indians who were present should explain to the rising generation where the true boundary ran."[11]

But there was an angry feeling among many Bloods that they had been victimized out of their rightful lands. People could not understand how their chief, who had proven himself to be honest, strong-willed, and utterly committed to the welfare of his people could ever have let it happen. It was almost as though he had betrayed them.

Some even looked to the supernatural for an answer, for they would not believe that Red Crow could ever willingly surrender their land. Missionary John Maclean paraphrased the comments of one of the Indians:

"Often in our lodges I had heard the chiefs say that a strong medicine man must have accompanied the white chiefs when they came to our camps to talk about our land, and that he must have used some secret incantations to steal the hearts and blind the eyes of Red Crow and the other chiefs, or they would never have sold any of it. . . . We had given away what did not belong to us, as the Great Spirit had given the land to the Indians, and it belonged to our children, and by selling it we had stolen our children's rights, and would never be able to repay them for the injury that we had done."[12]

Yet what choices did Red Crow have? He had protested to the Indian agent and to the Mounted Police. Colonel Macleod had ignored his pleas, and surveyor Nelson had proven that as a direct result of the treaty, a survey line actually had been laid a few years earlier. To the chief, a treaty was a solemn pact which had to be honored by both parties. In the end, he chose to believe the evidence before him, even if it was at variance with what he had requested.

But as far as the members of the tribe were concerned, the Bloods had simply been tricked out of a part of their reserve. "I knew Red Crow," said one informant. "I never liked him. He and the Mormons got together and made a deal for 99 years. He never got together with the other chiefs, he just did it himself. There were rumors that he got presents from the Mormons for doing it."[13] In later years, many believed that the chief had leased the land to the Mormons while others felt that somehow the settlers had been able to pressure Red Crow into abandoning his claim. Yet none of the stories were verified. It was likely that Red Crow had simply recognized the legality of a survey which had been made before the Mormons ever came on the scene.

By 1888, other problems were beginning to demand Red Crow's attention. Now that memories of the Riel Rebellion had faded, the government was resuming its efforts to reduce the rations, even though the Bloods felt these were already at a bare minimum. In addition, whiskey was again flowing into the reserve in increasing quantities, causing no end of problems, and a number of families were being encouraged to hang around Lethbridge and Macleod so that their wives or daughters could be pressed into prostitution.

At the same time, Red Crow was beginning to have second thoughts about the leadership of Blackfoot Old Woman. When the camps had divided in 1885, Red Crow had recommended that the downriver leader be considered the spokesman for that part of the reserve. In this way, the influence of war chief White Calf, who also lived downriver, was neutralized.

The ploy had been successful, but Red Crow had underestimated Blackfoot Old Woman's own ambitions. Fourteen years younger than Red Crow, he was leader of the Black Elks band and had considerable influence over the Many Tumors and Scabbies. Not satisfied with an unofficial role, he made several attempts to persuade the authorities to appoint him to the vacant head chieftainship. In 1886, he went to missionary Maclean and asked "whether or not he is going to have his share of the reserve, lower half, and be made head chief of the Lower Blood Indians."[14] And again in 1888, when he learned that Maclean was going to Regina, "he wished me to interview the Indian Commissioner about giving him a medal similar to the one given to Red Crow."[15] In the same year, Red Crow was offended when he was not consulted about Blackfoot Old Woman accompanying the official party examining the southern boundary of the reserve. As Nelson explained: "We also decided to take the Blackfoot Old Woman, who aspires to the chieftainship made vacant by the death of Sotenah, and is the most influential chief among the North Bloods."[16]

After his return from Brantford, Red Crow had considered grooming One Spot for the head chieftainship position. A young man and a relative, he would be no threat to the chief's authority. But it soon became evident that the importance of the role would go to the minor chief's head. Even with a minimal amount of encouragement, One Spot began to brag, "Red Crow is our Head Chief and I come next,"[17] and "The old men are nearly all dead and I am next [meaning leader] of the young men."[18] Besides, One Spot never did develop the qualities of leadership that the head chief hoped to see.

Yet Red Crow had no wish to see Blackfoot Old Woman made head chief. The man was a tough and determined leader who already had a sizable following and, with his camp located close to the Indian agent's headquarters, he might easily overshadow Red Crow in tribal affairs. As always, the chief was jealous of his position of sole leadership and he had no intention of surrendering it without a fight.

Red Crow surmised that although Pocklington admired Blackfoot Old Woman, he had no strong feelings about his appointment. Accordingly, the chief suggested an alternate for head chief: Day Chief, a forty-five-year-old man who had considerable influence with the young people.

The suggestion appealed to Pocklington, for as early as 1885 he had described the man as "one of the most infuential Indians among the Bloods."[19] He was a good farmer and had been active in trying to put down the liquor traffic. There was only one minor problem; Day Chief was a member of Red Crow's camp. Although not a Fish Eater, he was leader of a small group called the All Black Faces, which had allied itself to Red Crow's band when they had settled on the reserve.

The position of head chief was offered to Day Chief early in 1889 and, when he accepted, he moved his band from Bull Horn Coulee to a downriver location. Some of his followers protested and joined the Many Children band, but most were willing to stay with their leader now that he had suddenly been elevated from farmer to head chief. As for Blackfoot Old Woman, he simply bided his time; there was nothing else he could do. He was still recognized as an important leader of the Lower Indians, but not until 1907 did the elusive head chieftainship finally come to him. By that time, Red Crow was dead.

The appointment of Day Chief may not have been entirely selfish on Red Crow's part for the two men worked well as a team — even though the latter was undoubtedly the senior spokesman. They shared similar feelings about the need for education and self-sufficiency, decried whiskey traffic, and were outspoken in their defence of Indian rights. With Blackfoot Old Woman there was a danger of disagreements and confrontations; a scheming government agent could have played one against the other, effectively splitting the reserve and nullifying the influence of the chiefs. With Red Crow and Day Chief, this was impossible.

A demonstration of Day Chief's leadership came only a few months after his appointment. After the last war party had returned from Montana, bringing with it an Assiniboine scalp, three of the miscreants had been placed in the guardhouse, while another three were at large. When it became apparent that no one was coming from the United States to press charges, the trio were released and the other three voluntarily went into Macleod with Red Crow to receive a warning and reprimand.

Somehow, news that the charges were dropped had failed to reach the Mounted Police outposts, so when Staff Sergeant Chris Hilliard and two constables saw the horse raiders at the Sun Dance, they tried to arrest them. Instantly, cries of protest and indignation arose as the police forced their way into the sacred ceremonies. A scuffle followed, during which the policemen's guns were ripped away from them and their clothes were torn as the warriors vented their fury upon the hapless trespassers. Leading the demonstration were Day Chief, Red Crow's brother-in-law Sleeps on Top, and his son Crop Eared Wolf. However, before the situation got completely out of hand, Red Crow was able to calm his angry relatives and lead the policemen safely from the camp.

As a result of the incident, Day Chief and the others were arrested for obstructing the police, but when it was proven that there were no charges outstanding against the horse raiders, and that Hilliard did not have a warrant, the case was dropped.

In his own dramatic way, Day Chief had demonstrated that he did not intend to be a spokesman for the white man. He always maintained a secondary role to Red Crow, but like his leader, he would never willingly play a subservient role to the white man.

18

/ Encouraging Signs /

In his first ten years on the Blood Reserve, Red Crow had seen many changes. Warfare had virtually ceased, the wanderings of his people were being circumscribed by the Mounted Police, and more and more signs of the white man's way of life were evident. Trousers, shirts, and cotton dresses had replaced the traditional buckskin clothing; woollen blankets were worn instead of buffalo robes; and several families were using wagons instead of travois.

Around his reserve, the white people were arriving in increasing numbers. To the south, the Mormon town of Cardston nestled against the border of the reserve, while spanning out from it were small farms and sheep ranches. In the north, Macleod was a bustling community which still served as the Bloods' marketing centre, while to the east Lethbridge had become a large coal-mining town and terminus of the railway line. The open prairies to the west and east of the reserve were still virtually uninhabited, but they seemed like an alien country. Devoid of game, except along the Milk River or in the coulees, they offered little to the hunter or traveller.

After the Canadian Pacific Railway had been built across the Canadian West in 1885, westerners had expected a flood of immigrants to fill up the vacant prairies. Five years later, the movement was only a trickle and the land was still dominated by large ranches and older settlements. The Indians, particularly the Bloods with the largest reserve in Canada, were a significant part of the population. Although they remained aloof from the white man, both by edict and by preference, their activities as horse raiders and warriors were too well known to be ignored. Rumors were constantly afoot about possible uprisings, attacks on lone cowboys, or pilfering of ranch houses, but usually they were without foundation.

For ten years, Red Crow had labored to help his people survive. At first it seemed as though there was no hope, as every epidemic carried away the young and the old. In 1881, his tribe had collected treaty money for 3,560 persons, but by 1890 this figure had been halved to

1,703. A few had moved to the South Peigans, others had been stricken from the records as overpayments, but many had simply perished. In 1884, for example, there had been 46 deaths and 22 births; and in 1889 there were 148 deaths and 63 births. Each year, the mortality rate seemed to grow.

Some attempts had been made to raise grain and vegetables, but the rations of beef and flour were all that stood between the Indians and death. Even if the flour was, as Day Chief complained, "not black nor was it white,"[1] it was enough to prevent actual starvation. And at the age of sixty, Red Crow was still one of the best farmers on the reserve. With the help of his younger relatives, he planted crops of wheat, oats, potatoes, and turnips and in 1889, he set an example for the others when he broke two of his horses to the plough. Until that time, government oxen had been used.

The action was significant, for horses were still the basis of Indian wealth. They were herded and ridden and groomed, but had never been associated with the drudgery of farming. To some, the horse was still a symbol of the old way of life, but to Red Crow it was simply another means of gaining self-sufficiency.

Although the Indian agent really controlled the reserve, his power was not apparent. To the average Blood, Red Crow was the leader, for in their day-to-day lives they saw or heard little of the government officials. Policemen came by on patrol, farm instructors encouraged them to grow crops, and missionaries held services or school classes in their camps, but these activities seldom intruded upon everyday life.

Day Chief regularly rode upstream to the Fish Eaters camp to meet with his fellow chief, and if important business needed to be discussed, all the leaders were there. And it was done in the old traditional way.

"The aged chief arose and stepping outside the door of the lodge, gave a peculiar call, which was answered by two old men, who hastened to greet the chief. The criers of the camp, for such they were, received their instructions from Mikasto [Red Crow], and forthwith passed among the lodges, announcing a meeting of the Council in the lodge of the head chief."[2]

Gathering in his lodge, the business at hand was discussed, everyone expressing himself freely. Only the chiefs were there; the women and young men took no part in the proceedings. As in the past, decisions were usually reached by consensus, although if Red Crow had strong feelings on any subject, he stated them at the outset. Such was the respect he commanded that the matter was usually resolved in his favor.

Missionary Maclean, who knew the chief well, described his role in the camp. "Mikasto is a man of intellect, keen and critical," he said, "without any of the cunning of the low savages. His sense of honor prevents him from doing a mean act. I have never heard of a single action unworthy of the dignity of a statesman, who aspires to be an example of probity to his followers, and I never expect to hear anything detracting from the noble character of the man. He is essentially a leader of men. Not by force of arms, nor even through the influence of his position, does he rule, although his official dignity is a strong factor in maintaining his power over men; but it is his striking personality which enables him to command implicit obedience to the customs and laws of the tribe."[3]

His main opponents in the tribal council were White Calf, the truculent war chief, and Blackfoot Old Woman, angry because he had been bypassed for the chieftainship. And, interestingly, One Spot also turned on Red Crow for a while, upset because the chief had not followed through on his plans to make him a head chief. On one occasion, the three dissident leaders tried to circumvent Red Crow's authority by going to the Anglican missionary, Samuel Trivett, and asking him to write a letter to the Indian commissioner on their behalf. They told the missionary that their problems were not being heard and begged the commissioner to visit the reserve so he could hear their grievances. In particular, they complained about white men's cattle trespassing on the reserve, the mistreatment of Indians who were cutting timber in the mountains, and a shortage of rations. They also asked that the Indian agent and his employees be replaced.

When Pocklington heard about it, he wrote to the Indian commissioner himself. "One Spot, White Calf & Thunder Chief[4] are the principal growlers," he said. "They are inordinately jealous of Red Crow. The fact is they are too well treated & if they do not get everything they ask for there is no end to my meanness. I think perhaps it would be a good plan if you did come over & see them."[5]

But the attempt resulted in neither a visit from the commissioner nor a diminishing of Red Crow's authority. In fact, like many other grievances, their petition was ignored.

It was evident that agent Pocklington had great respect and admiration for Red Crow. He consulted with him frequently and obliged him wherever possible. In 1889, he built a new house for the chief, finishing it with shingles, floor, and ceiling. A short time later, he gave him a new brass bed and was pleased when the chief obtained "the sheets, pillow-cases, quilts, as white as snow."[6]

Maclean summed up the relationship between Pocklington and Red Crow when he said that the chief's influence "is no less among the white people who have learned to trust him, assured that he had always been friendly to their interests whilst guarding the rights of his own tribe."[7]

Yet the two men did not always agree. Not only was there the vexing problem of the reserve boundaries, but the rations were a constant source of complaint. Although the amounts of beef and flour given out had remained fairly constant since the Riel Rebellion, the striking of names from the register had materially reduced the amount of food issued daily. Early in 1888, for example, Red Crow complained to Pocklington: "Take pity on your children. We have had lots of trouble this winter over our grub. All Bloods and N. Peigans behave themselves and do what they are told. Why do they get such small rations? You always have some meat left in the ration house after issue. What are you going to do with it?"[8]

Pocklington tried to explain that the rations had not changed, but Red Crow cut him short, saying he didn't believe him. Angrily, the agent terminated his speech and refused to talk for the rest of the meeting.

Pocklington, therefore, was understandably concerned a few months later when a directive came from Regina, ordering him to reduce the meat ration by a quarter of a pound a day; that amounted to a 20 percent cut. In desperation, he explained that the rations were as small as they could safely be set and warned officials that "the Bloods will not go hungry for beef so long as they live in the centre of the Cattle country."[9] Nevertheless, the reduction went into effect, but because the winter of 1889-90 was a mild one, the young men were able to hunt deer and antelope. The following winter was just the opposite and when the blizzards drifted across the plains, cattle began to disappear.

The first to be arrested, early in 1890, was Different Person, a son of Blackfoot Old Woman; he received a stiff sentence of two years in prison. A few days later, when a couple of Cochrane Ranch cowboys caught some Bloods killing a calf, they were warned away at gunpoint. At about the same time, a yearling and calf were killed in Buffalo Hump Coulee, and a Blood named White Top Knot was nabbed for cattle killing but escaped.

Red Crow was concerned about the incidents and said the cattle were being killed by young men who were drawing rations only for themselves. As this did not give them enough food to sustain themselves, they had resorted to this extreme measure. He recommended that the rations be increased to their old level, and that the Bloods be permitted to have their own police force, just as some of the tribes were doing in the United States.

Initially, the recommendations fell on deaf ears in Regina, but in the autumn of 1890, when the cattle killings started again, the matter was revived. Before the end of the year, the government had approved the idea of a police force, as long as it was under the direction of the Indian agent. Red Crow agreed, and by spring the first six policemen had been appointed. At the same time, the government finally restored the meat ration to 1¼ pounds per day.

Although these actions did not wipe out cattle killing, the number of incidents fell dramatically. However, the ration level was still at a point which the Bloods considered too low and remained a point of concern and complaint until the end of the century. Although the various agents considered 1¼ pounds of beef and ¾ pound flour adequate for the tribe, they did not take into consideration that the meat ration included bone and fat, and that most Indians had no other food to supplement their diet. Some, like Red Crow, maintained a root cellar for potatoes and turnips, but others consumed their vegetable crops before the onset of winter.

Red Crow carried on a tireless campaign to increase the rations. He had the support of local missionaries who wrote letters to Regina on his behalf, but the government would not be swayed. Throughout the rest of the decade, low rations and semistarvation were constant sources of anger and frustration.

Yet in many ways, 1890 was a turning point for the Bloods. It was strange, but Red Crow's life seemed to have gone in ten-year cycles. He was born in 1830, became chief in 1870, and settled on his reserve in 1880. Now, in 1890, the decade of starvation and adjustment was replaced by an era of positive development.

His family was growing up, and the only child left was ten-year-old Shot Close, the adopted twin. He was both the pride and the hope of the old chief. Bright-eyed and fair-skinned, he was constantly being spoiled by his older brothers and sisters. Other boys had to make their own toy bows and arrows, but someone always made them for Shot Close. In return, Red Crow would give them a blanket.

Yet the boy, being half white, had his problems. On one occasion he was playing with his friends when an older boy called him *napipoka*

— a common term for "white boy" although it literally meant "Old Man's boy." Not realizing that he was adopted, Shot Close believed the playmate was accusing his mother of having sexual relations with a white man. In anger and humiliation, he ran to the old chief. To soothe him, Red Crow took him on his lap and said, "Shot Close, they are right that you are an old man's son. You see I am old."[10]

It was in Shot Close that the chief placed his faith in the future. Convinced that education was the key to advancement, he wanted the boy to get the best training possible. His older sons, Crop Eared Wolf and Chief Moon, were good men and potential leaders, but Red Crow believed that the Indian of the future would need to be able to work and compete with the white man on his own level. He had seen it happen on the Six Nations Reserve and he wanted it to happen at home.

The Anglicans, Methodists, and Roman Catholics all had schools on the Blood Reserve, and one small Anglican school was right in Red Crow's camp. However, the students were as wild as hares and seldom learned much. Often they came only because of the soup and hardtack which was served for lunch, and the teachers found it necessary to lock the doors at noon to prevent their pupils from running away after they had eaten.

The Methodist school, located in Bull Shield's village in the Lower Camp, was empty most of the time and the few students who attended were gradually drawn to the larger Anglican mission nearby. In fact, the Methodists lasted only until 1890, when they finally turned their labors over to the Anglicans. Although the latter church had small day schools at the camps of Bull Horn and Red Crow, its main facility was on an island adjoining the Lower Camp. There it eventually established a large boarding school for boys and girls.

The Roman Catholics, on the other hand, had been late arrivals to the reserve, with Father Emile Legal not establishing a school facility until 1888. It was located not far from the Upper Agency on Standoff bottom, with a small day school at Running Wolf's village.

Although Red Crow initially had two of his children baptized by the Anglicans, he had really supported none of the churches exclusively. However, as the Anglicans become polarized in the Lower Camp and the Roman Catholics in the Upper, the chief gradually came under the influence of Legal and other priests. But even when they opened a boarding school on the reserve, the chief did not want Shot Close educated there. Believing that there had to be a clean break from the family, he finally arranged in 1894 to have him sent to St. Joseph's

Industrial School at Dunbow, just south of Calgary. Here the Roman Catholics operated a school to teach farming and trades to young Indians. Upon arrival, the boy was given the name of Frank Red Crow, Number 166.

There were other changes in Red Crow's life too. At sixty, he was vigorous and healthy with a family which had survived the decade with only three deaths, two sons and a daughter. Another son, Chief Moon, reached the age of thirty in 1889 and married Different Iron and Two Spears Woman, the daughters of Wolf Sitting Down. However, the marriages were a failure and two years later he divorced them to marry White Wolf's daughters, Many Guns and Stole First. Willie reached the age of majority in 1890 and later moved to his own house when he married a widow named Taking Guns One After Another. In 1891, Red Crow's adopted daughter, Waiting Woman, married Longtime Squirrel and two years later the chief's South Peigan wife, Many Fingers, died and her children were taken to relatives in Montana. Within a matter of three or four years, Red Crow's family had been reduced from fourteen persons to just himself and four wives — Singing Before, Longtime Pipe Woman (who was blind), The Shield, and Spear Woman.

But even though the family was growing up, most of them stayed in his camp. Red Crow was rich and the Fish Eaters was the most influential band in the tribe so, according to custom, the sons stayed and the daughters' husbands camped nearby.

In the village, besides Crop Eared Wolf who was almost a sub-chief, there were Chief Moon, Willie, and the daughters who had married Many Mules and No Chief. Another daughter, Ground Diving Woman, was more rebellious; first married to the former farm instructor, John MacDougall, when she was only sixteen, she left the reserve for several years, only to return in the 1890s to marry another mixed-blood named Jack Wagner. They moved to Montana and never returned.

But Red Crow's relatives weren't just limited to his children. One of his wives' brothers, Sleeps on Top, lived in the village with his whole family, as did other close relatives like Making a Fire, Big Plume, and the aged *Natawista*, divorced wife of trader Alexander Culbertson. Two people who remained aloof from the camp and, in fact, lived at the other end of the reserve, were Sheep Old Man and Revenge Walker, brother and sister of Red Crow, who had never forgiven him for the tragic events of the 1870s.

Red Crow was generally pleased with his family. His sons Crop Eared Wolf and Chief Moon were hard-working farmers, while most of his sons-in-law were well respected on the reserve. He had never come to know his son Willie very well, for he had been raised by his wife's family, and he was the only one who had not profited by his father's steadying hand.

Besides his fine new house, Red Crow built a large stable in 1890 and had put up twenty tons of hay before the onset of winter. As the family adjusted to the new surroundings, his young wife Singing Before added a churn and sewing machine to their furnishings — the first ones on the reserve. On the neighboring hillsides, about 500 of the chief's horses grazed contentedly on the prairie grass.

The real milestone for Red Crow, however, was not his horse herds or his new house. Rather, it was Chief Moon, who proved that he was carrying his father's pride, energy, and independence to a new generation. In the autumn of 1890, he bought an old mower and took a contract from the local Mounted Police detachment to supply forty tons of hay. Hiring his own crew, he cut, raked, and delivered the order well before the onset of winter. It was, as the Indian agent explained, "the first attempt at this industry."[11]

A year later, the mower was smashed when the team ran away, but Chief Moon had earned enough to buy a new machine and began to seek further contracts from the Indian department, ranchers, and the Mounted Police. It was as though a dream of self-sufficiency was being realized.

And that wasn't all. Other Indians observed Chief Moon's success, and within a year Eagle Shoe, Bull Shield, Running Crane, and Heavy Gun had also bought their own mowers and rakes.

Encouraged by his haying experiment, Heavy Gun, who lived at the north end of the reserve, asked for permission to reopen an old coal mine which had been abandoned by white men after the reserve was established. Obligingly, the Indian agent gave him a contract to supply a hundred tons, hoping that he would be able to provide enough for winter use.

"This was rather a big undertaking for an Indian," commented the agent, "however, he went at it with a will and mined the coal far better than expected. He engaged Indians to do the freighting with their ponies, but it was very soon evident that they could not pull a load up the hill, which is rather steep. I therefore loaned them work oxen, when the coal came in regularly and quickly, averaging about 14 tons a week. When it is known that the round trip is upwards of 40 miles, it will readily be seen that no time was wasted. Having finished his contract satisfactorily, the same Indian mined 12 tons of coal for the schools. He also delivered coal for the Church of England mission."[12]

By 1894, the operation of the mine had been turned over to Black Horses who, with his son Chief Mountain, operated it successfully for the next twenty years. In their first year of operation, the father and son team supplied coal to the Indian agency, farm instructors, boarding schools, hospital, and several Mounted Police detachments. They also sold more then 100 tons to the big mining company in Lethbridge and 20 tons to neighboring settlers.

It seemed that the decade was offering the Bloods the opportunity for a new life. The great chief Crowfoot had died in the year of 1890, disillusioned and defeated, leaving his people dispirited and entirely dependent upon the government for their welfare. Red Crow, on the other hand, was quietly optimistic, as he saw individual Indians earning their own living. True, the numbers were small in comparison to the whole reserve, and the people generally had to rely upon rations to survive, but the good signs were there. And more important, the spirit of pride and independence had not been destroyed; it revealed itself in the willingness to work, in the ability to practise religious rituals in the face of government opposition, and in the attitude that the Bloods were inferior to no one.

When two warriors made a daring escape from jail, a Mounted Police officer commented ruefully, "The Bloods think that they are the cream of creation, and it is time for them to begin to imbibe some modification of the idea."[13] Even the Indian agent found he had to treat the Bloods with respect. On one occasion, police scout Calf Tail decided to oversee the rationing, in response to complaints that some Indians were being given less than they were entitled to. When the agent learned of the temerity of the scout, he angrily dashed down to the building.

"Upon my going to the ration house," he reported, "I found Calf Tail sitting there. I told him I did not want him there and to come out. I opened the door and asked him to go but he still refused, whereupon he was forcibly ejected. He was very insolent to me in the porch of the ration house and upon my telling him if he did not keep quiet I would put him under arrest, he then threatened to arrest me!"[14] In the end, the police sided with the agent, but no action was taken to quell the immovable Calf Tail.

It was this kind of arrogant pride which was able to sustain the tribe during their long period of unbelievable hardship, neglect, and suppression. It was the kind of pride which turned Chief Moon into a hay contractor and Black Horses into a coal miner. And it was a kind of pride which found its inspiration and example in the head chief of the tribe.

A strong supporter of Red Crow during these years was William Pocklington, the Indian agent. The English-educated ex-policeman was gruff and outspoken, but thoroughly frank and honest when dealing with his wards. He had won the confidence and respect of Red Crow over the years, just as he had come to admire the leadership of the chief. The arrangement was a happy one for both parties, but it came to a sudden end late in 1891, when Pocklington was transferred to the nearby Peigan Reserve. He was replaced by A. G. Irvine, former commissioner of the North-West Mounted Police, who had been discredited for his indecisive military role during the Riel Rebellion. He obviously considered the Blood Reserve appointment to be beneath him and a stop-gap until he found something better; in his first report he commented sardonically on the Bloods' "lazy habits and the filthy state in which they live."[15]

He spent only eight months on the reserve until he garnered an appointment as warden of Stony Mountain Penitentiary in Manitoba. During his short stay, he was more concerned with seeing Indian houses whitewashed, the camps cleaned up, and people vaccinated, than in any economic programs. In November 1892, he was replaced by James Wilson, who had been a farm instructor there for six years.

Where Pocklington had been effusive and friendly, Wilson was taciturn and autocratic. Red Crow got along with both men, but never established the same warm personal relationship with Wilson that he had shared with his predecessor. Yet Wilson was a good man who carried on most of the programs initiated by Pocklington. Indians were hired to do agency freighting, while coal mining and haying continued to be encouraged.

When the Bloods first settled on their reserve in 1880, the government had envisioned agriculture as their future means of livelihood. From the outset, Indians were encouraged to break the land and to plant small patches of grain and vegetables. However, by the 1890s the program was obviously a failure. Year after year, farming continued to be done by the most primitive means, the original plots of land were not enlarged, and one crop failure after another caused even the most optimistic farmer to become discouraged.

In 1892, for example, the Bloods planted only 250 acres of crops. The oats were an entire loss, the potatoes only fair, and the rest of the vegetables hardly worth harvesting. A year later the land was so dry that much of the seed never germinated.

Obviously there would never be enough coal mining or freighting to make the whole tribe self-sufficient. But what was the alternative?

Cattle.

For several years, Crop Eared Wolf and Red Crow had tried to convince the Indian Department that ranching should be introduced to the Blood Reserve. However, the commissioner's office in Regina was sure that the Bloods would become grain farmers and hence they rejected the idea. But during the winter of 1893-94, Red Crow renewed the plea and with Agent Wilson's support, the authorities grudgingly granted permission to provide some fifty head of cattle, in exchange for Indian horses.

Not surprisingly, Red Crow's family was the first to take advantage of the offer. While some Bloods were disdainful of any deal which meant parting with their prized horses, Red Crow was more pragmatic. At one time, horses were the basis of Indian wealth; they were essential for hunting buffalo and moving camp. Now, they were merely reminders of the past.

Red Crow and his son Crop Eared Wolf each asked for fifteen head of cattle, and his brother-in-law Sleeps On Top requested ten. The only Lower Indian to apply was Blackfoot Old Woman, who asked for ten head. It was a gala day when the exchange was finally made in June 1894.

"A movement like this naturally caused a great deal of excitement on the Reserve," said Agent Wilson, "and during the whole day large crowds of Indians visited the scene of operations. These four Indians gave very good horses in exchange for the cattle, and repeatedly expressed themselves as highly pleased with the trade."[16]

This exchange was the foundation of the livestock industry among the Blood Indians. The agent quickly discovered that while a person may reject the idea of scratching the earth and planting crops, he could be happy raising cattle. In some ways it was like their old life; in the saddle for hours at a time, following the four-footed cousins of the buffalo as they were watered, grazed, and protected from the prairie wolves. Within six years, the cattle population had risen to 2,000 head, with 100 being owned by Red Crow.

While the problems of the Bloods were far from solved, the introduction of cattle was the single most important event of the decade. Not until the turn of the century, and long after Red Crow's death, did farming finally become a viable reality. But ranching offered economic independence, and Red Crow had made it happen.

19

/ *The Sun Dance War* /

Red Crow was walking around his camp one day in July 1895, when he suddenly fell to the ground and began vomiting. He was carried to his house where Singing Before hurriedly sent for a medical student who was a teacher in the nearby school. He found that the chief had suffered a severe rupture and after settling him down, he had the Mounted Police doctor brought from Macleod.

It was the first time anyone could remember Red Crow being ill. He was a strong, hardy man who loved to ride for two or three days at a time to hunt blacktailed deer in the Sweetgrass Hills or antelope on the open prairie. He seldom complained about the hardships of life, except perhaps to tell his relatives about the demands of office. Only once could Agent Wilson recall that he had actually spoken about death. This had occurred at a meeting with a number of young men two years earlier, when he had commented, "In a few years, I may be dead, but I would like to help you so long as I am with you."[1]

The illness was serious, and for a while fears were expressed that the chief might not survive. He rejected suggestions that he be placed under the care of medicine men and followed the treatment prescribed by the police surgeon. By the onset of winter, he was well enough to resume his duties.

In the spring of 1896, Red Crow made a trip with Singing Before to see their son Frank at the industrial school. There they were pleased to see that the boy, hair cut short and dressed in a grey uniform, could speak perfect English. His complete isolation from the Blood Reserve had helped to transform him into the kind of person whom Red Crow hoped would lead his people in the future.

The price had been a high one. The chief had lost his only young son, for in many ways the boy whom he saw at school was a complete stranger. True, he had kept his language, for there were other Blood and Blackfoot boys with him, but there had been constant pressures from the priests for him to cast aside his "heathen" ways. In exchange, they offered to teach him the technical skills of farming, the language of the white man, and Christianity. Red Crow had realized the extent of the sacrifice when he made it, but just as warriors spent months away from home, gaining the prestige and knowledge needed to sustain them in later years, so did his son need the white man's education.

In spite of his illness, Red Crow continued to dominate the council and to hear the problems and grievances of his people. He tended to listen more and more to his son, Crop Eared Wolf, and although Day Chief was supposed to share the responsibilities of tribal leadership, the man always deferred to the elder statesman. Although Red Crow had virtually to give up hunting and travelling long distances on horseback after his illness, he still retained his vitality. He was no longer the seasoned warrior of his younger days, but neither was he an invalid. Rather, he quietly began to assume the role of the elderly patriarch, accentuating the dignity and pride which he had always possessed.

"He is a man of few words," commented missionary Maclean, "but when he speaks, everyone listens intently, as he indulges in no mean epithets, foolish jesting, or idle gossip. Reserved in speech, his language is chaste, and the burden of his addresses is the welfare of his people. Even the common talk of the lodge is weighted with wisdom when he is present."[2]

Late in 1896, the quietness of reserve life was disrupted when an attempt was made to kill Farm Instructor Edward McNeill. The culprit proved to be a Blood named Charcoal, who lived a short distance upstream from the Fish Eaters camp and who, in a fit of jealousy, had killed his wife's lover. The incident struck close to home for Red Crow in many ways, for not only was Charcoal a neighbor, but the murdered man was the chief's brother-in-law.

At the time of the shooting, Red Crow had come near death himself. After slaying the young Lothario, Charcoal had been determined to kill the head chief as well. He had approached the house in the darkness, but the barking of the chief's dogs had frightened the killer away. It was later that night that he had wounded Farm Instructor McNeill.

Thus began a manhunt which lasted for several weeks and crisscrossed the entire Belly River country. Dozens of Bloods spent hours in the saddle, following trails and searching for the wanted man. In his younger years, Red Crow would have been with them. Instead, he remained close to his house. Some Indians abandoned their places to form protective camps near the agency and one minor chief spent his nights in the loft. Red Crow, however, only took the precaution of sleeping on the floor, rather than in his bed, in spite of the fact that he was a prime target for the fugitive.

In the end, Charcoal was captured and hanged, but not before he had killed a Mounted Policeman in his flight. During his days of freedom, he had been pursued by every available Mounted Policeman and Indian scout in the district. It was almost like the buffalo days.

But Red Crow knew that the old days were gone. The days of warfare were past, the buffalo vanished, and a new life thrust upon them. He had tried to govern wisely, and there were signs that his people were gradually making the transition. But as each year passed, they were growing fewer in number, as tuberculosis and other diseases carried them off. By 1896 they were down to 1,300 people — a far cry from the 3,500 of fifteen years earlier. And the trend was continuing, as the deaths far outnumbered the births.

Most of the old treaty chiefs were gone; Medicine Calf, Many Spotted Horses, Bull Back Fat, Eagle Head, and Father of Many Children had all passed away. Even the irrepressible war chief White Calf was near death.

The old leaders had been replaced by a new breed of men, many of them good farmers and ranchers. There was Day Chief, Crop Eared Wolf, Strangling Wolf, Wolf Bull and Many Dust — all wise leaders, but some with no war records at all.

Even the face of the reserve had changed. The little villages along the river were gradually being broken up as the land was surveyed into eighty-acre lots. Some of the young farmers were moving far up the river, completely disregarding the old band groupings. A few — and Red Crow was among them — had established ranches far from their home camps, so that the cattle could graze without interference. The chief had built his ranch on the opposite side of the reserve, on the St. Mary River, where there was plenty of good land. But he still lived in his old house in the centre of his village.

Red Crow had cooperated with the white officials over the years because he had believed their work would benefit his tribe. He favored giving up horse stealing when the warring days were over, and he worked with those who wanted to bring education and agriculture to the reserve. As long as the changes helped his people, he was prepared to lead the way.

However, during the 1890s, after Agent Wilson was appointed, active efforts were made to suppress the Sun Dance, medicine pipe dances, and native religion generally. They were, the agent believed, in violation of the Indian Act. Red Crow was vehemently opposed to the action and his last years were spent fighting the agent on this basic religious issue.

During his tenure on the reserve, Agent Pocklington had made half-hearted attempts to discourage the Sun Dance but because it was not specifically covered by legislation, he chose to downgrade it in the eyes of his superiors, rather than to eliminate it. In 1891, for example, he refused to give Red Crow the beef tongues needed for the sacrament, but commented, "It really does not make much difference to us, because if we refuse, they can get them in the rations as usual."[3]

Agent Wilson was not so magnanimous. He saw the Sun Dance as a pagan ritual which kept the Bloods away from their fields for weeks at a time, interfered with the work of the missionaries, led young girls into immorality, and caused the graduates from Indian schools to go "back to the blanket." And in spite of the fact that the Indian Act prohibited only those rituals designated as potlaches or Tamanawa dances on the Pacific coast, he chose to apply the legislation to the Bloods.

Wilson realized that beef tongues were essential to the annual Blood ceremony but, more important, they had to be whole tongues. They could be dissected only by the holy woman who sliced them during a holy ritual and gave them out to be used as offerings by those who wished to reaffirm their faith in the Sun spirit.

The only readily available source of tongues was the ration house, so Wilson issued instructions that each one be cut in half as soon as an animal was butchered. In this way, they would be useless for the ceremonies.

In 1893 — Wilson's first year as agent — Red Crow asked for tongues but was refused. When he pressed the point, the agent promised to write to the commissioner for a ruling, but when he did so he urged that his stand be supported. In reply, the commissioner pointed out that there was plenty of work to be done on the reserve, but he would not interfere with any ceremony unless it involved giveaways which were specifically contrary to the Act. Wilson, unhappy that the response was not a firmer one, called Red Crow and the other chiefs together. "After communicating your views to them on the matter," he told the commissioner, "I showed them the amount of work to be done in the way of freighting supplies and immediately after that work is over haying would be on. They admitted they wanted the work in the worst way but asked that the young men do it and the old ones hold the Sun Dance."[4]

Wilson did not feel he was on strong enough ground openly to forbid the holding of the Sun Dance, but he restated his intentions of withholding the beef tongues. He told Red Crow that "the Department trusted to their own good sense to give it up but so far as I knew no steps would be taken to force them to give it up."[5]

In spite of this setback, the Bloods pitched a Sun Dance camp in July, but had to omit most of the sacred part of the ceremonies. The result, Wilson observed with some satisfaction, "was a miserable failure."[6]

The following year brought the same confrontation between Red Crow and Wilson. This time, Wilson not only refused, but he announced that he would issue an extra ration to those who boycotted the Sun Dance. The ceremony was to be held near the Upper Camp and when most of the Lower Indians agreed to stay away, the agent was sure the whole thing would fall through.

At this time, however, he was approached by Running Wolf, a minor chief and one of the leading supporters of native religion. He claimed that as a holy man, he had to go away by himself to make an offering to the Sun, but he needed six whole beef tongues to do so. Hoping to win the ceremonialist over to his side, Wilson gave him the tongues, but was shocked a few days later when he learned that they were to be used so that Eagle Child's wife could sponser the Sun Dance! Immediately, the opposition crumbled and the annual ceremony was held.

Agent Wilson, of course, was furious. He told Running Wolf that he would be denied any more freighting work and warned the others that he would reduce their rations if they attended. The effect, rather than discouraging the leaders, caused some of them to go when originally they had intended staying away. "White Calf," said the agent, "when he heard what was doing, immediately joined Running Wolf — not out of any strong desire for the Sun Dance but because he thought by supporting it he was annoying me."[7]

But that was the last time Wilson would be tricked. In 1895, the Indian Act was revised to prohibit any "festival, dance or other ceremony of which the giving away or paying or giving back of money, goods or articles of any sort forms a part."[8] Acting decisively, the agent ordered that the beef tongues be cut in half all season, effectively destroying any chance of holding a regular Sun Dance. That year was remembered in the Blood winter counts as the time "Indian Agent James Wilson stopped the Sun Lodge."[9]

Because of Agent Wilson's efforts, no Sun Dances were held for three years. Confident of his position, he prevented the Bloods from gathering into a single camp in 1896 and reported that "I think this Pagan ceremony had died out for good."[10] The Bloods tried in the following year but Wilson "was again successful in keeping these Indians from having a Sun Dance, but it is no easy matter."[11] He also organized July 1 sports days, on the assumption that this would be a wholesome alternative to the festival.

Heartened by his success, Agent Wilson decided in 1898 to extend his ban to include all types of giveaway dances. His first action was to arrest Running Wolf, Big Rib, and White Man's wife for putting on a medicine pipe dance, but he refused to press charges when the matter came before a magistrate. "I thoroughly recognize that this Medicine Pipe dancing is part of their religion," he explained, "and do not wish to insist at once that all this ceremony must cease. But I think it right, in view of the fact that so many children are being returned to the Reserves from Industrial & Boarding Schools where they have been given religious instruction, to begin to press the Indians a little upon the subject."[12]

Red Crow initially remained aloof from the controversy as there was a subtle division between purely political matters and religious ones. The chief tended to leave religious matters to the holy men, unless he was asked to intercede. But when Agent Wilson declared war on all giveaway ceremonies and threatened to arrest anyone taking part in them, he unknowingly involved the redoubtable head chief. While Red Crow was no longer a young warrior, he was still a formidable foe and an able fighter in the political arena. His direct cause for conern was the fact that his wife, Singing Before, had announced her intention of becoming the leader of the *Motokix*, the women's society, and of giving fifteen horses for the medicine bundle which belonged to Heavy Shield's wife. She had made the vow on behalf of Red Crow when he was ill and now that he was feeling better, it had to be fulfilled.

Without announcing his personal involvement, the chief went to Agent Wilson who explained that he was simply upholding the law and that violators of the Indian Act would be prosecuted. The rumor then swept through the reserve that Red Crow was going to be arrested!

The chief was aware that there had been a running feud for some time between Agent Wilson and R. B. Deane, the superintendent of the Mounted Police in Macleod. The latter was accused of meddling in matters dealing with rations, forwarding direct to Ottawa any complaints brought to him by the Indians. Deane was sympathetic to their plight and disagreed strongly with the officious and dictatorial manner of the agent. The result was that almost from the beginning of Wilson's appointment there had been bad feeling between the men.

Armed with this knowledge, Red Crow went to see the police.

"A picturesque bevy of both sexes paid me a visit on the 29th June," Deane reported. "It seems that some one had inadvisedly coupled the word 'arrest' with 'Red Crow's' name, and the old chief keenly resented the connection. He and his following came to ask me what he was to be arrested for. As a matter of fact I did not know, and it took me the whole of a long hot afternoon, with the aid of the best interpreter in the country, to get at the facts, and to pour oil on troubled waters."[13]

Red Crow explained the matter of his wife's vow and said that four separate ceremonies had to be held over a period of eleven days. The women's society had decided to have these in place of the usual Sun Dance.

"This naturally displeased the agent," said Deane, "who pointed to the clause in the Indian Act forbidding 'giving away' dances. Any one who knows anything of an Indian agent's difficulties must know that he is at times exasperated almost beyond endurance at the intractability of his wards, but it is an aphorism to say that in the last resort the application of a statute must perforce be referable to the courts of law, and it is a measure of common prudence to anticipate the verdict of a jury if possible. Whether this particular transaction on the part of the woman be looked upon in the light of a thank offering, from an Indian's religious point of view, or whether it be considered analogous to the initiatory fee payable on joining a secret society, the fact remains that there are the Indians' superstitions which cannot be eradicated in one generation — how are they to deal with it?"[14]

In response to Deane's request, the Bloods agreed to give up any plans for a Sun Dance that year, that no giveaways would occur other than the exchange of horses. With this commitment, the superintendent believed that "no court would hold that the Indian Act had been infringed,"[15] and agreed to ask Agent Wilson to allow the summer ritual "out of consideration for Red Crow and his advanced age."[16]

Immediately the Bloods interpreted the news as an indication that the Mounted Police had sanctioned the women's society ceremonies. The news passed through the camps like an electric shock and there was jubilation among the young and old. Red Crow called the Mounted Police scouts to his camp and, when he had informed them of their commander's decision, he instructed them to tell everyone to join the huge camp which was being established near the Belly River.

The Indian scouts were diligent in carrying out their instructions. "Some of the Lower Indians refused for a long time," claimed an angry Agent Wilson, "but after a good many threats such as that their children would be taken away, their houses pulled down under them, etc., they, with the exception of a few of those strong minded ones, joined them."[17]

Superintendent Deane did as he promised and wrote to Agent Wilson, asking that permission be given for the dance. By now this was a mere formality, but Wilson's vitriolic response left no doubt that he had not in any way altered his attitude. Not only that, but he pleaded for full support from his own superiors and when that was not forthcoming, he demanded that they seek a legal ruling on the application of the Indian Act.

Then he lashed out at Deane. "I have already told the Indians that these dances are prohibited," he wrote bitterly, "and I cannot allow them to think, as they most assuredly will, that I have been probably telling them an untruth. If the decision of the Crown Counsel is against my opinion I shall tell the Indians so, but if it supports my views, I will tell you so in writing and ask you to get some of these men who waited upon you to know what the law really is."[18]

Interestingly enough, while Agent Wilson was fuming about the law, he felt obliged to break it himself in order to combat the giveaway dances. In 1896, when he had been authorized to hold sports days to counteract the Sun Dance, he had been provided with government funds for the prizes. The games had been popular with many of the younger Indians and ex-students, so he promised that it would become an annual event. However, in the following year the commissioner refused to sanction the expenditure, so Wilson had dipped into the Bloods' own fund accumulated from grazing dues. After this had occurred for the second year, Wilson complained that "I do not care to go on year after year deceiving the Indians."[19]

Relations between Red Crow and Agent Wilson became extremely hostile during the controversy, the agent blaming the chief's adamant stand on old age and declining health. Although Red Crow had regained much of his activity and energy, he was consistently downgraded by the agent, as if to explain to his superiors how the head chief, who was so widely respected, could be so wrong.

When Red Crow first joined the fray in 1897, Wilson wrote directly to the superintendent general of Indian Affairs in Ottawa to say that the old chief "was being led and that he was talking in such a way that he was just losing control of the younger Indians."[20] When Red Crow persisted in the battle for religious freedom, Agent Wilson started a direct campaign to circumvent the chief's authority. He realized the great chieftain could never be deposed, but as long as he remained in office, he was both a hindrance to Wilson's policies and a threat to his position.

Finally he made a frontal attack. "At present," he wrote to the commissioner, "old Red Crow is of no use. He is 70 yrs of age and his memory is forgone and altho he will consent to anything being done today, tomorrow he is liable to change and in this way he cannot be counted upon. Of late he has given me a great deal of trouble in this and if a strong minded working man was appointed as Minor Chief with his understanding that he was to take charge of working parties, it would not only be a great convenience to the Farmers and myself but would be appreciated by the working Indians."[21]

When no action was taken upon his recommendation, Wilson tried to exclude Red Crow from the council meetings. But he had not counted on the chief's great fighting spirit. The attempt occurred in August 1899, when Agent Wilson asked for a petition to be signed requesting that the grazing money be turned over to him for buying farming equipment for individual Indians. The only prominent member of the Fish Eaters band to sign was Willie Red Crow, the chief's errant son. As soon as the incident occurred, Red Crow and a delegation of supporters went directly to Superintendent Deane.

"When the Treaty was made," reported Deane, "he was duly elected chief and was told that the Indians of his tribe should make any representations through him. He says a meeting was lately held on the Reserve and was called without his knowledge. He was not notified of it until the day of the meeting. He was not there himself because when the Agent sent for him at the last moment he thought he was not being treated properly. The Agent is reported to have said to Eagle Bear that it did not matter whether Red Crow was there or not, provided a majority of the Indians were present and that Red Crow was getting too old to act anyhow. He wishes to have a new meeting called after due notice given, to discuss matters of which he will give notice."[22]

When news of the complaint was communicated to Wilson, via Ottawa, the agent launched another violent attack on the head chief.

"Red Crow, who is now an old man, has lately been very hard to do anything with. His memory is failing and falls back upon what some Indian says. Lately he has got very exaggerated ideas of his own importance and forgets he is merely Head Chief of the Southern Bloods (Upper Reserve) while Day Chief is Head Chief of the Northern Bloods

(Lower Reserve) and sits and talks as if his word should be law to the whole tribe, forgetting all the time his advice lately has been against the best interests of the working men."[23]

In spite of Red Crow's efforts, the suppression of the Sun Dance continued. The encouragement given by Superintendent Deane enabled the Bloods to gather into a single camp again in 1899, this time to permit the Horn Society to transfer memberships. Wilson did all he could to prevent the encampment, but increasingly he found that he was standing alone. The agents on the Blackfoot and Peigan Reserves were letting the Sun Dances go on without molestation and when the ceremony was suppressed at home, many Bloods simply travelled to the reserves of their fellow tribesmen.

The Mounted Police had shown a marked sympathy for leaving the Sun Dance alone, and Wilson's superiors had taken a hands-off attitude. Even the churches seemed sympathetic, with Anglican Bishop W. C. Pinkham making an effort to intercede on behalf of the Bloods.

But Wilson remained single-minded about stamping out the Sun Dance, and his campaign was not limited to personal attacks on Red Crow. It included the threatening of anyone who openly campaigned for the resumption of the ritual and, alternatively, resulted in the favoring of the younger farmers who showed no interest in religious matters. In one instance, the agent tried to depose Running Wolf, a minor chief and leading ceremonialist on the reserve. In Wilson's eyes, the chief was incompetent, for "any head man who so persistently refuses to obey the wishes of the Department cannot be said to be competent."[24]

As the summer of 1900 approached, it was obvious that there would be another major confrontation. The Bloods had not held a real Sun Dance for six years, but during the winter, Yellow Buffalo Stone Woman, wife of Eagle Child, had promised to sponsor one. Her husband had been ill for several weeks and the vow to the sun had been made in the hopes that he would be restored to health.

Lined up against Agent Wilson were Red Crow and the leading holy men on the reserve. In addition, the Mounted Police scouts sided with their head chief and, almost like the old days, they acted like a warrior society under his control.

The first salvoes were fired in May, when Red Crow, Running Wolf, and White Buffalo Chief visited the agency office. As a leading ceremonialist, Running Wolf announced that the Bloods wanted to hold the summer festival, but Agent Wilson refused to discuss the matter. When he persisted, Wilson had him arrested but when the minor chief was brought before the magistrate, he was released with a caution.

The action angered Red Crow and the others, who immediately rode to Macleod, where they saw their old friend Superintendent Deane. Disgusted with the stiff-necked attitude of the agent, the police officer elicited a promise from the chief that there would be no major giveaways, except for the legitimate exchanges of horses for medicine bundles. When Red Crow agreed, the superintendent said he would not authorize a Sun Dance, *per se*, but approved eleven days of summer ceremonies.

The Bloods were elated by the news as Agent Wilson frantically tried to intervene. He called for the sergeant of the local Mounted Police detachment to force the Indians to abandon the big camp and to go home, but the ploy was unsuccessful. Instead, the Mounted Police scouts scoured the reserve, rousing Indians from their beds and hauling them in from their fields, ordering them to gather at the camp. It was a banner year which went down in the winter counts as the time when "Yellow Buffalo Stone Woman put up the Sun Dance by force."[25]

In the meantime, no beef tongues had been secured, for the Blood rationers still followed the practise of despoiling each tongue after an animal was slaughtered. Although unable to come to the office himself, Red Crow sent three leading chiefs — Bull Shield, Calf Shirt, and Eagle Ribs — to inform the agent that the Mounted Police had authorized their dance and the release of a quantity of whole tongues to them.

"I pointed out to these Head Men," said Wilson, "that the Police had no jurisdiction over Indian Affairs, that they were in the Country for the protection of life and property and to arrest all law breakers, that the Indian Dept was the only one able to give them instructions and that Indian Agents were appointed for the purpose of letting them know the law. I then repeated what I had told Running Wolf and said I had definitely made up my mind to insist upon each family returning to their own farms and this was absolutely necessary as Red Crow and some others had been camping away from their own places for four weeks and the rest of them for from two to three weeks."[26]

He adamantly refused to provide the necessary beef tongues, but when Red Crow heard the news, he announced that he would slaughter some of his own herd for that purpose. However, the move proved to be unnecessary, for arrangements were quietly made for the scouts, who received their rations directly from the Mounted Police, to take their meat allotment in whole tongues.

Bitterly, the agent made a last-ditch stand by refusing to issue rations to any Indian who attended the Sun Dance, but the threat lasted only one day, for Red Crow responded by saying that he would kill his whole herd, if necessary, to feed the camp.

At that point, Wilson's opposition crumbled; he was completely and utterly defeated. The Bloods put on their biggest Sun Dance in more than a decade, and never again was the ceremony denied to them. Red Crow, with the help of the Mounted Police, had won perhaps the greatest victory of his life.

Back in 1877, when he had signed the treaty, Red Crow had said, "Everything that the Police have done has been good."[27] Now, twenty-three years later, they had helped him save the very basis of his tribe's religion from destruction.

It was a fitting end to Red Crow's career, for just two months after the Sun Dance ended, the great chief died. He had crossed the Belly River on August 28, 1900, to round up his horses and, when he did not return, his favorite wife became worried.

"Singing Before went to look for him," recalled a woman who was living in the Red Crow tepee at the time, "and she found him laying on the gravel at the edge of the river. I saw her crying and we knew what had happened. We all went across with Red Crow's wagon and brought his body over. Pretty soon both the religious denominations were there, together with many white people. Then we started to move camp.

"Red Crow had used some stones between his tepee pegs. When the lodge was moved, this circle of stones was completed and then we placed four radiating lines on the four sides of the tepee ring. We did this because it was the custom as far back as the days when we used dogs. They were the marks of a warrior chief.

"That night, Bull Horn moved his camp to the next bottom. He had not heard about Red Crow's death. Next morning he went to the camp site and saw the marks around Red Crow's tepee stones. He began crying, for he knew that Red Crow was dead. He went back to his tepee and said, 'We have lost our chief.' "[28]

20

/ Red Crow's Legacy /

Red Crow had won most of the battles of his life. As a young warrior he had defeated and scalped his enemies; as a chief he had guided his people through their difficult years on the reserve; and as an elder statesman he had led them in the direction of better education and self-sufficiency, at the same time retaining their fierce independence and pride.

It was a strange anomaly that a people could become wholly destitute and completely reliant upon a government for their food, yet remain unbroken. When they had been lords of the plains, their stance had been understandable, for the buffalo gave them the means to be independent and free. In theory, this sense of arrogance and well-being should have been destroyed during the reservation years, just as it was among many other tribes.

But the Bloods were different, and their attitudes in part can be traced directly to Red Crow's leadership. It helped that they had a large reserve where they could be isolated from the white man's world around them, and there was no denying that their location near the International Boundary permitted them to be reckless and daring when they could easily slip beyond the clutches of the law. More than anything else, however, there was one factor which made the Bloods distinctive. It was the attitude that they were the "cream of creation;" they felt inferior to no one — not to a Cree, a Mounted Policeman, or an officious Indian agent. That was why the Bloods did not hate the white man; they did not have the deep burning hostility of a subjugated people. For that reason Red Crow had no difficulty in keeping his people out of the Riel Rebellion. They did not jump at a chance to kill white men; they would rather have attacked their old enemies, the Crees. They had no interest in a grand alliance to destroy the burden of the white man's yoke, for they did not feel it pressing heavily upon their shoulders.

These were the attitudes held by Red Crow, and they were ones which he shared with his tribe. He was fiercely possessive of what was his but was always ready to adopt the knowledge or the teachings of others if he felt they would help. After his trip to Brantford, he became convinced that education was the answer to his tribe's problems. After seeing the Six Nations Indians at work, he wanted his young men trained to run factories, farms, and ranches.

To gain these ends, he was willing to cooperate with the white man, but there were limits beyond which he would not go. He permitted the missionaries to come on his reserve, but he adamantly refused to cast aside his religion. He was willing to lease hay lands to the white ranchers, but he would never willingly give up the land itself.

The story is told of one attempt which was made to convince Red Crow to surrender part of his reserve. This occurred in 1893, when the Mormons first agitated that a strip of land "ten or fifteen miles of the Blood Indian Reserve, should be thrown open for settlement."[1]

According to the tale, Red Crow was standing on the prairie when he was approached about the land surrender. Bending down, he picked up a piece of sod, and pulling the grass from it he said, "Here, you can have this." Then, clutching the sod to his heart, he added, "but this is for me and my people forever."

And his lessons were learned well by his followers. In the twenty years after Red Crow's death, several attempts were made to force the surrender of tribal lands, but the chiefs opposed them with a vengeance. By the time the pressure had eased, the Blackfoot had lost half their reserve and the Peigans a quarter, but the Bloods had not given up a single acre.

Before his death, Red Crow made it clear that he wanted his adopted son, Crop Eared Wolf, to succeed him. Similarly, when Crop Eared Wolf was on his deathbed in 1913, he chose his son Shot Both Sides. And before Crop Eared Wolf died he "called his minor chiefs and people together and made them promise that they would never sell their land to the white man."[2]

The Blood tribe has been dominated by the Fish Eaters clan ever since Seen From Afar wrested control from the Buffalo Followers in the 1840s. There it remained under the guidance of Red Crow, his adopted son Crop Eared Wolf, his grandson Shot Both Sides, and in 1956 his great-grandson Jim Shot Both Sides. With only a two-year break[3] the leadership has been firmly in the hands of the Red Crow clan for more than a century.

Frank Red Crow, the young boy in whom the old man placed so much of his faith in the future, left school shortly before the turn of the century and went on to become a prosperous rancher. He was elected a minor chief of the tribe and served faithfully until he retired in the 1950s. And, interestingly, his twin brother who had been taken north to the Blackfoot Reserve also became successful, his son[4] eventually becoming head chief of that tribe.

Agent Wilson, Red Crow's main antagonist during the reserve years, did not stay with the Bloods for long after the chief died. In many ways he was a good agent but he could never grasp the problems created by the collision of two alien cultures. He left in 1903 to become a brand inspector in Medicine Hat, his replacement being Robert N. Wilson, a former Mounted Policeman and amateur anthropologist.

Two days after the death of Red Crow, a funeral service was held in the little Roman Catholic church near the Upper Agency. Strangely enough, during the very period when the chief was fighting to restore the Sun Dance, he was persuaded by a priest to become baptized and married. Until that time, it had been a firm rule of the priests not to marry people until they cast aside their other wives. But in Red Crow's case an exception was made. On December 22, 1896, he was baptized John Mikahestow, while his youngest wife, Singing Before, was named Frances Ikaenikiakew.[5] They were married immediately after the ceremony.

Agent Wilson was aghast.

"During the month, the Rev. Father Legal put Red Crow and one of his wives through a form of marriage, but as he has *three* other wives living with him, each of whom has been his wife for a longer period than the married (?) one, I fail to see what good this ceremony had done. The Indians on the other hand say it has been done so that his wife may claim all the old man's property to the exclusion of the others."[6]

The rumor was correct, of course. Singing Before was the adopted mother of Frank, who was in the industrial school; and the priest, by solemnizing the marriage, created a situation whereby Red Crow's only baptized Catholic son stood to gain the inheritance.

At the time of his death, Red Crow owned about 500 horses, 100 cattle, a fully-equipped ranch on the St. Mary's River, and his home ranch on Standoff bottom. When the estate was settled, most of the property went to Frank and his mother, as they were the legal heirs.[7]

Red Crow was buried in the Catholic cemetery on a little hill overlooking Standoff bottom. Standing by the grave, the mourners could see the ragged line of the Rocky Mountains to the east, with Chief Mountain jutting out by itself. To the north, the Belly River wound its peaceful way to the buttes, where it was lost among the steep cliffs and tall cottonwoods. To the south and east, the land stretched out like a rolling tide, sweeping to the slopes a few miles away, then bounding off again over the vast miles of reserve land.

Today, the hills and rivers are still there, but everything else has changed. A small stone monument beside a busy asphalt highway commemorates the chief's death, while scattered through the nearby cemetery are many fresh mounds, some decorated with little clusters of plastic flowers. There is a pleasant smell of spring in the air, just as there was in Red Crow's time, and the same wind whips along the prairie grass, the flies buzz, and the butterflies bob and dart among the tombstones.

To the east, a huge orange-colored factory with a silvery metal roof sits like a giant protuberance on the prairie landscape. Owned by Red Crow Developments, it is run by the Blood tribe and manufactures prefabricated homes. Partially finished houses cluster around the building in neat rows, while behind them, grazing land sweeps eastward and disappears over a ridge two miles away.

To the northeast the Belly Buttes lose their prominence to an Indian housing development. Low buildings, yellow, green, pink, and brown, on paved crescents and streets, hug the hillside while above them a tall yellow watertower is thrust towards the sky, its bulbous head emblazoned with the word "Standoff." Still farther away the Shot Both Sides building — administrative headquarters of the Blood tribe — projects its brick frame and yellow box-like roof over the whole area.

Beside the building stands a life-size bronze figure of Red Crow himself, unveiled by Prince Charles in 1977 to commemorate the signing of Treaty Number Seven. It gazes, symbolically, towards the Belly Buttes, the landmark chosen by Red Crow when the reserve was surveyed.

To the north, just over the hill and out of sight, is the modern Kainai Sports Centre, while beside it are the Red Crow Memorial rodeo grounds, and across the highway is the Red Crow Park where the Indian Days are held each summer. An Alberta Government highway sign nearby pays tribute to the exploits of the great Blood chief.

To the west, a wooden Roman Catholic church is surrounded by farming land that stretches to the nearest horizon. Farther away, the mountains still dominate the skyline, but their image is muted by haze and smoke. To the south, the highway follows the edge of a coulee to a ridge four miles away; all along its flanks are fences, highway signs, farm houses, and metal granaries.

Within two miles of Red Crow's monument there are farms, ranches, schools, a community hall, pool hall, service station, and shopping centre, all run by Blood Indians. They are evidence that the people have changed with the land. The education which was a dream in Red Crow's time has become a reality for his grandchildren and great-grandchildren.

The Bloods, whose population had slipped to 1,111 by 1920, now number more than 5,000 and the reserve is becoming crowded. Some Indians are involved in irrigation while others run sizable herds of cattle, work as teachers or teachers' aides in the reserve schools, or as reporters in the office of the *Kainai News,* an Indian-run newspaper. Others work for the tribal administration as accountants, road foremen, welfare officers, policemen, and secretaries.

The feeling of pride instilled by Red Crow a century earlier still remains. They were then, and are now, the "cream of creation."

/ Notes /

1. / The Fish Eaters /

1   John C. Ewers, interview with Weasel Tail, 1942. Personal communication from author, 1 February 1954.
2   More correctly, *Natoyist-siksina'*.
3   James Willard Schultz, *Signposts of Adventure*, p. 113.
4   Interview with Percy Creighton, 17 July 1954.
5   Interview with Frank Red Crow, 10 May 1954.
6   Interview with Percy Creighton, 17 July 1954.
7   Ibid.
8   John C. Ewers, *The Blackfeet, Raiders on the Northwestern Plains*, p. 60.

2. / Early Years /

1   Philip H. Godsell, ed., "The R. N. Wilson Papers," 1958, unpublished manuscript in Glenbow-Alberta Institute archives, p. 140.
2   *Miksiksipoksapowowa*, or literally "Angry Walking Towards You."
3   In 1886, Paper Woman married Crowfoot, head chief of the Blackfoot.
4   Interview with Frank Red Crow, 10 May 1954.
5   Interview with Charlie Pantherbone, 24 July 1954.
6   Bull Collar and White Wolf were the names of the two chiefs at the time of the incident. Most Blood warriors had several names during their lifetimes.
7   John C. Ewers, *The Blackfeet, Raiders on the Northwestern Plains*, p. 64.
8   James T. Bradley, "Affairs at Fort Benton from 1831 to 1869," p. 69.
9   Ibid.

10   John Rowand, Edmonton House, to Governor George Simpson, 25 December 1839. Hudson's Bay Company Archives, Winnipeg, reel 3M58. This and other excerpts from the H.B.C. Archives are published by permission of the Governor and Committee of the Hudson's Bay Company.

3. / Novice Warrior /

1   Unless otherwise cited, Red Crow's war experiences are based upon the chief's own account given to trader R. N. Wilson in December 1891, and contained in Philip H. Godsell's "The R. N. Wilson Papers," 1958, pp. 140-227.
2   Winter count of Bull Plume, Peigan Indian. Fort Macleod Museum.
3   Godsell, "The R. N. Wilson Papers," p. 178.

4. / On The Warpath /

1   Through common usage, linguistic origin, and legal definition, both terms Blackfoot and Blackfeet are correct. However, the native people themselves in Canada and the Canadian government prefer Blackfoot, so this term is generally used throughout the text. Similarly, the spelling Peigan is official Canadian usage, while Piegan is preferred in the United States.
2   Cited in John C. Ewers, *The Blackfeet, Raiders on the Northwestern Plains*, p. 125.
3   Philip H. Godsell, ed., "The R. N. Wilson Papers," p. 217.
4   Cited in Ewers, *The Blackfeet*, p. 125.
5   Ibid.
6   Godsell, "The R. N. Wilson Papers," p. 152.
7   James T. Bradley, "Lieut. James H. Bradley Manuscript," p. 248.
8   *Benton Record*, 18 October 1878.
9   Anne B. MacDonnell, "The Fort Benton Journal, 1854-1856, and the Fort Sarpy Journal, 1855-1856," p. 66.
10   Alfred Sully to E. S. Parker, commissioner of Indian Affairs, Washington, D.C., 16 July 1870, enclosing census of the Blackfoot nation, in the National Archives, Washington, D.C.

5. / A Seasoned Warrior /

1   Philip H. Godsell, ed., "The R. N. Wilson Papers," p. 159.
2   Ibid.

3   Ibid., p. 164.
4   Ibid., pp. 124-35.
5   Ibid., p. 175.
6   Ibid., p. 184.
7   Ibid., p. 192.

6. / Treaty With the Long Knives /

1   Mildred W. Schemm, "The Major's Lady," p. 11.
2   John C. Ewers, *The Blackfeet, Raiders on the Northwestern Plains,*
    p. 212.
2   James Doty, "A Visit to the Blackfoot Camps," pp. 12-16.
3   Ewers, *The Blackfeet,* p. 220.
4   Two other Bloods, The Feather and White Eagle, signed the
    treaty but they were not band chiefs.
6   Ewers, *The Blackfeet,* p. 227.
7   Philip H. Godsell, ed., "The R. N. Wilson Papers," p. 208.
8   Ibid.
9   Ibid., p. 211.
10 Ibid., pp. 210-11.
11 No informants could recall the name of Red Crow's second
    wife.
12 Godsell, "The R. N. Wilson Papers," p. 116.
13 Ibid., p. 117.
14 Cited in "Decorated Buffalo Hides," in *Exhibits on Display,* Royal
    Canadian Mounted Police Museum, Regina, mimeographed.
    n.d., pp. 17-18. This booklet contains an account of Crop Eared
    Wolf's war experiences which were painted on a buffalo robe
    in 1882.

7. / Unsettled Years /

1   Father Nicholas Point, *Wilderness Kingdom: The Journals & Paintings
    of Father Nicholas Point,* p. 116.
2   John C. Ewers, *The Blackfeet, Raiders on the Northwestern Plains,*
    p. 231.
3   Fort Edmonton journal, entry for 25 September 1860, in
    Hudson's Bay Company Journals and Correspondence (HBC
    Arch. B.60/a/31).
4   Ibid., entry for 18 October 1860.
5   William J. Christie to Governor A. G. Dallas, 28 March 1861.
    Edmonton House correspondence book (HBC Arch. B.60/a/31).

6   Ibid., 31 December 1863 (HBC Arch. B.60/6/1).

7   *Benton Record,* 31 January 1879.

8   Fort Edmonton journal, *op. cit.,* entry for 17 June 1865.

9   Philip H. Godsell, ed., "The R. N. Wilson Papers," p. 121.

10   Ibid., pp. 166-67.

11   Fort Edmonton journal, entry for 17 March 1865.

12   Godsell, "The R. N. Wilson Papers," pp. 166-168.

13   Hugh A. Dempsey, *Crowfoot, Chief of the Blackfeet,* pp. 49-52.

14   Interview with John Cotton, 15 July 1954.

15   Cited in Dempsey, *Crowfoot,* p. 56.

16   Interview with John Cotton, 15 July 1954.

17   There is considerable confusion about the names and relationships of Red Crow's wives, but the most authoritative sources have been the chief's adopted son, Frank, the baptismal register in the Oblate Papers, Box 44, File X5, Provincial Archives of Alberta, and the annuity paylists of the Department of Indian Affairs, 1887-1901. The latter are on microfilm in the Glenbow-Alberta Institute archives, Calgary.

18   Jim White Bull, "Records by the Blood Indians & Blackfoots," unpublished manuscript in author's possession.

19   *Helena Weekly Herald,* 27 February 1868.

8. / Whiskey /

1   Interview with Laurie Plume, 24 October 1955.

2   William F. Butler, *The Great Lone Land,* pp. 367-68.

3   Interview with John Cotton, 26 December 1953.

4   Interview with John J. Healy in Tappen Adney Papers, Montana Historical Society.

5   Alfred Sully to E. S. Parker, commissioner of Indian Affairs, Washington, D.C., 16 July 1870, enclosing census of the Blackfoot nation, in the National Archives, Washington, D.C.

6   Butler, *The Great Lone Land,* p. 370.

7   For a detailed account, see Alex Johnston, *Battle at Belly River,* Lethbridge: Historical Society of Alberta, 1966.

8   Morris, *The Treaties of Canada with the Indians of Manitoba and the North-West Territories Including the Negotiations on Which They Were Based, and Other Information Relating Thereto,* p. 248.

9   *The Manitoban,* Winnipeg, 14 March 1874, reprinted from the *New York Sun.*

10   James W. Schultz, "Raven Quiver, The Trader," p. 43.

11 Gerald L. Berry, *The Whoop-Up Trail,* p. 49.

12 Hugh A. Dempsey, ed., "Narrative of Donald Graham, 1872-73."

13 Esther S. Goldfrank, *Changing Configurations in the Social Organization of a Blackfoot Tribe During the Reserve Period,* p. 12.

14 Interview with John Cotton, 26 December 1953.

15 Interview with Percy Creighton, 1 August 1939, by Esther S. Goldfrank. Goldfrank Papers, Glenbow-Alberta Institute archives, BC/243, p. 185.

16 My older sister.

17 Interview with Percy Creighton, by Goldfrank, p. 186.

18 Ibid.

19 Dempsey, "Narrative of Donald Graham, 1872-73," p. 17.

20 Ibid.

21 R. B. Nevitt, *A Winter at Fort Macleod,* p. 83.

22 *Lethbridge Herald,* 15 November 1924.

23 Ibid.

24 Ibid.

25 Constance Kerr Sissons, *John Kerr,* p. 167.

26 Morris, *The Treaties of Canada,* p. 248.

27 Philip H. Godsell, ed., "The R. N. Wilson Papers," pp. 277-78.

9. / Red Coats /

1 Rodney C. Macleod, *The North-West Mounted Police and Law Enforcement, 1873-1905,* p. 11.

2 Hugh A. Dempsey, "Robertson-Ross' Diary, Fort Edmonton to Wildhorse, B.C.," p. 11.

3 R. B. Nevitt, *A Winter at Fort Macleod,* p. 17.

4 *The Macleod Gazette,* 1 November 1888.

5 Bull's Head died during the winter so the one-year limit was never discussed again by these two men.

6 James F. Macleod to A. G. French, 1 December 1874, in *Annual Report, North-West Mounted Police,* 1874, p. 64.

7 Alexander Morris, *The Treaties of Canada with the Indians of Manitoba and the North-West Territories Including the Negotiations on Which They Were Based, and Other Information Relating Thereto,* p. 270.

8 Ibid., p. 272.

9 Hugh A. Dempsey, "A Mountie's Diary," p. 13.

10   H. A. Kennerly, Birch Creek, to Maj. J. S. Wood, U.S. Indian
     Agent, 29 January 1875. Blackfoot Agency Archives, Browning,
     Montana.
11   Nevitt, *A Winter at Fort Macleod*, p. 48.
12   John Maclean, "Social Organization of the Blackfoot Indians," p. 253.
13   Ibid.
14   Interview with Mrs. Frank Red Crow, 7 August 1977.
15   Petition forwarded by Assistant Commissioner A. G. Irvine to
     Lieutenant-Governor A. Morris, 12 June 1876. No. 1265, Morris
     Papers, Public Archives of Manitoba.
16   Ibid.
17   Ibid.
18   Ibid.
19   Morris, *The Treaties of Canada*, p. 245.
20   Ibid., p. 249.
21   Ibid.
22   *Manitoba Free Press*, Winnipeg, 31 July 1876.
23   James F. Macleod to Secretary of State, 17 November 1876. Fort
     Macleod letter-book, 1875-76, 165-66. RCMP Museum, Regina.
24   Ibid., pp. 170-71.
25   *The Montana Post*, 9 December 1865.
26   Morris, *The Treaties of Canada*, p. 270.
27   Macleod to Secretary of State, 21 November 1876, pp. 191-92.
28   Ibid.
29   Norman T. Macleod, undated article, ca. 1924, from the
     Lethbridge Herald, in the Higinbotham Papers, Glenbow-Alberta
     Institute archives.
30   *Benton Record*, 24 August 1877.
31   Interview with George Calling Last, December 1954.
32   Interview with Mortimer Eagle Tailfeathers, 29 December 1954.
33   Letter. P. R. Neal to commissioner, North-West Mounted
     Police, 4 February 1888. RG-18, vol. 19, file 249, Public
     Archives of Canada.
34   Information from Archie Big Swan, a grandson.
35   Richard Hardisty Jr. in the *Calgary Herald*, 18 November 1933.
36   Ibid.

10. / The Blackfoot Treaty /

1   Alexander Morris, *The Treaties of Canada with the Indians of
     Manitoba and the North-West Territories Including the Negotiations on
     which They Were Based, and Other Information Relating Thereto*, p. 254.

2 Cecil Denny, *The Riders of the Plains*, p. 97.

3 Morris, *The Treaties of Canada*, pp. 267-68.

4 See Chapter 9, notes 27-28.

5 *The Globe*, Toronto, 30 October 1877. A fairly accurate copy of this newspaper account was reprinted in Morris, *The Treaties of Canada*, pp. 263-75. Unless otherwise cited, all quotations dealing with the treaty negotiations are from *The Globe*.

6 In spite of Laird's promise, he met with a delegation of half-breeds immediately after the treaty and told them "that the notice having been short, the law would not be very strictly enforced for the first winter."

7 Denny, *The Riders of the Plains*, p. 98.

8 Morris, *The Treaties of Canada*, p. 258.

9 Hugh A. Dempsey, *A Blackfoot Winter Count*, p. 16.

10 "Treaty with the Blackfeet Indians. Governor Laird's Negotiations Successfully Terminated. Valuable Territory Acquired," *The Globe*, Toronto, 8 October 1877, and "The Blackfeet Treaty. How It Was Made. The 'Talk' on Both Sides, the Indians and N.W.M. Police," *Manitoba Free Press*, Winnipeg, 8 November 1877.

11 John Maclean, *The Indians of Canada: Their Manner and Customs*, p. 152.

12 Hugh A. Dempsey, *Crowfoot, Chief of the Blackfeet*, p. 106.

13 Printed in full in Dempsey, *Crowfoot*, p. 103, and Morris, *The Treaties of Canada*, p. 272.

14 *The Globe*, Toronto, 9 October 1877.

15 Ibid.

16 Immediately prior to the treaty, veteran trader John Healy considered the two head chiefs of the Bloods to be Red Crow and Hind Bull. See *The Daily Independent*, Helena, 26 September 1877.

17 Red Crow also arranged for a minor chieftainship for Stolen Person in a diplomatic move, as that man's son, Otter Robe, was a leading war chief of the Assiniboines in Montana.

18 *The Daily Independent*, Helena, 26 September 1877.

19 Letter. P. R. Neale to commissioner; North-West Mounted Police, 4 February 1888. RG-18, vol. 19, file 249, Public Archives of Canada.

20 Morris, *The Treaties of Canada*, p. 275.

11. / Last Days of Freedom /

1   *The Globe*, Toronto, 27 December 1877.
2   *Benton Record*, 8 February 1878.
3   Ibid., 24 May 1878.
4   John Maclean, *The Indians of Canada: Their Manners and Customs*, p. 152.
5   *Benton Record*, 12 December 1879.
6   Letter. Jean L'Heureux to Lieutenant-Governor Edgar Dewdney, 24 September 1880. Indian Affairs archives, file no. 34527.
7   Letter. Constantine Scollen to A. G. Irvine, 18 April 1879. Indian Affairs archives, file no. 14924.
8   *Benton Record*, 7 November 1879.
9   Report of Superintendent L. N. F. Crozier, in *Annual Report North-West Mounted Police*, 1880, p. 30.
10   Letter. P. R. Neale to commissioner, North-West Mounted Police, 4 February 1888. RG-18, vol. 19, file 249, Public Archives of Canada.
11   Hugh A. Dempsey, "Story of the Blood Reserve," p. 1.
12   Norman T. Macleod, undated article, ca. 1924, from the *Lethbridge Herald*, in the Higinbotham Papers, Glenbow-Alberta Institute archives.
13   Letter. Norman T. Macleod to commissioner, 15 October 1880. Blood letter-book, RG-10, 1427:36, Public Archives of Canada.
14   Register of Baptisms, St. Paul's Anglican mission, entry for 23 October 1881. Later, the Catholics baptized Samuel again, re-naming him Joseph.
15   *Benton Record*, 1 September 1881.
16   Letter. Edgar Dewdney to John A. Macdonald, 26 October 1881. Letter 358, vol. 210, Macdonald Papers, Public Archives of Canada.
17   Letter. N. T. Macleod to commissioner, 1 June 1881. Blood letterbook, RG-10, 1427:234-35, Public Archives of Canada.
18   Letter. Neale to commissioner, 4 February 1888.

12. / A New Life /

1   Oblate Papers, Box 44, file X5, Provincial Archives of Alberta, and baptismal register, St. Paul's Anglican mission. It has not

been possible to correlate the baptismal names of the girls with the Indian ones which are known. These include Shaggy Hair Woman, who married No Chief, and the wives of Many Mules and Longtime Squirrel.

2   The Bishop of Saskatchewan's Report of his Visitation to the Society's Mission at the Blood Reserve, 12 December 1885. Church Missionary Society Papers, Reel A-113.

3   Appreciation is extended to Ted J. Brasser, ethnologist at the National Museum of Man, Ottawa, for sharing his research on tepee designs.

4   Jim White Bull, "Records by the Blood Indians & Blackfoots," unpublished manuscript in author's possession. Entries for 1884, 1897, and 1891 respectively.

5   *Annual Report, North-West Mounted Police,* 1881, p. 17.

6   John Maclean, *Canadian Savage Folk: The Native Tribes of Canada,* p. 555.

7   *Benton Record,* 25 August 1881.

8   Letter. Cecil Denny to commissioner, 1 November 1881. Indian Affairs archives, no. 29506.

9   *Benton Record,* 22 December 1881.

10   *Annual Report, North-West Mounted Police,* 1881, p. 15.

11   *Benton Record,* 22 December 1881.

12   Letter. Denny to Commissioner, 1 November 1881. Indian Affairs archives, no. 29506.

13   Letter. Denny to W. C. McCord, 4 April 1882. Blood letter-book, RG-10, 1428:27, Public Archives of Canada (PAC).

14   Article by Waseecha Hoska (pseud.), in *Scarlet and Gold,* 2nd annual, 1920, p. 103.

15   Letter. Edgar Dewdney to John A. Macdonald, 24 February 1883. Indian Affairs archives, vol. 211, no. 111.

16   Letter. Denny to commissioner, 1 June 1882. Blood letter-book, RG-10, 1428:183, PAC.

17   Monthly diary of W. C. McCord, entries for January 19 and 23, 1884. Blood letter-book, RG-10, 1551:102, PAC.

18   Denny, monthly report for May 1882. Blood letter-book, RG-10, 1428:165, PAC.

19   Report of Cecil Denny, *Annual Report, Department of Indian Affairs,* 1882, p. 171.

20   Letter. Denny to Superintendent J. M. Walsh, 17 May 1882. Blood letter-book, RG-10, 1428:154, PAC.

21   Cecil Denny, *The Law Marches West,* p. 289.

22 Letter. Denny to commissioner, 5 September 1883. Blood letter-book, RG-10, 1550:578, PAC.
23 Ibid., 28 July 1883, RG-10, 1550:415, PAC.
24 Ibid., 28 July 1883, RG-10, 1550:415, PAC.
25 Ibid., 28 September 1883, RG-10, 1550:670, PAC.
26 Ibid., 28 September 1883, RG-10, 1550:671, PAC.
27 Ibid., 30 November 1883, RG-10, 1550:842, PAC.

13. / Unsettled Conditions /

1 Hugh A. Dempsey, *A Blackfoot Winter Count*, p. 17; see also *Fort Macleod Gazette*, 14 August 1883.
2 Report of Cecil Denny, *Annual Report, Department of Indian Affairs*, 1882, p. 176.
3 R. G. Mathews in *Lethbridge Herald*, 18 February 1922.
4 Report of Cecil Denny, *Annual Report, Department of Indian Affairs*, 1882, p. 176.
5 *Fort Macleod Gazette*, 8 July 1882.
6 *Indian Treaties and Surrenders*, Ottawa, 1905. II:134.
7 Dempsey, *A Blackfoot Winter Count*, p. 3.
8 Letter. William Pocklington to commissioner, 30 September 1884. Blood letter-book, RG-10, 1551:221, Public Archives of Canada (PAC).
9 Monthly diary of W. C. McCord, entry for 20 February 1884. Blood letter-book, RG-10, 1551:221, PAC.
10 Ibid., entry for January 1884, RG-10, 1551:100, PAC.
11 Letter. Denny to commissioner, 25 December 1883. Blood letter-book, RG-10, 1550:930, PAC.
12 Ibid., 13 January 1884, RG-10, 1551:47, PAC.
13 Monthly diary of W. C. McCord, entry for 1 February 1884. Blood letter-book, RG-10, 1551:220, PAC. See also report from Rev. Samuel Trivett, 2 February 1884, Church Missionary Society Papers, Reel A-112, PAC.
14 *The Regina Leader*, 14 February 1884.
15 Hugh A. Dempsey, *Crowfoot, Chief of the Blackfeet*, p. 160.
16 Letter. P. Williams, farm instructor, to commissioner, 30 June 1884. Blood letter-book, RG-10, 1551:712, PAC.
17 George H. Ham, *Reminiscences of a Raconteur*, p. 116.
18 Ibid.
19 John Maclean, *Canadian Savage Folk: The Native Tribes of Canada*, p. 417.

20   Letter index, summary of letter, Dewdney to John A. Macdonald, 19 July 1884. Macdonald Papers, North-West Rebellion, file 14624, vol. 1, p. 95. PAC.
21   Pocklington, monthly report for September 1884. Blood letter-book, RG-10, 1552-55, PAC.
22   Ibid., RG-10, 1552:57, PAC.
23   *Fort Macleod Gazette*, 21 March 1885.
24   Letter. Pocklington to commissioner, 18 March 1885. Blood letter-book; RG-10, 1552:469, PAC.
25   Maclean, *Canadian Savage Folk*, p. 415.

14. / Riel Rebellion /

1   John R. Craig, *Ranching With Lords and Commons*, pp. 158-59.
2   Letter. W. F. Cochrane to his father, Senator H. M. Cochrane, 6 April 1885. Cochrane Ranch letter-book, Glenbow-Alberta Institute archives.
3   Letter. Pocklington to commissioner, 8 April 1885. Blood letter-book, RG-10, 1552:525, Public Archives of Canada (PAC).
4   Desmond Morton and Reginald H. Roy, *Telegrams of the North-West Campaign, 1885*, p. 137. In the published version the telegram's meaning was altered by a misplaced comma. It should have read that the Bloods "wanted to fight Crees, stopped them," but it came out "wanted to fight, Crees stopped them."
5   Pocklington to commissioner, 6 April 1885. Blood letter-book, RG-10, 1552-521, PAC.
6   *The Macleod Gazette*, 18 April 1885.
7   Telegram, John A. Macdonald to Dewdney, 10 April 1885.
8   Hugh A. Dempsey, *Crowfoot, Chief of the Blackfeet*, p. 167.
9   John Maclean, *Canadian Savage Folk: The Native Tribes of Canada*, pp. 540-41.
10   Interview with James Gladstone, 19 June 1954.
11   Letter. Pocklington to commissioner, 10 May 1885. Blood letter-book, RG-10, 1552:601, PAC.
12   Morton & Roy, *Telegrams*, p. 119.
13   *The Macleod Gazette*, 23 May 1885.
14   Letter. Pocklington to commissioner, 25 May 1885. Blood letter-book, RG-10, 1552:637, PAC.

15   Report of William Pocklington, *Annual Report, Department of Indian Affairs*, 188, p. 74.

15. / Old Life And The New /

1   Report of Inspector Alex McGibbon, *Annual Report, Department of Indian Affairs*, 1886, p. 151.
2   Letter. Pocklington to commissioner, 9 November 1885, Blood letter-book, RG-10, 1553:265-66, Public Archives of Canada (PAC).
3   Ibid.
4   Ibid., RG-10, 1553:267, PAC.
5   Ibid., 22 January 1891, RG-10, 1558:143, PAC.
6   John Maclean, diary entry for 5 October 1886, Maclean Papers, United Church Archives.
7   Thomas R. Clipsham, in *Christian Guardian*, 30 December 1885, p. 820.
8   George H. Ham in *Toronto Mail*, 28 January 1886.
9   Ibid.
10   Ibid.
11   John Maclean, "Apokena Among the White Savages," unpublished novel in Maclean Papers, United Church Archives, pp. 104-05.
12   Ibid., p. 113.
13   Ibid., pp. 91-92.
14   *Ottawa Free Press*, 11 October 1886.
15   Ibid., 9 October 1886.
16   Ibid., 11 October 1886.
17   *The Globe*, Toronto, 12 October 1886.
18   Ibid., 19 October 1886.
19   *The Daily Expositor*, Brantford, 18 October 1886.
20   Jean L'Heureux, undated matter accompanying expense account. Indian Affairs archives, no. 32864.
21   *Brantford Daily Courier*, 14 October 1886.
22   *The Globe*, Toronto, 14 October 1886.
23   *Brantford Daily Courier*, 15 October 1886.
24   *The Globe*, Toronto, 15 October 1886.
25   *Brantford Daily Courier*, 14 October 1886.
26   *The Globe*, Toronto, 19 October 1886.
27   Ibid., and *Brantford Daily Courier*, 16 October 1886.

28 *The Globe*, Toronto, 19 October 1886.
29 *Brantford Daily Courier*, 22 October 1886.
30 *The Daily Expositor*, Brantford, 16 October 1886.
31 Letter. Jean L'Heureux to Dewdney, no date. Indian Affairs archives, no. 32864.
32 Pocklington, monthly report for October 1886. Blood letter-book, RG-10, 1554:740-41, PAC.

16. / Another Treaty /

1 Letter. Pocklington to commissioner, 24 October 1886. Blood letter-book, RG-10, 1554:704, Public Archives of Canada (PAC).
2 Ibid, 20 January 1887, RG-10, 1555:174, PAC.
3 John Maclean to his wife, 25 January 1887. Letter-book in Maclean Papers, United Church Archives.
4 Letter. Pocklington to commissioner, 23 March 1887. Blood letter-book, RG-10, 1555:270, PAC.
5 Ibid., 3 April 1887, RG-10, 1555:310, PAC.
6 Actually, Big Rib was the adopted son of Crop Eared Wolf who in turn was the adopted son of Red Crow. But in the eyes of the Indians, Big Rib was the chief's grandson.
7 Letter. Pocklington to commissioner, 27 June 1887. Blood letter-book, RG-10, 1555:480-81, PAC.
8 Hugh A. Dempsey, "A Treaty of Peace," p. 11.
9 Ibid.
10 Ibid., p. 12; also "Peace Council held between the Bloods, Gros Ventres & Assiniboines," in Blood letter-book, RG-10, 1555:457-58, PAC.
11 "Peace Council," RG-10, 1555:458, PAC.
12 Ibid., RG-10, 1555:459, PAC.
13 Ibid., RG-10, 1555:460, PAC.
14 Dempsey, "A Treaty of Peace," p. 15.
15 Letter. Pocklington to commissioner, 17 May 1889. Blood letter-book, RG-10, 1557:40, PAC.
16 John Maclean, day book entry for 26 August 1888, Maclean Papers, United Church Archives.

17. / The Boundary Conflict /

1 John Woolf, "Story of Cardston's First M.L.A.," in *Lethbridge Herald*, 19 June 1937.

2   Letter. Pocklington to commissioner, 31 January 1888. Blood letter-book, RG-10, 1556:240, Public Archives of Canada (PAC).
3   Letter. P. R. Neale to commissioner, North-West Mounted Police, 4 February 1888. RG-18, vol. 19, file 249, PAC.
4   Ibid.
5   Ibid.
6   Ibid.
7   Ibid.
8   Report of John C. Nelson, *Annual Report, Department of Indian Affairs*, 1888, p. 190.
9   Ibid.
10 Letter. Pocklington to commissioner, 30 August 1888. Blood letter-book, RG-10, 1556:646, PAC.
11 Macleod Detachment, monthly report for July 1899. RCMP Papers, RG18, vol. 161, file 86/99, PAC.
12 John Maclean, "Apokena Among the Savages," unpublished novel in Maclean Papers, United Church Archives, p. 105.
13 Interview with Mrs. Rosie Davis, 1 August 1977. The informant was married to Revenge Walker's son.
14 John Maclean, day book entry for 1 December 1886. Maclean Papers, United Church Archives.
15 Ibid., 19 August 1888.
16 Report of John C. Nelson, 1888, p. 190.
17 "Peace Council held between the Bloods, Gros Ventres & Assiniboines," in Blood letter-book, RG-10, 1555:459, PAC.
18 Letter. P. R. Neale to commissioner, North-West Mounted Police, 4 February 1888, RG-18, vol. 19, file 249, PAC.
19 Letter. Pocklington to commissioner, 8 December 1885. Blood letter-book, RG-10, 1553:346, PAC.

18. / Encouraging Signs /

1   Report of Alex McGibbon, *Annual Report, Department of Indian Affairs*, 1891, p. 94.
2   John Maclean, "Apokena Among the Savages," unpublished novel in Maclean Papers, United Church Archives, p. 37.
3   John Maclean, *Canadian Savage Folk: The Native Tribes of Canada*, pp. 414-15.
4   Another name for Day Chief.
5   Letter. Pocklington to commissioner, 4 April 1891. Blood letter-book, RG-10, 1558:222-23, Public Archives of Canada (PAC).

6 Report of Alex McGibbon, p. 94.

7 Maclean, *Canadian Savage Folk*, p. 415.

8 Letter. P. R. Neale to commissioner, North-West Mounted Police, 4 February 1888, RG-18, vol. 19, file 249, PAC.

9 Letter. Pocklington to commissioner, 7 September 1888. Blood letter-book, RG-10, 1556:678, PAC.

10 Esther S. Goldfrank Papers, Glenbow-Alberta Institute archives.

11 Report of William Pocklington. *Annual Report, Department of Indian Affairs*, 1891, p. 81.

12 Ibid., 1892, p. 183.

13 Report of Superintendent R. Burton Deane, *Annual Report, North-West Mounted Police*, 1889, p. 42.

14 Letter. James Wilson to commissioner, 29 September 1894. Blood letter-book, RG-10, 1560:528-29, PAC.

15 A. G. Irvine, monthly report for February 1892. Blood letter-book, RG-10, 1558:716, PAC.

16 Letter. Wilson to commissioner, 18 June 1894. Blood letter-book, RG-10, 1560:229, PAC.

19. / The Sun Dance War /

1 Letter. James Wilson to commissioner, 22 November 1893. Blood letter-book RG-10, 1559:570, PAC.

2 John Maclean, *Canadian Savage Folk: The Native Tribes of Canada*, p. 417.

3 Letter. Pocklington to commissioner, 21 May 1891. Blood letter-book, RG-10, 1558:570, PAC.

4 Letter. Wilson to commissioner, 21 June 1893. Blood letter-book, RG-10, 1559:325-26, PAC.

5 Ibid., RG-10, 1559:326, PAC.

6 Ibid., 3 August 1893, RG-10, 1559:398, PAC.

7 Ibid., 9 July 1894, RG-10, 1560:268, PAC.

8 Sec. 114 of "An Act to further amend the Indian Act," 22 July 1895. *Statutes of Canada*, 58-59 Victoria, 1895, p. 121.

9 Jim White Bull, "Records by the Blood Indians & Blackfoots," unpublished manuscript in the author's possession.

10 Wilson, semi-annual report, 25 July 1896. Blood letter-book, RG-10, 1561:791, PAC.

11 Ibid., semi-annual report, 11 February 1898, RG-10, 1563:628, PAC.

12   Letter. Wilson to commissioner, 29 April 1898. Blood letter-book, RG-10, 1563:804-05, PAC.

13   Report of Superintendent R. Burton Deane. *Annual Report, North-West Mounted Police*, 1898, p. 27.

14   Ibid.

15   Ibid.

16   Ibid.

17   Wilson, monthly report for June 1898. Blood letter-book, RG-10, 1723:7, PAC.

18   Letter. Wilson to Deane, 5 June 1898. Blood letter-book, RG-10, 1564:16, PAC.

19   Letter. Wilson to commissioner, 7 June 1899. Blood letter-book, RG-10, 1719:360, PAC.

20   Letter. Wilson to A. E. Forget, Superintendent General of Indian Affairs, 4 June 1897. Blood letter-book, RG-10, 1563:69, PAC.

21   Letter. Wilson to commissioner, 5 May 1899. Blood letter-book, RG-10, 1719:322-23, PAC.

22   Macleod Detachment, monthly report for July 1899. RCMP Papers, RG18, vol. 161, file 86/99, PAC.

23   Letter. Wilson to commissioner, 4 August 1899. Blood letter-book, RG-10, 1719:429-30, PAC.

24   Ibid., 24 July 1899, RG-10, 1719:421, PAC.

25   Jim White Bull, "Records by the Blood Indians & Blackfoots."

26   Letter. Wilson to commissioner, 12 June 1900. Blood letter-book, RG-10, 1719:781-82, PAC.

27   *The Globe*, Toronto, 9 October 1877.

28   Interview with Mrs. Bruised Head, 12 August 1955.

20. / Red Crow's Legacy /

1   *Cardston Record*, 3 September 1893.

2   *Calgary Daily Herald*, 22 April 1913.

3   In 1965, Rufus Goodstriker was elected head chief and served a two-year term of office. In the next election, Jim Shot Both Sides resumed the leadership.

4   Clarence McHugh.

5   Baptismal register, vol. X5, box 44, Oblate Papers, Provincial Archives of Alberta.

6   Wilson, monthly report for December 1896. Blood letter-book, RG-10, 1562:224, Public Archives of Canada.

7   Esther S. Goldfrank, *Changing Configurations in the Social Organization of a Blackfoot Tribe During the Reserve Period*, p. 65.

/ Bibliography /

/ Unpublished Sources /

"Correspondence from the Blood Indian Reserve and Treaty Seven, 1880-1900." Typescript, 4 vols. In author's possession.

Dempsey, Hugh A. "The Band System of the Blood Indians." 1955. In author's possession.

Maclean, John. "Apokena Among the Savages." In Maclean Papers, United Church Archives, Toronto.

"The R. N. Wilson Papers," edited by Philip H. Godsell. 2 vols. Glenbow-Alberta Institute, Calgary.

Royal Canadian Mounted Police Papers, in Record Group 18, Public Archives of Canada, Ottawa.

White Bull, Jim. "Records by the Blood Indians & Blackfoots." In author's possession.

/ Published Sources /

Annual Reports, Department of Indian Affairs. Ottawa: Queen's Printer, 1882-1900.

Annual Reports, North-West Mounted Police. Ottawa: Queen's Printer, 1874-1900. Some of these were reprinted by Coles Publishing Co., Toronto, in 1973 under the titles: *Opening Up the West* (1874-81); *Settlers and Rebels* (1882-85); *Law and Order* (1886-87); and *The New West* (1888-89).

Berry, Gerald L. *The Whoop-Up Trail.* Edmonton, Applied Art Products, 1953.

Bradley, James T. "Affairs at Fort Benton from 1831 to 1869." *Contributions, Historical Society of Montana,* III. Helena, 1900.

———"Lieut. James H. Bradley Manuscript." *Contributions, Historical Society of Montana,* IX. Helena, 1923.

Butler, William Francis. *The Great Lone Land.* London: Sampson Low, Marston, Low & Searle, 1874.

Craig, John R. *Ranching With Lords and Commons.* Toronto: William Briggs, 1903.

Dempsey, Hugh A., ed. "Narrative of Donald Graham, 1872-73." *Alberta Historical Review,* Winter 1956, pp. 10-19.

———"A Mountie's Diary." *The Early West.* Calgary: Historical Society of Alberta, 1957.

———"Robertson-Ross' Diary, Fort Edmonton to Wildhorse, B.C." *Alberta Historical Review,* Autumn 1961.

Dempsey, Hugh A. "A Treaty of Peace." *Alberta Historical Review,* Winter 1962.

——— *A Blackfoot Winter Count.* Calgary: Glenbow Foundation, 1965.

———"Story of the Blood Reserve." *The Pioneer West II,* pp. 1-8. Calgary: Historical Society of Alberta, 1970.

——— *Crowfoot, Chief of the Blackfeet.* Norman: University of Oklahoma Press, 1972, and Edmonton: Hurtig Publishers, 1976.

——— *William Parker, Mounted Policeman.* Edmonton: Hurtig Publishers, 1973.

Denny, Cecil. *The Riders of the Plains.* Calgary: The Herald Printers, 1905.

——— *The Law Marches West.* Toronto: J. M. Dent, 1939.

Doty, James. "A Visit to the Blackfoot Camps." *Alberta Historical Review,* Summer 1966, pp. 12-16.

Ewers, John C. *The Blackfeet, Raiders on the Northwestern Plains.* Norman: University of Oklahoma Press, 1958.

Goldfrank, Esther S. *Changing Configurations in the Social Organization of a Blackfoot Tribe During the Reserve Period.* New York: J. J. Augustin, 1945.

Ham, George H. *Reminiscences of a Raconteur.* Toronto: The Musson Book Co., 1921.

Indian Treaties and Surrenders. 2 vols. Ottawa: King's Printer, 1905.

McDonnell, Anne B. "The Fort Benton Journal, 1854-1856, and the Fort Sarpy Journal, 1855-1856." *Contributions to the Historical Society of Montana,* X, Helena, 1940.

Maclean, John. *The Indians of Canada: Their Manners and Customs.* London: Charles H. Kelly, 1892.

———"Social Organization of the Blackfoot Indians." *Transactions of the Canadian Institute,* Toronto, vol. 4, no. 8, pt. 2, 1895.

——— *Canadian Savage Folk: The Native Tribes of Canada.* Toronto: William Briggs, 1896.

Macleod, Rodney C. *The North-West Mounted Police and Law Enforcement, 1873-1905.* Toronto: University of Toronto Press, 1976.

Morris, Alexander. *The Treaties of Canada with the Indians of Manitoba and the North-West Territories Including the Negotiations on Which They Were Based, and Other Information Relating Thereto.* Toronto: Willing & Williamson, 1880.

Morton, Desmond and Reginald H. Roy, eds. *Telegrams of the North-West Campaign, 1885.* Toronto: Champlain Society, 1973.

Nevitt, R. B. *A Winter at Fort Macleod.* Calgary: Glenbow Museum, 1974.

Point, Father Nicholas. *Wilderness Kingdom: The Journals & Paintings of Father Nicholas Point.* London: Michael Joseph, 1968.

Schemm, Mildred W. "The Major's Lady." *Montana Magazine of History,* 2:1, January 1952.

Schultz, James Willard. "Raven Quiver, the Trader." *Forest and Stream,* 18 July 1903.

——— *Signposts of Adventure.* New York: Houghton Mifflin Co., 1926.

Sissons, Constance Kerr. *John Kerr.* Toronto: Oxford University Press, 1946.

/ Index /